ABSTRACTING PRACTICES IN LIBRARIES

ABSTRACTING PRACTICES IN LIBRARIES

By

Dr. B.J.Ankuya
In-charge
University Librarian & Head of Dept.
Library & Information Science
Veer Narmad South Gujarat University
Surat (India)

DISCOVERY PUBLISHING HOUSE PVT. LTD.
NEW DELHI-110 002

Published by:
Namit Wasan
DISCOVERY PUBLISHING HOUSE PVT. LTD.
4383/4B, Ansari Road, Darya Ganj
New Delhi-110 002 (India)
Phone : +91-11-23279245, 23253475, 43596065
E-mail : discoverypublishinghouse@gmail.com
sales@discoverypublishinggroup.com
web : www.discoverypublishinggroup.com

Reprinted: **2019**

First Published: **2013**

ISBN: 978-93-5056-365-6

Abstracting Practices in Libraries

Printed at:
Infinity Imaging Systems
Delhi

Contents

Preface

Abstracting practices are vital links in the string of communication between the originator of information and the ultimate user. Huge development in published literature, diversity of publications, language barrier and scatter of published information, etc., are some of the factors that have contributed the launching of abstracting practices. This has made abstracting practices in libraries become important. The conventional function of libraries is to collect, process, disseminate, store and utilize information to provide service to the university community. However, the environment in which libraries operate today is changing. Libraries are part of the university and its organizational culture. Whatever affects universities has an impact on libraries. As a result, the role of libraries is changing to provide the competitive advantage for the parent universities. The success of libraries depends on their ability to utilize information and knowledge of its staff to better serve the needs of the academic community.

—Author

1

Information Science Abstracts

Information science and the industry associated with it have changed so radically in recent years that they bear little resemblance to their appearance. The changes are dramatic, striking, and simply amazing. And not only do the changes continue unabated, but the *rate* of change has increased so much in recent years that it is a gargantuan task to keep abreast of the changes and their effects.

One excellent way to track the changes that have occurred in a field is to consult its *Abstracting and Indexing* (A&I) publications. Such publications not only record the history of a discipline by collecting and indexing its literature but they can serve as 'watchdogs' of changes. This chapter presents a brief historical review of one of the major A&I publications in information science—*Information Science Abstracts* (ISA)—and then in more depth it reviews much of the past work that sought to define 'Information Science.' From this review, a new working definition of 'information science' and a subject mapping of the field have been derived.

The definition and map are suitable tools that can be used to guide the selection of material for inclusion in ISA. Finally, some of the distinctions between information science and its most closely related discipline, librarianship, are discussed. The ultimate goal of this research was to develop a new subject classification for ISA; however, before one can classify the subjects making up a discipline, one must first develop the foundational definitions. I first became involved with ISA in 1996 as Sr. Technical Editor, and was astonished to learn that a working definition of information science had never been developed for this major A&I publication. This chapter rectifies that deficiency. It reviews the various definitions of information science that have been promulgated over the years and derives a definition consistent with the present environment that will guide the coverage of ISA.

HISTORY OF ISA

EARLY HISTORY

ISA began publication in 1966 under the name *Documentation Abstracts,* and assumed its present title in 1968; before that, A&I coverage of the literature of information science was scattered in various other publications. ISA was the first A&I publication to focus on information science, and it has published continuously since, then, making it the oldest A&I publication in the field. In the early 1980s, a non-profit consortium consisting of representatives of eight professional societies in the library and information science field was founded under the name *Documentation Abstracts, Inc.* (DAI), whose sole purpose was to ensure the continuation of ISA as a viable A&I publication.

DAI's assets were the name, copyright, and content of ISA. DAI entered into a contract with Plenum Press, Inc., a major publisher of books and journals, to publish ISA. Plenum provided an editor, and production was done by Plenum's subsidiary, IFI/Plenum Data Corp. DAI maintained loose oversight of ISA through periodic Board meetings with the Plenum staff. As on-line databases developed, IFI/Plenum Data established contracts with the Dialogue service, which mounted the ISA database as File 202, and with SilverPlatter Information, Inc. to distribute it on CD-ROM. ISA was marketed by Plenum on behalf of DAI, with a significant marketing effort for the online and CD-ROM versions being done by Dialogue and SilverPlatter, respectively. Revenues were collected by Plenum, and DAI received a portion of them as the database owner.

Because DAI was a non-profit organisation, it retained the revenues and used some of them for professional purposes, one of which was the sponsorship of a yearly grant awarded to an information science professional to conduct research. In 1995, Pe´ter Jacso´ of the University of Hawaii received the DAI grant. Jasco´ studied the journal coverage of ISA, compared it to other A&I information science databases, and reported that the quality of ISA was significantly lacking in several areas. Jasco´'s report ultimately led to the termination of DAI's contract with Plenum and the acquisition of ISA by *Information Today, Inc.* (ITI) on June 1, 1998. With the sale of its only publication, DAI is in the process of disbanding and distributing its assets to the eight sponsoring societies. ITI quickly addressed and corrected the quality deficiencies identified by Jacso´, and began to market ISA through its own marketing channels. Plans are currently underway to make ISA available on the Internet.

ISA TODAY

ISA is structured as a conventional bibliographic database. A typical record from the ISA on-line database as it appears on the Dialogue service.

```
DIALOG(R)File 202:Information Science Abs.
(c)  Information Today, Inc. All rts. reserv.

00223964   9803964
ISA Document Number in Printed Publication: 9803233
   Visualizing a discipline: an author co-citation analysis of
information science, 1972-1995.
Document Type: Journal Article
Author (Affiliation): White, H.D.  (Drexel Univ, Philadelphia, PA);
McCain, K.W.
Country of Affiliation: United States
Journal: Journal of the American Society for Information Science
Publication Language(s): English
Source: Vol. 49 Issue 4 p. 327-355 Apr 1, 1998 58
        An extensive domain analysis of information science is presented
    in terms of its authors. Among the findings revealed in tables and
    graphics are: (1) the disciplinary and institutional affiliations of
    contributors; (2) the specialty structure of the discipline over 24
    years; (3) authors' memberships in one or more specialties; (4)
    inertia and change in authors' positions on two-dimensional subject
    maps; (5) the two major subdisciplines of information science and
    their evolving memberships; (6) "canonical" authors who are in the
    top 100 in all three subperiods; (7) changes in authors' eminence
    and influence over the subperiods; (8) authors with marked changes
    in their mapped positions over the subperiods; (9) the axes on which
    authors are mapped, with interpretations; (10) evidence of a
    paradigm shift in information science in the 1980s; and (11)
    evidence of the general nature and state of integration of
    information science.
Descriptors: AUTHORS; BIBLIOMETRICS; CITATION ANALYSIS; INFORMATION
    SCIENCE
Subject Class Header (Number):Information Science and Documentation,
    Primary and Secondary Sources (01.01)
```

Fig 1.1 Ty pical ISA Record

ISA records are indexed using a controlled vocabulary containing approximately 1,200 'Descriptor' terms that was originally based on a version of the *ASIS Thesaurus*. Additional terms were added to ISA's vocabulary more or less randomly over the years. Because ISA's controlled vocabulary has long outlived its usefulness, ITI has decided to update it and, hopefully, reindex the entire database. Although there are several potential sources for a new vocabulary, it has been felt appropriate to base it on the revised and updated second edition of the *ASIS Thesaurus*. Abstracts in ISA are organised into seven broad subject classifications, each of which is further subdivided. Each abstract in the printed version appears under the most relevant classification; in the electronic version of the database, all subject headings are searchable.

WHAT IS 'INFORMATION SCIENCE'

HISTORICAL REVIEW

Before developing a new subject classification and index terms, it was necessary to define ISA's subject coverage. This process began by turning to some of the early definitions of information science for guidance. Attempts to define information science appear to have begun in the late 1960s. The *American Society for Information Science* (ASIS) changed its name from the "American Documentation Institute" to its present name in 1970; the name of its journal was also changed at the same time. Shortly thereafter, Harold Borko, then president of ASIS, challenged the membership to develop a definition of information science. Several authors responded to Borko's challenge, and others have expanded on the topic in succeeding years.

The following discussions were helpful:

- Hoshovsky and Massey suggested an 'output oriented' societal definition, in which information science was regarded as a body of knowledge providing an understanding of the means through which society's information needs are met. They differentiated between data, knowledge, and information as three steps in a process, each building on its predecessor, with information at the highest level. They also observed that knowledge exists in three places besides the minds of people—documents, computer tapes, and memories—and they suggested that market research, economics, and information ecology are three neglected areas of information science. Finally, they state that the 'documentation industry' is different from information science. Hoshovsky and Massey's definition is well reasoned, and includes many elements of information science that were relevant not only at the time their article was written, but continue to be relevant today. Their distinction between data, knowledge, and information is especially attractive. Their definitions of the three knowledge repositories are also relevant.

Klempner analysed the intellectual content and activities of information science, starting with the definition then published in ASIS brochures, which described information science as "investigating the properties and behaviour of information, the forces governing information transfer, and the technology necessary to process information for optimum accessibility and use." Klempner divided the field into three segments—conceptualisation, storage and transmission, and utilisation—and he listed the technologies or activities needed in each segment.

Conceptual framework for information science:

- Conceptualisation segment
  - Indexing
  - Abstracting
  - Classification
  - Thesaurus building
  - Subject heading work
  - Document selection
  - Development of interest profiles
- Storage transmission segment
  - Analysis of storage transmission channels
  - Networks
  - Efficient organisation and administration

- Utilisation segment.
  - Relevance assessment
  - Management appraisals
  - Evaluation of community satisfaction
  - Satisfaction of national or international cultural, ethical, recreational, or sociopolitical goals.

He also discusses the important distinction between libraries and librarianship on the one hand and information science on the other—a distinction of importance to ISA in the effort to differentiate it from its competing databases. Klempner's concluding statement, "The field of information science is concerned with the study of both men and machines," is one of his most important, and is a major consideration that should not be lost sight of.

- Giuliano provides a helpful differentiation between information science and librarianship. Giuliano suggests that librarianship should be defined in terms of knowledge transfer, rather than in terms of a place or a building. He then enumerates some of the basic concepts of what we have come to regard as information science: "assembling of knowledge, its systematic organisation, its storage, its retrieval and dissemination," and he also states, "Information science comprises the set of research and development undertakings necessary to support the profession of librarianship." In defining ISA's subject coverage, Giuliano's work is illuminating, especially his analogy to the medical profession, in which he points out that the people who work in hospitals are not called 'hospitalitarians' but 'medical professionals.' Giuliano states that the field of librarianship developed along different lines, concentrating on institutional library procedures rather than knowledge transfer. This observation has provided helpful guidance in deciding what areas should or should not be covered by ISA.
- Harmon reviewed earlier work that contrasted documentation and information retrieval, and concluded that information science is an

interdisciplinary field that includes such topics as behavioural science, classification, transfer, and language and linguistics. He concluded that information science is closely related to communications and behaviour.

- Farradane in response to a letter suggesting that information science is not a discipline in its own right but a branch of cybernetics, linguistics, and psychology, rightly pointed out that this is not true, stating that information science encompasses much more and is therefore not a 'non-starter,' He suggested that information science is concerned with the "nature of thought and its expression and communication... determining and matching the communications to the needs or thought patterns of users."
- Diener enumerated some of the fundamental characteristics of information: it is an entity, it is not consumed when it is used, and can be reproduced without loss of content or meaning, it is societal, and it is intangible.
- In response to Diener, Bohnert suggested that the name for the field used from 1950 to about 1970—information retrieval—be retained. She also observed an increasing trend to combine 'library' with 'information science' in the names of bibliographic services and academic departments as well as in the titles of publications. Figure shows the results of a search on the June 1999 CD-ROM version of ISA for articles having both terms in the title. Bohnert's observation was true as of the date of her article, but since, then, the number of articles with both terms in the title seems to be decreasing over time rather than increasing.
- Williams also compared information science to medicine, observing that both are amalgams of a variety of other disciplines and listing 14 disciplines that relate to information science. She suggested that these disciplines help solve problems relating to the

generation, organisation, representation, processing, distribution, communication, and use of information.

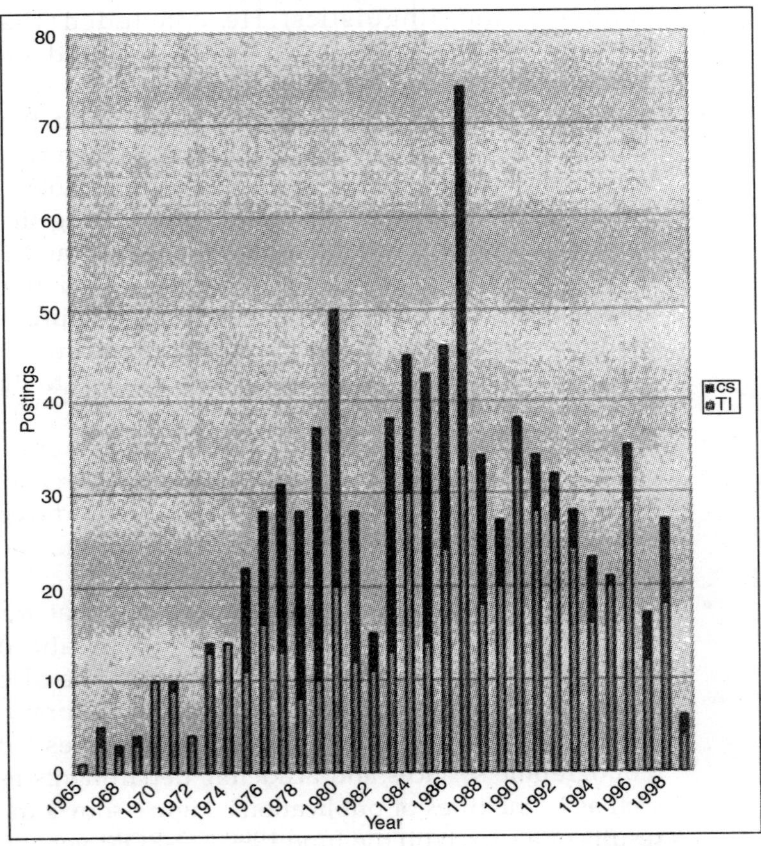

Fig 1.2 Postings with Both 'Library' and 'Information Science' in ISI's Title (TI)

The works cover the time period through the late 1980s. Interest in defining information science seems to have waned following Williams', but recently, several highly relevant articles have appeared.

They are discussed separately below because of their significance:

- Rayward in an introduction to a special issue *of Information Processing and Management*, reviewed some of the history of information science and some of the early disagreement as to what comprises information science. He quotes at length from Machlup and Mansfield, who describe a 'narrow' discipline of information science that might become part of either library science or computer science. In fact, this 'narrow' definition is an excellent list of many of the disciplines and technologies that are currently at the forefront of information science: communication, classification, bibliometrics, information exchange, access control, regulation, user behaviour, and human factors. Rayward suggests that information science is really a composite of 'chunks' of other disciplines such as those listed by Machlup and Mansfield.

- Bates discusses many of the indexing issues involved for digital libraries in the current Internetdominated era. Much of her work will be relevant to ISA in the future when the proposed reindexing of the database occurs, but it is of note here that she mentions several fields closely related to information science, among which are cognitive science, computational linguistics, and artificial intelligence. Bates followed up her initial work by describing some of the less obvious characteristics of information science, making the following cogent points:
  - Information science cuts across several conventional academic disciplines;
  - The domain of information science is the universe of recorded information;
  - Information science is the study of the gathering, organising, storing, retrieving, and dissemination of information.
- Morris and McCain derived the structure of the medical informatics literature and in the process mentioned the following topics relevant to that field: "cognitive, information processing, and information management tasks," logic, mathematics, computer science, behavioural science, decision theory, artificial intelligence, systems analysis, and industrial

psychology. Their topic list is remarkably similar to that of Bates.

- Ding, Chowdhury, and Foo used author cocitation analysis to study changes in information retrieval between 1987 and 1997. They examined the works of 39 highly cited authors, from which they were able to group together those working in similar areas. For the last half of the decade, they found that the authors could be grouped into the following clusters:
  - Information retrieval (IR) model;
  - IR techniques;
  - User perspectives of IR;
  - User (on-line) information seeking and retrieving behaviour;
  - Information seeking and retrieving model;
  - General IR theory;
  - IR system design and evaluation. These are all topics relevant to the area of basic information science research.
- McCreadie and Rice in the first of an extraordinarily detailed pair of articles, derived a general model of access to information. As part of their analysis, they have described the concept of 'information,' addressing not only the underlying concepts, but also the access-related issues, the common concepts of the information seeking process, and the influences and constraints on access to information. They characterise information in the following four ways:
  - A resource or commodity consisting of messages that can be produced, purchased, and distributed;
  - Data such as objects or tactile phenomena;
  - Representation of knowledge in the form of books and other media; and
  - A part of the process of communication, including human behaviour relating thereto. This work is extremely helpful in formulating a

general definition of information science because it characterises the raw material with which the discipline is concerned, *i.e.*, information.

- Summers, Oppenheimer, Meadows, McKnight, and Kinnell present the Institute of Information Scientists' criteria for information science, which is divided into three major areas: the information science core area, information management, and information technology. They comment that this viewpoint shows 'a relative lack of emphasis on understanding or knowledge of a theoretical basis to the profession," a sentiment with which we strongly agree. However, they go on to assert "it is probably unprofitable to try to draw a boundary around information science: the limits are constantly changing," and they feel that the best we can do is "point to major themes that fall within the scope of information science." Recall that our purpose here is a practical one: to define the discipline of information science so that it can be used on a daily basis by those tracking the field and its literature. This is a point of disagreement with Summers *et al.*; drawing a boundary around information science so that one can make intelligent decisions about what is and is not part of the field is exactly what should be done. When confronted with an article on basic research in information science that was refereed and published a respected journal such as *JASIS*, an Editor's decision requires little thought, and a boundary around the field is hardly needed. However, the decision is much more difficult when considering a paper from an area on the borders of the field. Having a good idea of the boundary can be extremely useful in this case. It must be stressed that a decision to exclude an article from inclusion in a publication such as ISA is no reflection on its intrinsic quality or of the quality of the journal in which it is published; it is simply a decision based on its relevance to the subject. We do appreciate and agree with the depiction by Summers *et al.* of the multidisciplinary nature of information science and their list of core activities in the field and the related fields that contribute to information science.

- Buckland feels that we should not argue over the meaning of 'information science,' but should recognise that information becomes important because of its relationship to knowledge. He notes that the field has strong historical roots in documentation and methods for handling, managing, and manipulating documents. He lists a number of subjects as appropriate for a graduate programme in information science, some of which, such as economics of information, information policy, and law, are outside the traditional research areas of the field.
- Finally, Saracevic, one his acceptance address for the 1997 ACM/SIGIR Gerard Salton Award for Excellence in Research, and the other an essay prepared for one of the 50th anniversary issues of *JASIS*, analysed and described many of the basic aspects of the information science field. Both of these stages are highly relevant to our subject here, and could be quoted extensively. I will resist this temptation, however, and give only some highlights. In his 1997 address, Saracevic argued that information science is a branch of computer science, with computer science providing the infrastructure, and information science the context. He emphasised that content is the most important property of literature, and that information science is concerned with the interface between people and literatures. Saracevic had expanded and refined these ideas, listing three general characteristics of information science: it is interdisciplinary, it is connected to information technology, and it has a strong social and human dimension. He suggested that today's information science discipline has developed from three major ideas—information retrieval, relevance, and interaction—and recommends that the following

newly emerging areas be included in today's concept of information science: interaction studies, multimedia and multilanguage information retrieval, digital libraries, and Internet searching. He specifically excludes such information systems as record or document management, decision support systems, as well as direct communication between persons from information science. Saracevic also comments that information can be treated narrowly, as messages, or broadly, as cognitive processing or understanding. He distinguishes between computer science and information science, placing algorithms relating to information under computer science and the nature of information and its use under information science. Saracevic's work, drawing heavily on some of the same work we have reviewed, is an excellent elucidation of the field of information science, and it has helped us greatly in our formulation of a working definition of the field suitable for ISA.

A recent proposal by ASIS president, Eugene Garfield, to change the name of ASIS is relevant to this study. Garfield's proposal is currently under considerable strong debate. It is not the purpose of this object to summarise or enter into that debate; however, the comments from the ASIS-L Listserv discuss the nature and definition of the field of information science:

- "Information science... is a fruitful meeting ground for those interested in both human and technological factors, and for both researchers and practitioners."
- "Information science should include a strong social science component—the sociology of information use and the economics of publishing."
- "We live in an information society in which more people must manage more information, which in turn requires more technological support, which both demands and creates more information. Electronic technology and information are mutually reinforcing phenomena, and one of the key aspects of living in

the information society is the growing level of interactions we have with this complex and increasingly electronic environment."

- "The core problem is the tight coupling of library science and information science—library science and libraries are the primary concrete reference points for assessing information science—rather than using many such reference points, including communications, information systems and computer sciences..."
- "There are few cognate disciplines that connect systems view with human view, and have practical experience in consciously assisting people to become informed, to the extent that library and information science does."
- "Social informatics is a part of information science... There is a huge body of understanding on how people relate to information, in various forms and channels, including computer-mediated, that is enormously valuable to any consideration of the social role of information technology."
- "There has been a tendency in both the academic and popular press to computer technology with automated information, that is, to assume that the 'information' part of information technology is supplied by the fact that computers are involved. This stance ignores the information itself that is stored within the computer and fails to note the many ways in which the character of that stored information interacts with the design of the computer information system and with how human beings process information and the acts of information seeking."

The foregoing comments are valuable because they represent the current thinking of professionals working in the field, many of whom feel passionate about their chosen discipline. Several of the comments clearly show that the field of information science is broadening, and the area of the social and behavioural interactions between information users is appropriate for inclusion into it.

A WORKING DEFINITION OF 'INFORMATION SCIENCE' FOR ISA

The picture that emerges of the discipline of information science is that of a field drawing some important concepts from a number of closely related disciplines and becoming a cohesive whole focussing on information. Williams' definition, Saracevic's discussion, Buckland's suggestions, and Rayward's historical derivations provide the most encompassing overviews of the field and well summarise the areas that ISA should cover.

The disciplines listed by Machlup and Mansfield are also particularly significant. However, we also agree with the thoughts of Harmon and Farradane, both of whom feel that information science should also concern itself with communications and behaviour among information users, and finally, we appreciate Giuliano's helpful distinction between information science and librarianship. Bates has quoted a long-standing definition of information science, observing that it has existed for at least the past 30 years. One might logically ask, therefore, why the present work was undertaken instead of simply adopting this definition for ISA.

Primarily, the reason is because the field has radically changed in the past 30 years. Thirty years ago, there were no on-line databases, no industry based on producing and selling them to users, and certainly no Internet. In today's world of the Internet and the World Wide Web, the concept of information has undergone a revolutionary transformation. We now must deal with new ways that information is recorded: HTML, XML, e-journals, e-books, 'zines, etc. Even the fundamental concept of a 'document' has been challenged by the Web. In such a radically changed environment, a new definition of information science is highly relevant. Particularly in today's Internetdominated culture, information science must concern itself with the behaviour of users and the means they use to satisfy their information needs. A large industry has grown up based on the selling of information and related products; although some pure researchers may contest the point, it seems apparent that the economics, markets, and players of this industry are also rightfully part of the practical side of the discipline of information science.

These concepts have been brought together into the following definition, to serve as the coverage statement for ISA:

- Information Science Abstracts covers the world's literature on information science—an interdisciplinary field concerned with the theoretical and practical concepts, as well as the technologies, laws, and industry dealing with knowledge transfer and the sources, generation, organisation, representation, processing, distribution, communication, and uses of information, as well as communications among users and their behaviour as they seek to satisfy their information needs.

LIBRARIANSHIP AND INFORMATION SCIENCE

Perhaps the greatest difficulty one faces in deriving a definition of information science is how to distinguish it from 'librarianship.' Saracevic concludes that information science and librarianship "are two different fields in strong interdisciplinary relations." He notes that current research on OPACs has had the effect of drawing the fields closer together because OPACs are increasingly using some of the principles developed by researchers in information science, and he also suggests that the emerging area of digital libraries will have a similar effect. Bates takes a similar view, noting that the phrase 'library and information science' has become common. She also notes that librarianship has a more service-oriented value system. Summers earlier work suggesting that information science is an academic discipline rather than a professional activity.

They also suggest that 'information scientists' add value to their work by evaluation, and that 'librarian' has a somewhat more negative image. These points can be hotly debated at length; we do not enter into such a debate here. To help resolve this question, the subject classification of *Library and Information Science Abstracts* (LISA) was examined. Table

1.1 lists some of the differences. The left column lists the subjects that LISA covers that ISA does not. They are more related to librarianship.

The right column lists the subject areas covered by ISA but not by LISA. These terms are more focused on 'pure' information science. In general, ISA concentrates on the theoretical and practical aspects of the knowledge transfer process and its supporting technologies, while excluding coverage of basic librarianship issues such as library facilities, budgeting, personnel management, etc.

Table 1.1 Librarianship *vs.* Information Science

Librarianship subjects	Information science subjects
Archives	Artificial intelligence, expert systems
Buildings	Basic information science research
Exhibitions	Behavioural sciences
Furniture	Fuzzy logic/fuzzy searching
Library organisation	Information industry/ marketplace
Library use and users	Information professionals
Loans	Information technologies technical aspects (*i.e.*, computing, Internet, telecommunications)
Management, budgeting, finance	Law/legislation/regulation
Materials	Natural language processing
Microforms	Reading (literacy)
Museums	Subject area databases
Non-print materials	Types of literature
Old and rare materials	
Promotions	
Removals	
Types of library staff	
Users (various types)	
Vehicles	
World librarianship	

INFORMATION SCIENCE MAP

Having arrived at a definition of information science, one can then enumerate the specific subjects that should be included in it, as well as the closely related fields, to yield a selection guide for ISA. It was helpful to express the results as a 'map' of the field, in which the basic subjects comprising information science are shown in a 'core' at the centre, with related fields surrounding the core.

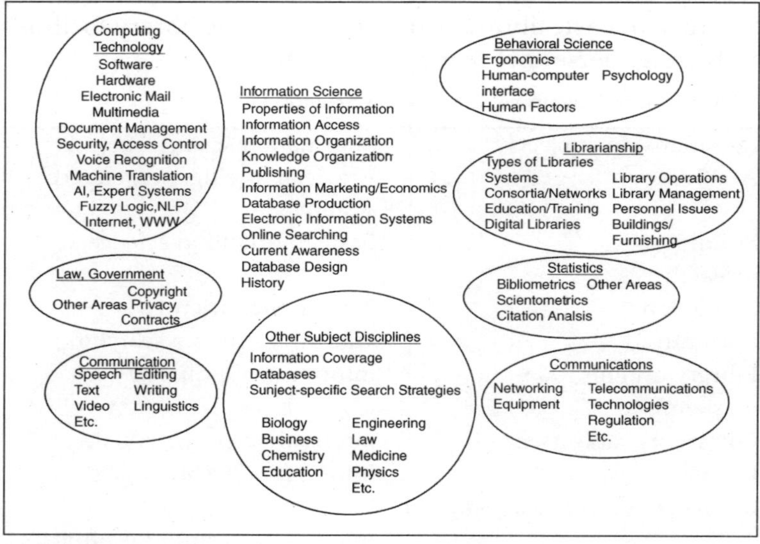

Fig 1.3 Information Science Map

The fields most closely related to information science are: computing technology, behavioural science, librarianship, statistics, communications, law and government, communication, and other subject disciplines. Each of these related disciplines, of course, has its own subject map, a portion of which would overlap information science. It is important to distinguish the subdisciplines that fall within the scope of information science and those that fall outside of it.

LITERATURE REVIEW

This is by no means the first use of a map to portray the relationships between a field and its related disciplines. For information science, several investigators have used bibliometric and other techniques to develop maps showing the relationship of information science to other fields.

The following studies are relevant and provide helpful background in this area:

- McCain used a codescriptor analysis of the 1993 issues of ISA and derived a mapping of the topics it covered. She concluded that ISA's subject coverage centers on three major areas: databases and information retrieval, information management, and implementation of information technologies in libraries. Mc- Cain also noted that the 1993 issues of ISA contain an unusual preponderance of patents.
- In an outstanding and extremely thorough study, White and McCain used author cocitation analysis to derive the subdisciplines of information science. They divided the field into two major specialties: experimental and practical information retrieval, and scientific communication as exemplified in bibliometrics, citation studies, and the like. Of special interest here are White and McCain's 12 subdisciplines, or specialties, in information science:
  - — Experimental retrieval;
  - — Citation analysis;
  - — On-line retrieval;
  - — Bibliometrics;
  - — General library systems;
  - — Science communication;
  - — User theory;
  - — OPACs;
  - — Imported ideas;
  - — Indexing theory;
  - — Citation theory; and
  - — Communication theory.

  White and McCain went on to map the authors working in each of these areas and also the changes in the maps that have occurred over the years. Two of their conclusions are especially relevant:

  - Information science is a versatile discipline that provides breadth and focus; and
  - It concentrates on 'the human—literature barrier.' Perhaps more than any other study, this work has helped crystallise the concepts presented here, especially in preparation of the map.
- Using citation analysis and ISI's *Journal Citation Reports*, Rice derived a list of 77 core journals in communication and library/information science. He then ranked and clustered the journals at several points during the decade 1977 to 1987, and concluded that there were two distinct subdisciplines in communication and three in library/information science. He also observed that changes occurred within each discipline but not across them.
- Using data from 1973 to 1975, Small also derived a list of core journals in information science and listed several of the most highly cited objects in the field, clustering them by subject. Using multidimensional scaling techniques, he was able to map information science and develop a citation network with closely related fields. He concludes that information science is relatively isolated from the social sciences.
- Yerkey and Glogowski studied the appearance of abstracts on library and information science topics in a range of bibliographic databases covering other subjects. They grouped the articles into seven major subject categories: librarianship, libraries, library materials, organisation and administration, reader services, technical processes, and information storage and retrieval. The largest number of postings they identified were concerned with library materials, organisation and administration, and reader services. They listed the most productive databases in each category and the search strategies they used for each of the seven categories. Because their study focused on non-information science databases, ISA and its competing databases were not included, although they obtained their search terms from

the subject classification used by *Library and Information Science Abstracts* (LISA).

MAP DERIVATION

In figure, the map of the field of information science, was derived using the definition of information science, some of the results of the studies, and empirical knowledge of the field as gained from lengthy experience. In the central core of the map, the major subjects and subdisciplines of information science are listed. Disciplines outside the central core overlap the core concepts of information science. The boundary between the core and external disciplines passes through the related fields; subfields relevant to information science are placed inside the boundary. All the central subjects and many of the related ones are appropriate for coverage in ISA.

A NEW TAXONOMY FOR INFORMATION SCIENCE

Abstracting and indexing (A&I) services have long provided their users with aids to retrieving information from their databases. The initial products of many A&I services were printed publications organised in separate parts similar to chapters in a book and containing helpful author and subject indexes. Each part contained abstracts of articles on a broad subject. Users could therefore simply scan a part to find items of interest. The subject index portions of such A&I publications were generally based on controlled vocabulary terms developed at considerable cost and effort by information professionals with expertise in the discipline covered by the publication.

Controlled vocabulary terms were frequently organised hierarchically into a thesaurus; the titles of the parts often became top-level terms in the thesaurus. When A&I publications became available as searchable on-line databases, the controlled vocabularies and main headings were usually made searchable by the search service vendors. These added-value features provided valuable assistance to searchers, especially before the full text was available on-line. Many database producers expended considerable resources in training searchers in how to use their thesauri.

TAXONOMIES IN THE WEB ENVIRONMENT

One of the concerns a database producer must address is whether to expend the considerable resources required to produce a taxonomy and then to index the information using it. When commercial on-line databases first appeared, professional searchers clamored for the inclusion of thesauri and subject classifications to help them formulate their searches. Database producers responded favorably, and many of the early on-line databases included controlled vocabulary fields drawn from thesauri, as well as fields containing subject classification codes. The experiences of the past few years in the Internet world have made it clear that the effort to include such data is still worth while.

When databases of information first became available on the Internet, many users felt that thesauri and subject classifications were no longer needed and would go the way of horseless carriages. After all, the theory ran, if everything is available on-line in full text, one would only need to enter the appropriate terms into a search engine, and the desired information would be retrieved. Inexperienced searchers quickly discovered the fallacy of this approach to information retrieval when they were faced with result sets numbering in the millions of hits, with the desired information buried somewhere in them.

It was soon recognised that, far from fading away in the Web environment, subject classifications and thesauri have become more important than ever, and organising information into subjects, or *taxonomies*, provided users with a significant improvement in retrieval. One of the earliest examples of the use of taxonomies was Yahoo!, which used trained information professionals to organise and categorise Web sites. Presently, in addition to a simple search box, most other search engines now provide an optional taxonomy that one can use for retrieval. The use of taxonomies has also spread to many large company intranets.

INITIAL CONSIDERATIONS

Hawkins described some of the history of *Information Science Abstracts* (ISA) and the development of a new definition of information science as well as a 'map' of the field showing the subjects central to it and their relationships to those on the periphery. The work described here is an implementation and a practical application of the definition of information science and its relationship to related disciplines. We have used his portrayal of the discipline to develop a new taxonomy for information science—and for ISA in particular—which accurately reflects the field as it exists today. These concepts have also been actively used to select relevant articles for abstracting in ISA.

ISA's subject classification scheme and controlled vocabulary last underwent modification in 1993, when minor revisions were made. Since, then, as the information field experienced many major and traumatic changes, the taxonomy became outdated. It contained many outmoded terms, and it was no longer able to accommodate the rapid technological and market changes affecting the information industry. ISA's editors and indexers found it difficult to use; consequently, one can infer that users had even more difficulty. A major flaw in the previous taxonomy was that each top-level part contained a subsection entitled 'General.' Over time, many abstracts had been placed in those subsections because the field had advanced and the taxonomy had not kept up with the changes. The result was that the taxonomy became virtually useless as an information retrieval tool.

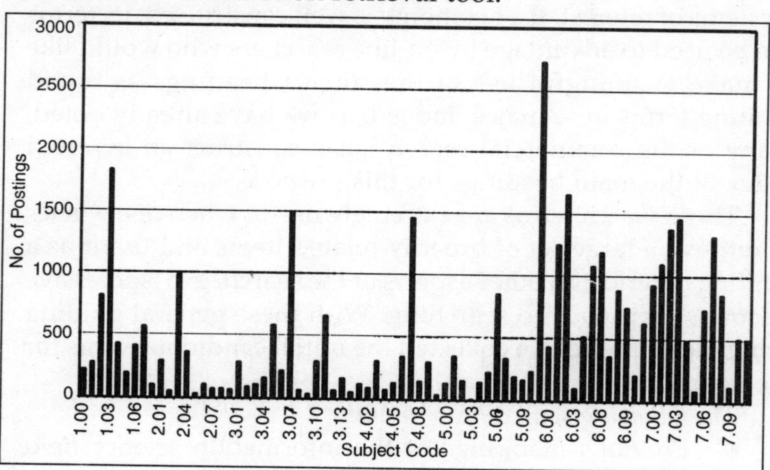

Fig 1.4 Subject Code Distribution—Former Taxonomy

Figure containing data taken from the master ISA production database, illustrates these observations. It shows the number of items posted in each part between 1992 and 2001. Note the wide variation in the number of items in the various parts.

The part with the most postings had over 2,700 items in it, and the one with the fewest had just four postings. Twelve parts had over 1,000 postings each, and 15 had fewer than 100 postings. These data provided strong evidence of the need for a new information science taxonomy, and the definition and map previously developed provided an excellent conceptual foundation for it.

TAXONOMY DEVELOPMENT PHILOSOPHY AND METHODOLOGY

In these days of Internet search engines that are widely used by end users, the structure of a taxonomy must be clear and logical, and the taxonomy must be easy to use if there is to be any hope of its enjoying significant acceptance. It must also be dynamic, easily updated, and able to reflect rapid changes and technological advances.

These principles are especially important for those users who scan the printed version of an A&I publication looking for items of interest. If a taxonomy is well constructed, its terms can be used to advantage by on-line searchers who would like to make meaningful use of the subject headings as broad limiting terms in searches. Indeed, as we have already noted, many of the commercial search hosts construct an inverted index of the main headings for this purpose.

These search terms are extremely useful when one wishes to retrieve a large set of broadly related items and use it as a limiting criterion on other aspects of the search, in a 'successive fractions' approach to searching. With these general guiding principles in mind, we collected the initial candidate terms for the taxonomy.

The following sources were useful:

- Previous mappings of the information science field by Hawkins and others;

- ISA's then-current list of descriptors;
- Lists of subject terms used by two other databases covering information science: R.R. Bowker's *Library and Information Science Abstracts* (LISA) and H.W. Wilson's *Library Literature;*
- The *ASIS Thesaurus of Information Science and Librarianship* compiled by Milstead;
- Scope outlines for two of the central publications in information science, the *Journal of the American Society for Information Science* (JASIS) and the *Annual Review of Information Science and Technology* (ARIST); and
- Appropriate parts of thesauri used by several other non-information science databases that contain information science terms.

Candidate terms were grouped and organised into a preliminary taxonomy containing 13 main headings. Before being accepted, many of them were checked by searching for them in the ISA database and observing the number of postings retrieved as well as the context in which the terms were used.

VALIDATION OF THE TAXONOMY

These six issues of ISA contain a total of 3,004 abstracts, so approximately 9,000 index assignments were made. Each abstract was assigned to the subject classification judged most relevant by the indexer. To simplify and speed this process, abstracts were given only a single classification number; in real life, of course, many abstracts have multiple classifications. Classification numbers were of the form *x.y,* where *x* is the 'main heading' and *y* is the 'subheading.' Abstracts for which the indexer felt that no appropriate classification existed were noted separately.

The classification assignments were assembled into a Microsoft Access database. If at least two of the indexers agreed on the classification of an abstract, then that assigned classification number was accepted as its correct indexing. Abstracts that were placed in different classifications by all three indexers as well as those that had been noted separately were reviewed, and the different points of view were either reconciled or appropriate modifications were made to the taxonomy to accommodate them. Using the Access database, we were able to quickly obtain data on the distribution of abstracts in each of the parts.

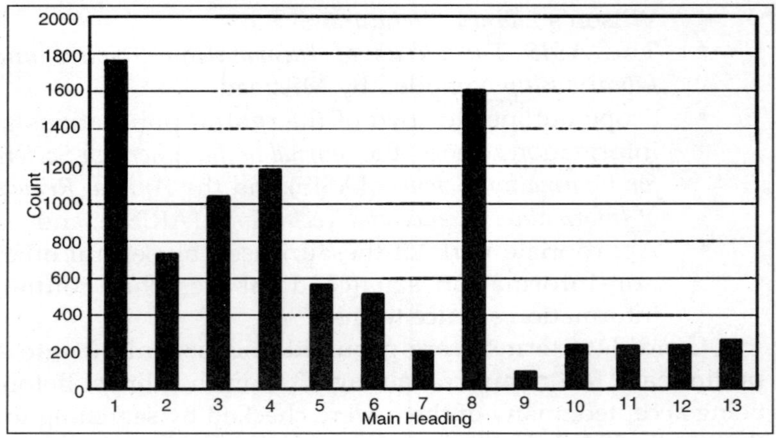

Fig 1.5 Results of First Verification Test

As a result, we were able to identify some extraneous categories and make the taxonomy more consistent by combining closely related categories into one. The distribution of part assignments falls into three broad groups. Which were concerned with basic information science research and electronic information systems, received over 35per cent of the assignments.

A second group of parts taken together, received about 45 per cent, and the remaining 20 per cent of the assignments fell into one of the other parts. This exercise was extremely helpful and revealing. The abstracts that could not be indexed pointed out several gaps in the preliminary taxonomy and the distribution shown in figure showed that further refinement of the parts would be appropriate.

INDEXING CONSISTENCY

The validation exercise also allowed us to measure consistency among the three indexers, shown in table.

Table 1.2 Overall Indexer Consistency

Indexer Agreement	Main and Subheadings		Main Headings Only	
	Number of total	Per cent	Number of total	Per cent
All 3 Agree	793	26.4	1069	35.5
A-B Agree	402	13.3	443	14.7
A-C Agree	424	14.1	434	14.4
B-C Agree	484	16.1	482	16.0
Only 2 Agree	1310	43.6	1359	45.2
All Disagree	901	30.0	576	19.2

Considering the full classification of each item, consisting of both main and subheadings, at least two of the indexers agreed on the classification of 70 per cent of the 3,004 abstracts from these issues of ISA. Because the distinction between many of the subheadings may be rather small, we also looked at the consistencies when only the main headings are taken into consideration. On that basis, consistency rose significantly, with 81 per cent agreement among the three indexers.

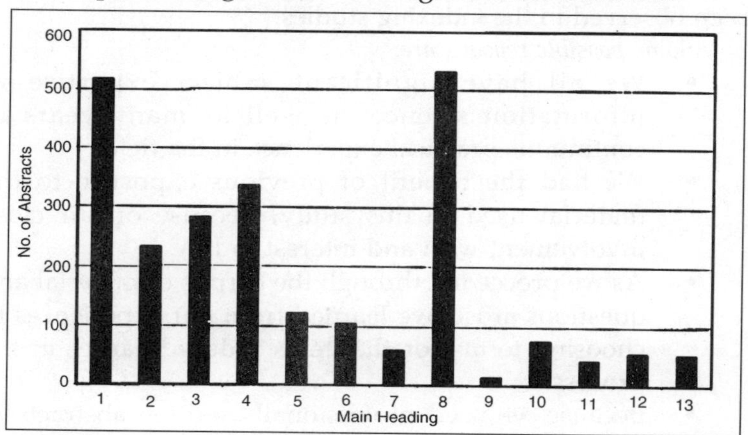

Fig 1.6 Main Heading Distribution—Two Indexers Agreed

Figure 1.6 shows the distribution of the classifications for the 2,428 abstracts where at least two indexers agreed on the main headings. This distribution confirmed our results from figure, showing that some parts could be combined and others should be considered for subdivision. A number of studies have observed that indexer consistencies generally do not exceed 50 per cent, and it has not changed significantly in the past 30 years. Sievert and Andrews found that 71 pairs of duplicate records in ISA had the same descriptors in about 48 per cent of the cases. Reich and Biever compared the descriptors assigned by different indexers from the same thesaurus in two agriculture databases and found that they averaged between 24 per cent and 45 per cent agreement in different samples.

Our results show significantly higher consistencies than those found previously—in 35 per cent of the cases, all three of us agreed on the assignment, and in an additional 45 per cent of the cases two of us agreed. Only in 19 per cent of the cases did all three of us disagree on the main heading assignment of an abstract. It is of interest to note that in this work, we assigned headings based on the abstracts alone, in contrast to most indexing studies. Despite indexing from the abstracts, the level of agreement among us is significantly higher than has generally been observed in the indexing studies.

Some possible reasons are:

- We all have significant subject expertise in information science, as well as many years of continuous practical experience in the field.
- We had the benefit of previous exposure to the material used in this study. Because of our close involvement with and interest in ISA.
- As we proceeded through the corpus of material and questions arose, we learned from our experiences in choosing terms for the items indexed earlier in the process.
- Because we used professionally written abstracts in our tests, we could be confident that each abstract clearly identified the main concepts of the articles they represented. Because the abstracts were brief and focused, there was less uncertainty as might have occurred if we had used complete articles.

FINAL TAXONOMY DEVELOPMENT AND USE

As we were proceeding through the first taxonomy validation, we began drafting revisions to correct deficiencies that were uncovered. Besides using our practical experience gained in the field and the experience of the validation test, we also examined the concepts propounded in Hawkins' ensured that they were incorporated into the taxonomy. A large part of this work was done empirically because ISA production continued as this research proceeded. We were thus able to take advantage of what authors in the field were publishing at that moment.

In the 'final' taxonomy, the 13 main headings were consolidated into 11, and a number of the subcategories were realigned as well. We also conducted a second validation test. Two of the authors manually indexed the May, June/July, and August 2001 issues of ISA, containing a total of 1,265 abstracts. The abstracts were copied from the master ISA production database to a separate Microsoft Access database, and the taxonomy was also converted to an Access database. A simple form displayed the title and abstract fields of each abstract and also provided an interface to the taxonomy, thus facilitating searching the taxonomy and entering the appropriate subject code.

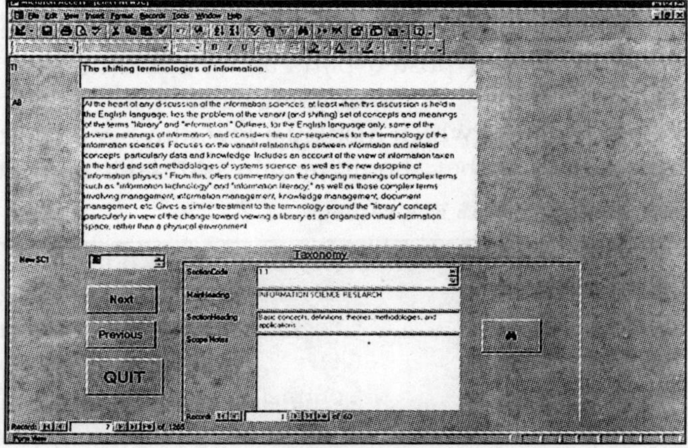

Fig 1.7 Indexer's Taxonomy Interface Form

This second test resulted in the taxonomy which became the 'ISA Taxonomy' at the beginning of 2002. To date, six issues of ISA, containing a total of 2,692 abstracts have been produced using it. Each ISA abstract is required to be assigned to at least one subject classification, and it can be assigned to up to three subject classifications. For the 2,692 abstracts, a total of 3,504 subject classification assignments were made. Their distribution is shown in figure.

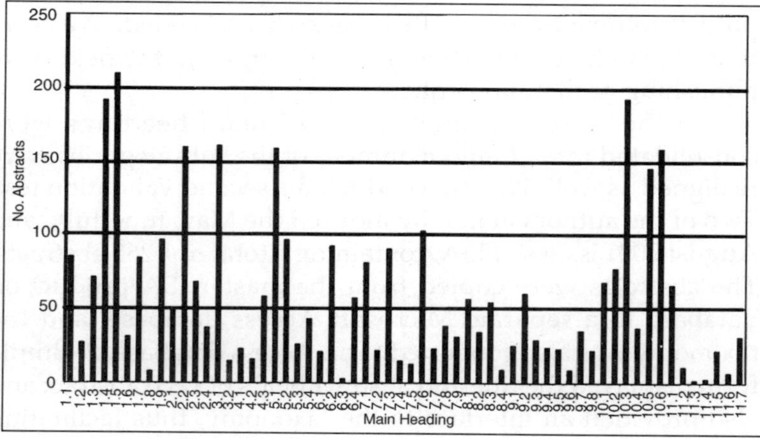

Fig 1.8 Classification Distribution Using New Taxonomy

Figure shows that the abstracts are well distributed over the 11 main parts and subsections of the taxonomy. There are a number of heavily posted parts as well as a number with only a few postings. We examined each of the subsections shown below, all of which display a low number of postings, and concluded that they should remain as discrete subsections.

Table 1.3 Subsections with Few Postings

1.8	Operations research/mathematics
6.3	Secondary publishing
8.4	Geographic information systems
9.6	News
11.3	Contracts and licensing
11.4	Liability issues
11.6	Information policies and studies

Most of these subsections represent significant or growing areas of information science or, because of the focus of the field, they are important, even though not many articles concerning them are currently being published. We must remember that our sample for this test included only 3 months' worth of data from the then most recent issues of ISA. In one or two cases, our years of experience in the field influenced our decision. We also considered the three most highly posted subsections to determine if they should be subdivided.

Table 1.4 Highly Posted Subsections

1.4	Information retrieval research
1.5	User behaviour and uses of information systems
10.3	Library automation, operations, and strategic planning

It is hardly surprising that these subsections are highly posted; because they represent the essence of the field. We therefore decided not to subdivide them.

ABSTRACTION, LIBRARIES, AND EFFICIENCY IN C++

Typically, the aim of a responsible programmer is to reasonably quickly produce a programme that correctly performs its task, does so with reasonable efficiency, and is maintainable. The key to fast development, correctness, efficiency, and maintainability is to use a suitable level of abstraction supported by good libraries.

Doing anything significant using only basic language features—that is, without the use of libraries—is unpleasant and unproductive. The key to elegant code and productivity lies in the production and use of libraries. That's true in any language. C++ provides features, such as classes, class hierarchies, templates, exceptions, and namespaces, to directly support library building and use.

The design of C++ favours systems programming and applications where performance is essential or where resources must be carefully managed. Consider a very simple example:

To read an unknown number of characters from a keyboard, file, or network connection, we need to set aside a fixed size buffer, read individual characters into that buffer, check that we are not overflowing our allocation, expand the buffer as needed and finally report the number of characters read back to the application. Doing all this 'by hand' is tedious and error prone. The C++ standard library provides types, such as string and istream that makes such operations trivial to write. For example:

```
string s;
in >> s; // 'in' is an input stream connected to a
data source
cout << 'I read'  << s.length() << 'characters';
```

A library provides a vocabulary for saying things directly and simply, correctly handling difficult low-level details in the implementation. For an istream, >> means read into; for an ostream, << means write to.

Typically, we want to read data with more complicated structure and store it in a form suitable for processing. For example, you might find code like this in software used for managing a movie theatre:

```
typedef map<string, vector<double> > Sales;// a data
structure for recording sales
Sales sales // sales of named movies
string movie; // name of movie
double take; // sales amount for movie
while (cin>>movie>>take) // read name and sales amount
sales[movie].push_back(take); // add sales amount
to movie record
```

This reads sales figures like this:

- Casablanca 123.75
- Tom-Jones 234.00
- Casablanca 79.45

and produces a map, that is a data structure that store elements so they can be accessed by indexing with a name string or by traversing the structure. Typically, a map is implemented by a red-black tree. Here each element in the map is a string with a vector of its associated sales figures.

You could illustrate the structure of resulting sales map like this:

- (Casablanca, (123.75, 79.45)) (Tom-Jones, (234.00)).

Given that, you can easily and efficiently compute all kinds of useful information, such as total sales for a movie, a list or all movies in alphabetical order, average sales for a set of movies. For example:

```
void print_totals(const Sales& s)
{
for (Sales::const_iterator p = s.begin(); s!=s.end();
++p)
cout << p->first << ': '
          << accumulate(p->second.begin(),p-
>second.end(),0.0) << '\n';
}
```

The for-statement visits each element of the map in order. The accumulate function is a standard library algorithm adding the elements of a sequence.

A call looks like this:

- print_totals(sales).

The output would be:

- Casablanca: 203.20
- Tom-Jones: 234.00

Maybe it's unrealistic to use a file title as a key when we could use a simple unique integer instead.

That would require minimal change to the code:

```
typedef map<int, vector<double> > Sales;
```

Only code that specifically relies on the key being a string would require further modification. In particular, the code fragment reading input and print_totals() remains unchanged.

The point of this simple example is to demonstrate to the flexibility and power of C++'s type system. When used in a well-designed library, such as the C++ standard library, the results can be simultaneously elegant and efficient. By elegance, I mean the ability to say things directly without lots of spurious notation. This is a major component of maintainability. Once a type is known, appropriate operations can be applied and appropriate notation defined. It is essential that a user – in particular a user writing a library – can define such types and operations on them. That's the basis of data abstraction, object-oriented programming, and generic programming.

C++ supports each of these programming styles, sometimes called 'programming paradigms' and allows a programmer to choose between them to best express solutions to various problems. This is often called 'multi-paradigm programming' and rests on the observation that many problems have more elegant or efficient solutions using one style than another, that no one style is superior in all cases, and that some problems are best solved using a combination of techniques. In particular, library writers benefit from the efficiency and flexibility offered my multi-paradigm programming.

In the example, I used simple generic programming as supported by the standard library. For example, the map and vector types are parameterised on their element types offer a variety of common useful operations, such as accumulate() and the iteration mechanism used. The elegance of such code comes from the compiler's ability to automatically choose the correct implementation of operations based on the declared type of each object. I did not have to litter my code with complicated names or inelegant type conversions to correctly select appropriate operations for each type of object. To compare, try rewriting the example in some other language or in some other style of C++.

Like elegance, efficiency comes from knowing the type of each object at compile time. Performance is probably not an issue. However, C++ is used in application areas where performance is essential, such as high-energy physics, gaming, and some embedded system applications. In such applications, programmes usually rely on highly tuned libraries providing fundamental operations. For example, there are vector and matrix libraries that make the performance of standard scientific and numeric computations as good as that of Fortran while significantly improving notation. For example, given a suitable library (such as Blitz++, MTL, uBLAS, or POOMA), you can write code such as this without loss of performance compared to Fortran:

```
Matrix<double,100,50> m;
Vector<double,100> v,v2;
// initialise m, v and v2
Vector<double,100> v3 = m*v+v2;
```

Furthermore, such libraries can express more advanced concepts, such as:

```
Matrix<int,sparse,10000,500> m2;
Matrix<complex<double>,UpperTriangular,100,50> m3;
```

The key to performance is that the declared types are used to guide the selection of implementations. The techniques used are standard part of C++ generic programming. In addition to being keys to ease of use, correctness, and performance, libraries are key to portability.

Like C, C++ contains many constructs that are implementation defined; that is, they detailed meaning varies from platform to platform. This is essential for low-level work and often essential for performance at the lowest level. However, if a programmer directly relies on such a feature, the result is clearly a non-portable programme. The obvious solution for most programmers is to use a library that provides an elegant and efficient platform independent to needed services.

There are many such libraries. Examples are BOOST and ACE. Using such libraries, a C++ programmer can use a range of systems unmatched by any other language except C, while retaining whichever degree of platform independence is desired.

To actually get work done, you need more than a language specification. For example, you need a compiler that works for your particular computer and operating system, libraries, manuals, tutorial material, and a technical community. This is one of C++'s strengths. C++ is supported by all major platform vendors and implemented according to its international (ISO) standard. It is therefore less vulnerable to changes of fashion and the whims of commercial organisations than proprietary languages.

How do you decide if the strengths of C++ are applicable to your particular problems? You basically have to listen to people who have tried it and try for yourself. In doing so, it is most important to seek out good libraries and use them, rather than making the—unfortunately common—mistake of trying to write everything yourself from the bare language features or using only a few functions remembered from the C standard library. In particular, for most people it is essential to raise the level of programming style from the tradition C and Fortran styles to a more abstract, yet still efficient, level relying on libraries. If no other library is relevant, the C++ standard library can often be used.

2

Innovative Practices in Library Services

INTRODUCTION

There has been a sea change in the concept of library and its similar institutions in this knowledge society. Information and Communication Technology (ICT) has been considered as the most instrumental factor for the change in the mode of delivery of library services.

General and traditional services of the library have been influenced with the introduction of new innovative practices, because of application of new ICT–based products and services. As a result, a new trend is observed in the process of delivery of services by the library organisations around the world. Most of the traditional services have also been replaced by new ICT-based services.

Majority of the libraries have been automated, while remaining ones are in the process. An attempt has been made in this chapter to highlight the innovative practices adopted in the delivery of the services at Manipur University Library.

MANIPUR UNIVERSITY LIBRARY

MANIPUR

Manipur is one of the smallest border states situated on the North-eastern part of India having an area of 22,327

Sq.Kms. which is divided into 9:1 ratio of Hill and Valley. The population of the state is 23, 85,634. The overall literacy rate of this multi-coloured and pluralistic society is 68.87 per cent. The number of educational institutions of lower and higher standards is increasing leaps and bounds at present throughout the state. These are run either by the Government or private individual. There are two Universities in Manipur *viz* Manipur University, Imphal and Central Agricultural University, Imphal.

MANIPUR UNIVERSITY

Manipur University was established on June 5, 1980 under the Manipur University Act, 1980 as a teaching cum affiliating University at Imphal with territorial jurisdiction of the whole of the state of Manipur. It is located at Canchipur an outskirts of Imphal, the Capital of Manipur. It is easily accessible by National Highway-39 and by Mayai Lambi Road. The primary objective of the University is to pursue higher education and research. The University has been upgraded to the status of a central university by an act of Parliament since, 13th October, 2005.

MANIPUR UNIVERSITY LIBRARY

The Library of the Jawaharlal Nehru University Centre of Post Graduate Studies, Imphal, which was established in 1972, was amalgamated to Manipur University in 1981. The Manipur University Library is at the centre of the University Campus.The MU Library was declared as one of the INFLIBNET nodes in the first phase in the year 1993.

The Library has completed the works related to creation of Database of Books, Serials, Thesis and new entries are added to the existing databases from time to time. It also became a part of the UGC-INFONET: e-Journal Consortium since, 2003.

Building

The library building is of three storied to carry out all the functions and services of the same.

Collection

The library collection is growing steadily covering both in the form of published and unpublished materials. As on 31st July, 2007 the collection of the library was as follows;

- Total No. of Books 1, 31,368
- Total No. of Journal Title: 228
- Newspapers: 21
- Magazines 5
- Bound Volumes 1000
- e-journals title 4000
- Manuscripts 33
- Other e-resources (Floppy, CD, DVD etc.,) 200
- Theses/Dissertations 2587

User Community

The teachers, research scholars, PG students, officers and non-teaching staff of the University are the regular members of the library.There are a total of about 3550 regular members of the library. Besides a number of visitors who are not registered are also visiting the library to avail the facilities. The library has become the referral library of the state. About 300 visitors visit the library daily.

Library Staff

The present staff positions of the library are as follows:

- Top level professionals 3
- LIS professionals (Permanent) 16
- Other Staff (Permanent) 9
- Other Casual/Part time staff 7

AUTOMATION STATUS

Manipur University Library initiated its automation process since, 1993.Also it was declared as one of the INFLIBNET nodes in the first phase in the same year.

The present automation status of the library is as follows:

- Creation of Database of Books, Serials, Theses and new additions.

- Retro conversion of the databases created in CDS/ ISIS into SOUL package.
- Total database contains records of about 95,000 materials.
- About 35 computers including 18 meant for staff are used for automation work.
- Installation of OPAC (Online Public Access Catalogue);
- Installation of Bar code system in circulation system;
- Other Administrative aspects of the library.

MU LIBRARY SERVICES

The teacher, research scholars, students and the staff are the main users of the library.The majority of the Post Graduate students of the University depend on the collection and the services of the library. For convenience of the readers, the service of the library is made available from 9AM to 7 PM on all working days and from10 AM to 3.30PM on Sundays. Besides the books in the stacks for lending, the library has a special collection of textbooks for issue and reference purpose in the reading room. Reprographic services are provided to the readers on nominal charges to enable them to copy the required materials. The library provides Internet services to the readers for browsing the required materials.

GENERAL SERVICES

The general services of the library include:

- General administrative works
- Procurement of information resources to serve the users
- Room setting making more conducive to the users
- Infrastructure development in the tune of the demands of the users
- Issue and return of books, circulation of reference and journal materials and other materials for reading room service
- Basic training on the handling of new services as a part of users education programme

- Reservation of documents
- Reprographic services and other bindery works
- Stack arrangement and maintenance

TRADITIONAL SERVICES

The following traditional services have been prevailing in the library till date:

- Organisation of Knowledge resources
  - Classification following CC 6th Edition
  - Cataloguing adopting CCC
- Circulation of reading materials following Browne charging System
- Reprographic Service
- Reading Room Service
- Reference Service
- Referral Service

INNOVATIVE PRACTICES

Since, the very beginning of the starting of automation work when the library became a node of INFLIBNET in 1993, new innovative practices have been introduced in the delivery of services by the library.

Such practices can be summed up in the following ways:

- E-commerce and its application in the general administrative activities of the library with the use of new ICT enabled services, such as—
  - Contacting people, vendors, publishers, suppliers, etc;
  - Submitting requirements of the holding to be procured electronically;
  - Replacing manual clerical works by computers, etc;
- Creation of databases of the boou using library application packages like CDS/ISIS and SOUL;
- Automation of different house keeping operations of the library;
- Provision of services in electronic environment;
- Developing Local Area Network.

- Participation in network programmes and enhancement in the resource sharing activities, providing reliable access to the Online Union Catalogue of documents of different libraries.
- Internet connectivity enabling the users access to global information resources.
- *Joining the UGC*: INFONET-e:journal Consortium enabling the academic and research community access to more than 4000 foreign journal.
- Improving existing service conditions.
- Helping towards promoting e-learning as well as e-literacy among the scholars.
- Improving the efficiency and effectiveness of the library.
- Making library management more systematic to serve the users conducively.
- Changing towards overall development of the library.
- Adopting Barcode System in circulation system.

Currently, users of the MU Library are getting in following Services:

- Access to the full text of the journals.
- Easy access to the journals.
- Assistant from the professionals to use the e-resources made available through consortium.
- Provision of up to date information.
- Saving time in searching desired information.
- Fulfilling the need of the users.
- More information on career opportunities and jobs.

3

Reinventing the Reference Librarian

Librarianship is a profession which strives to link people with information in ways which are efficient, equitable, timely and meaningful. Along with the strong focus on access, it also boasts an extensive tradition of educating users to find, use and evaluate the information they require from a diverse palette of sources via an equally diverse range of formats, i.e.: to teach people how to become information literate.

As the world races towards an information explosion of unprecedented magnitude, this role becomes more critical than ever before. Academic librarians are, and always have been, an inherent part of the teaching and learning cycle in their institutions. However, as the emphasis shifts from discipline-rich teaching to one of processoriented learning, librarians now find themselves at a critical juncture—do they maintain the status quo of tried and tested academic librarianship or seize the new and somewhat ambiguous responsibility of pedagogical leadership?

With information literacy as their ticket, librarians have an opportunity to enter a different teaching and learning arena and to carve out a challenging, unique role in the world of academia—in point of fact, to reinvent themselves in a new image. It is this principle which forms the premise of this paper. Nonetheless, it would be foolhardy to suggest that such a change could or would come easily, or occur unchallenged. Resistance is an anticipated by-product of any change to the status quo, particularly if and when a condition is perceived as unchangeable, or the change deemed unnecessary. Therefore, as librarians undertake a more proactive teaching and learning role, the change will affect all those in the higher education arena as surely as it will affect the microcosm of librarianship itself. As librarians strive for different outcomes, the traditional beliefs, understandings, expectations and practices of all involved will be challenged. The ways in which these challenges are managed will determine the success of librarians' educational re-engagement at personal, professional and institutional levels in terms of perception, satisfaction, challenge, advancement and reputation.

With the emphasis upon pedagogical integrity and cohesiveness, the development of information literate students with the capacity to become lifelong learners will be the ultimate marker of success. If academic librarians *are* to exert a dynamic influence on the teaching and learning agenda, what are the challenges to be faced, by whom, how and to what end? This chapter seeks to unpick, rather than resolve, the issues - indeed, many of these issues have no simple solutions and will no doubt be the source of much further discussion and debate for some time to come.

WHAT CHANGES

What are the actual 'unchangeables' of the academic librarian's role and what do we believe to be non-negotiable functions of an academic library? What are the *true* boundaries of our role as librarians and how far can, and should, they be tested? Which values, beliefs and services are anchored in a chapter of time and experience which has passed, and which retain little relevance in the new information dimension which confronts higher education today? These are questions which need to be answered. As Starr asserts, the politics of success demand only that librarians possess a high level of esteem, have the courage to be idealistic and see themselves in broad conceptual terms.

PROFESSIONAL CHANGES

A transformation of the academic culture within tertiary institutions is essential. Such a transformation will necessarily need to promote academic librarians as intrinsic members of the teaching and learning process with knowledge and skills comparable to that of their academic colleagues and the capacity to make equal contribution. Broadly, this process should involve the identification of those barriers which are practical and those which are purely historical and/or philosophical.

Specifically, it requires a reassessment of the ways in which labels such as 'support service' and 'general staff' affect perceptions of value and pathways to participation, and how the conferring of faculty status opens up new opportunities to librarians. It also involves a review of pay scales. It is necessary to explore these issues afresh against the backdrop of the role of the academic librarian and information literacy. For the purpose of this discussion, the term 'faculty status' will encompass any category of employment in tertiary institutions which places librarians within an industrial bracket equivalent to, but not necessarily the same as, that conferred upon academic teaching staff.

Accredited Status

The debate regarding the industrial status of librarian's features periodically in the literature of librarianship but with little consensus of opinion. Argument ranges over conditions of employment, alignment to standards and criteria, job satisfaction and performance, and the affect of status on the attitudes, expectations and perceptions of faculty with regard to their library peers. It also ranges over issues relating to organisational and functional difficulties, the economic ramifications of such status and the commitment of time and effort in academic endeavours not viewed as fundamental to librarianship.

Institutional acknowledgment, of an industrial nature, that academic librarians are partners in the educational process varies considerably in form from country to country and, indeed, from institution to institution. In Australia, the status of academic librarians is predominantly that of 'general staff' which aligns with the *Higher Education Worker* (HEW) levels in academic institutions. However, despite the best of intentions, levels of employment for, and remuneration of, librarians across the Australian higher education sector are not standardised. The same is true for the United Kingdom and the United States.

The antagonists, while quite vehement in their opposition to the idea of faculty status for academic librarians, rarely look beyond traditional arguments which have at their core somewhat erroneous logic and subjective opinion. Cronin argues that the "tenure and the paraphernalia of the academic calling have nothing whatsoever to do with the praxis of librarianship", a view supported by Kehde who asserts that "history has shown that it's impossible and a waste of time and effort for librarians to compete on this field", stating that librarians "aren't scholars, intellectuals, teachers, or writers". Cronin goes even further by suggesting that the conferment of faculty status upon librarians actually invites a mockery of the academic professoriate and consumes an unacceptable amount of institutional resources in the process.

He contends that: "If all the time spent writing unforgettable articles for journals of often questionable quality and compiling bloated dossiers were converted into service delivery" everyone would be much better off. It is to this issue of service delivery and librarianship as a service profession that the argument consistently returns. Analysts maintain that faculty status provokes competing expectations and responsibilities and that greater demands on time make it difficult to reprioritise library-related activities and tasks which are consistent with librarian's jobs during a standard working day.

Time, in short, would be better spent buying, cataloguing and issuing books. Despite objections of this nature, there is little evidence or substantive data to indicate that the possession of academic or faculty status is, or would, be detrimental to the information literacy efforts of the emerging academic librarian. For every negative argument, there is an oppositional view which asserts that faculty status creates greater opportunities for developing teaching and learning partnerships and establishing collaborative relationships between librarians and academics. Furthermore, the protagonists' view contends that librarians become more active participants in the governance of teaching and learning and the educational communities in which they work, and that faculty status, owing to research and publishing expectations, creates the potential for intellectual vibrancy in academia and librarianship.

Riggs and Oberg believe that librarians with faculty status and rank are generally more likely to be perceived as peers by their academic colleagues. Oberg argues that it gives librarians "the wherewithal to relate to faculty and administrators as colleagues and peers, not as subalterns and handmaidens...". He further states that "student and faculty contacts may be seriously degraded when librarians are perceived as clerks and not as experts and coequals", a view supported by Muronaga and Harada, who argue that, in these relationships, "a sense of parity is critical where each person's contribution to an interaction is equally valued, and each person shares power in making decisions".

For Schroeder, faculty status for librarians provides "entree into the educational process on an equal footing, as an invited or occasional guest. She argues that it provides a link for "working cooperatively together and for improved communication to promote the educational process", acknowledges 'membership' to the sphere of educational authority and practice at the most elementary level, and creates a climate of trust and mutual respect. Schroeder also believes that in no way does faculty status detract from, or debase the position of, academic librarians on campus.

Salary and Remuneration

Schroeder also reasons that equal remuneration is essential to the survival of the academic librarian of the future, and links status and salary to political power and institutional influence, a position which echoes the long-held belief of the UK Association of University Teachers (AUT) that the salary and grading of academic-related staff should be linked to that of academics. Nevertheless, while linked classifications may be desirable, the issue of individual and institutional remuneration is one which cannot be viewed in isolation of broader industrial conditions.

In Australia recent moves have indicated that a change may be forthcoming, and sooner rather than later. In December 1998, the New South Wales (NSW) Pay Equity Enquiry found that "there had been no full work value consideration of librarianship for the past 25 years historical resistance to the recognition of librarianship as a profession which meant that rates for librarians were, and had been for a long time, lower than for other public sector professionals". The Report concluded that the evidence established that librarians' work was underpaid.

After a major test case of the principle, lodged by the Public Service Association, the NSW Industrial Relations Commission ruled that librarians' responsibilities have been historically undervalued despite significant increases in their skills. In response, the Commission granted substantial pay rises of up to 26 per cent and "formalised the professional status of librarians by placing them industrially on an equal footing with lawyers, engineers and other professional categories". While the response from within the profession was predictable, the backlash from outside the profession is indicative of the general misperceptions of librarians and their requisite expertise. The disagreeable but enduring stereotype of the genteel, helpful librarian was expressed clearly by a journalist for the Sydney Morning Herald.

McGuiness described librarianship as a sedentary and comfortable occupation based on a mixture of elementary skills and 'soft' science. He concluded his portrait by categorising these 'easy to learn' skills as "quite trivial matters of classification and indexing, simple book handling, book issuing and searching databases". Not surprisingly, Mr McGuiness was the worthy recipient of a barrage of censure and, although it is easy to dismiss his comments as ignorant and uninformed, it is a position which echoes a widespread view. Regrettably, it is a view such as this which nurtures a disadvantageous status quo for academic librarians by keeping them tied to conventional processes and procedures, and out of reach of new roles and responsibilities.

DEVELOPMENTAL CHANGES

At Think Tank III, Dupuis and Watts re-evaluated the teaching role of academic librarians in light of the major information literacy initiatives witnessed in higher education over the past ten years. The key conclusion arising from that forum stressed that "librarians are still struggling for validation in ... roles as educators, both within and outside of profession". This 'struggle' is destined to continue unless some significant attitudinal and organisational changes take place. As an acknowledgment of the extensive role librarians play in teaching in academic institutions, and on the strength of their key role in teaching and learning, the Institute of Learning and Teaching (ILT) in the UK strongly encourages the involvement and membership of librarians.

Membership to the ILT requires evidence of involvement in 5 key areas:

- Teaching and the support of learning;
- Contribution to the design and planning of learning objectives;
- Assessment and giving feedback to students;
- Developing effective learning environments and students' learning support systems; and
- Reflective practice and personal development.

That academic librarians in the UK are eligible for membership in an association based on such criteria sends a clear signal regarding the future of teaching and learning in higher education. With a powerful and critical role to play as educational leaders, librarians must equip themselves with the skills and knowledge to proactively engage in these five areas.

Pedagogical Skills

Schroeder, predicts that universal acceptance within tertiary institutions that librarians not only 'teach in the traditional sense' but also 'inspire, guide, and support students and peers' as well will lead inevitably to an appreciation that reference librarians are, or should be, the most qualified people to lead in the education of information literate students.

The question remains: Will academic librarians be ready, willing and able to pick up the mantle? Until recently, any curriculum development has been traditionally viewed as the sole province of the teaching academic. It needs now to be presumed likewise for the academic librarian, by academia at large, library administration and by librarians themselves. However, while the concept of curriculum development is neither difficult to grasp, nor necessarily to accomplish, librarians themselves have not traditionally posed this role to themselves *in these terms*. The time has come for librarians to embrace the responsibility and work to engender trust and merit in their contribution to curriculum design, delivery and evaluation. In this way, they will be able to work with faculty 'to introduce information literacy education at the point of greatest relevance". It is not enough to support the concept in principle; rather, libraries, the profession and librarians themselves must strive to transform the principle into practice. As a stronger nexus develops between the two traditionally distinct areas, librarians must be strongly positioned as key educators in the teaching and learning environment, and empowered with an educational competence and professional confidence equal to that of their academic peers.

The latter is as critical to their own well being as it is to increasing their influence in the educational arena. The pressure is mounting on faculty teaching staff to refashion the academic curriculum in order to meet the new learning needs of students, including the embedding of process-based generic skills. As academics ask less 'what *is* information literacy?' and more 'how do I *teach* it?' the librarian's position as a consultant and proactive participant in the teaching and learning cycle becomes more critical than ever before. Academic librarians, therefore, need to not only be conversant with pedagogy and practice—they must be *ahead* of the game. The most pressing issue still to be universally addressed is the fundamental need for training for academic librarians themselves, and for training which is proactive and responsive to specific needs of librarians.

Information Literacy Research

Design and delivery of instructional programmes relating to the use of libraries and information has long been an accepted role for libraries. However, as the nature of the contribution changes, the accepted role of the academic librarian becomes increasingly ambiguous. Rather than being seen as a negative consequence, this ambiguity should be considered as a positive opportunity for librarians to recreate themselves within a unique professional framework which includes knowledge creation. As the territory expands, Bruce believes that the 'directions being established will potentially make information literacy research a significant source of knowledge for information professionals and educators".

The reasons generally cited as barriers to the conduct of comprehensive research by practitioners in the field relate to issues of time management, time allocation, workload, financial remuneration and recognition of the worth of the endeavour to the organisation. As the work of Boice, Scepanski and Wilson concludes, lack of time is not the essential issue; rather, they noted that 'the publishing efforts of librarians... suffered less from actual lack of time than for insecurities, entrenched work habits, inefficient use of time, and unsupportive workplace cultures".

Mitchell and Reichel believe that librarians who regularly undertake research are 'more receptive to change and have more effective relationships with other faculty than do those who do not do research" and that research 'promotes advancement and recognition for librarians". While it may be difficult for librarians to match the quantitative production and delivery standards of academics, they do possess the requisite skills to conduct quality research and are in a unique position to do so if given the time, encouragement and recognition for undertaking this professional pursuit.

STRUCTURAL/ORGANISATIONAL CHANGES

Akeroyd believes that it is critical for libraries to create a 'leaner, meaner workforce which is well paid, occupies the high ground of knowledge transfer", and which undertakes to outsource and/or automate the mundane and routine tasks of the academic library. The challenge is how to build a 'new-look information organisation which comprises of a mixture of professionals for whom information literacy dictates changing boundaries and alliances". If the driving information literacy force is the reference librarian, then it is specifically the realm of reference service that one must interrogate more closely, with a view to identifying ways to better facilitate the efforts of the teaching librarians.

While many believe that reference and information desk services will continue to be important, some people believe that the services should function simply as specialised add-ons to basic teaching in information literacy, a view supported by Kohl who maintains that the emphases on reference services and instruction should be reversed with 'instruction seen as the primary means of providing intellectual access to the collection". He predicts that current and future educational, economic and technological pressures will demand that academic libraries move beyond the traditional model and argues that traditional reference services, in fact, undermine information literacy goals as they encourage dependent rather than independent users, and force reference librarians to mediate a system continually disrupted by the traditional reference desk service.

There is a concern that organisational restructuring and more functionally defined remuneration will create variant 'classes' of staff within one library with differing working conditions and compensation. This view highlights the potential for internal organisational friction and disharmony between reference librarians and their library colleagues who, by virtue of their role in the organisation do not have similar opportunities. However, while these are certainly issues with which organisations may need to struggle in the short-term, the experience of many organisations would illustrate that they are not insurmountable.

WAYS AND MEANS

As the design and delivery of tertiary education changes, so will academic-related staff increasingly become involved alongside academic staff in making a direct contribution to the provision of higher education. In this capacity, the academic librarian must become a proponent of exemplary practice in the design, delivery and evaluation of effective curriculum and quality teaching and learning experiences. They must also become confident, competent practitioners and leaders in not only information literacy education but also in those areas associated with broader generic skills development.

This reconceptualisation of oneself as directly involved in, rather than as an ancillary supporter of, the educational process requires support, courage and, to some degree, a leap of faith. As Oberg states, to survive in an era of rapid change, librarians must become 'quickwitted, creative risk-takers'. It is timely for academic libraries to now review and re-evaluate their traditional roles and services in order that they may firmly establish their new place in the educational continuum.

These roles can be categorised in three main areas with three main keys to success:

- *Attitudinal:* Pertaining to those areas which relate to raising the status and profile of teaching librarians in higher education;
- *Behavioural:* Pertaining to those areas which relate to engaging the teaching librarians in the decisionmaking processes within tertiary institutions; and
- *Relational:* Pertaining to those areas which relate to building collaborative and cooperative curricula partnerships with academic staff.

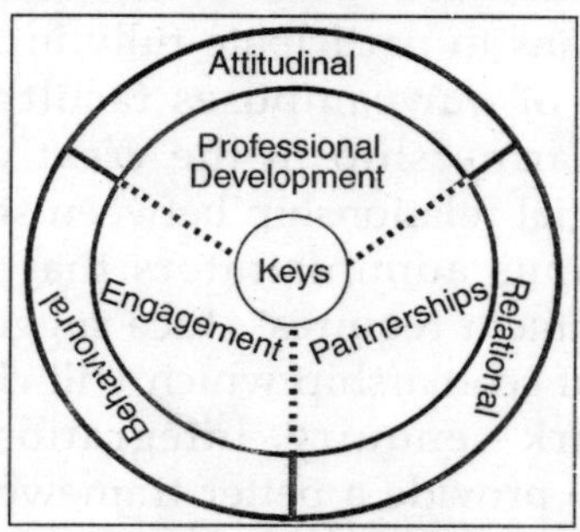

Fig 3.1 Keys to Change for Teaching Librarians

ATTITUDINAL CHANGES

Attitudinal changes must first take place *within* the profession. Until academic librarians cease to *question* their rightful place in the educational process and begin to see themselves as educators who are integral to the educational process, it will be impossible to convince others that they have anything of value to offer. If the academic community, and society at large, has a narrow definition of librarianship, then it might be argued that it is the profession itself which is responsible for altering this view by producing, enabling and supporting librarians who can function intellectually and creatively.

It could also be argued that the change must first happen philosophically and practically at an individual level. However, as academic librarians do not work in a vacuum, Peacock sees that some responsibility must rest with parent organisations to provide adequate, appropriate and timely support for a cultural and functional shift of this nature and to 'open pathways to accreditation which recognise the contribution made by academic librarians to teaching and learning". This chapter argues that faculty status provides a link for librarians and academics to work more effectively and cooperatively together to elevate the educational process. It acknowledges 'membership' to the sphere of educational authority and practice at the most elementary level and creates a climate of trust and mutual respect.

Oberg concludes that "tiered reference and faculty status encourage librarians to participate fully in the scholarly life and governance of our campuses faculty status accords librarians full partnership in the creative, cooperative, synergistic, collegial relationship between students, teaching faculty and campus administrators that today's volatile academic environment requires". Rice suggests that the four emerging types of scholarship which will change the nature of academic work—enquiry, integration, teaching and application—may provide a better framework within which academic librarians with faculty status can work. However, if, as Kingma suggests, the academic model is judged *unsuitable* for librarians, then perhaps it is time to develop a new model that more appropriately serves the needs of librarians, students and academics in an era where information literacy has become a critical element in the learning cycle. Regardless of the form or label given to such a status, academic librarians must be viewed as partners with academic staff in providing higher education, and equivalent pay and grading be an assumed consequence of such an outcome. It is naive to presume that salary increases and a change in status alone will open pathways to participation in teaching and learning. The issues do, however, raise many fundamental questions regarding the impact of the academic librarian upon information literacy initiatives and learning outcomes in higher education which require closer scrutiny.

To summarise:

- Do academic libraries exist just to 'support' the educational missions of universities, or to actively contribute to and/or participate in them?
- Is the work of a teaching librarian essentially different from that of an academic?
- Does parity of status and salary necessarily ensure librarians will be viewed and treated as equal partners and contribute to their influence in curricula reform and development, or does it have a negative impact on library service levels and performance?
- Would the assignation of faculty status upon one particular group of librarians create divisive and disharmonious working relationships and environments?
- Can librarians be teachers, scholars and service providers without compromising either?
- Are the achievements of teaching librarians afforded equal prominence, significance and prestige in the academic environment, and should they be?
- Will life on the academic periphery become increasingly more difficult for libraries, particularly in economic rationalist times, when funding and personnel are hard to come by?

Regardless of official contracted status—academic or otherwise—institutions of higher education must begin to recognise the changing role of the academic librarian, acknowledge the critical nature of their contributions to teaching and learning, and encourage, facilitate and reward their participation in scholarly pursuits.

To this end, it may be timely to review such areas as:

- Performance criteria and promotional incentives;
- Pay structures and renegotiation of employment classifications;
- Sustained and timely professional development opportunities;
- Workload and renegotiation of duties; and
- Equal access to fringe benefits such as bursaries, scholarships, release time etc.

Along with individuals and organisations, professional library associations also have a role to play in advancing the role of academic librarians in higher education. Ideally, too, academic librarians will vie for entry into broader educational associations, and participate proactively in wider educational forums and debates.

For all groups—individuals, organisations and associations—extensive, creative and targeted marketing and promotion can serve to raise client awareness, inform or alter opinion, and open new opportunities for all teaching staff, academic or otherwise. Such action will provide the opportunity to 'professionalise our practice and to advertise our role in the teaching and learning context".

Key—Professional Development

The key to affecting attitudinal change, both internal and external to the library organisation, is professional development and rigorous self-evaluation. Librarians must embrace and undertake stringent individual and organisational self-development and self-evaluative processes and procedures which strengthen their credibility, substantiates their educational role and instils the trust of the academic community in their educational ability.

Such processes may include:

- Peer review of teaching;
- Ongoing contribution to information literacy and teaching and learning research;
- Ongoing contribution to the literature across multiple disciplines;
- Commitment to ongoing postgraduate study, such as graduate certificates and doctoral studies, in disciplines such as adult learning, and teaching and learning in higher education.

Librarians require a new palette of tools, skills and conceptual understandings to move beyond the traditional model of library instruction, and an increasing variety of options are now being developed which meet the specific needs of teaching librarians. This is a view also clearly stated by Dr Alan Bundy, President of the Australian Library and Information Association (ALIA), in an address to LIS students:

- It is an issue for all librarians... as they assert their role as full partners in the teaching and learning process... This means that librarians need to become conversant as early as their preservice education with pedagogical concepts, issues and how people learn. They may also need to develop the capacity to teach.

Todd believes that, although the development of systematic and explicit teaching strategies is complex, time-consuming and challenging, it is by developing these skills that librarians will "contribute to qualitatively different learning experiences and positive learning outcomes". Professional development courses such as *EduLib* and *TSISL* deliver curricula designed to respond to the condition of being a teacher without a cohort. Specifically, these courses address those key areas of teaching competency which require a degree of training and/or additional support, summarised by the ILT as reflective practice, professional development, variant teaching methods, the planning of teaching and learning events and assessment, and the creation of learning environments. Also required is education and training in pedagogical theory, evaluative practices and effective presentation methods. Such content is often accessible to librarians via graduate certificate programmes in adult learning or higher education, and library teaching staff should be encouraged to take part in professional development alongside their academic colleagues; indeed, more librarians are now availing themselves of the opportunity. Such courses will become increasingly relevant to librarians as the curriculum developers respond to changing client demographics, needs and expectations.

In some cases, these opportunities have spawned significant gain for librarians. At QUT, as part of a recent human resources initiative regarding linked classifications, the University's *Graduate Certificate in Higher Education* can now be used to demonstrate attainment of a high level of knowledge in teaching and learning by those librarians who wish to achieve 'soft-bar' promotion from a Level 6 to a Level 7.

Provision of, and access, to sustained and specialised professional development will require:

- Considered planning.
- Access at time of need.
- Design, development and delivery by qualified teachers/facilitators with appropriate expertise; and, last but not least.
- Organisational support in the form of release time and funding.

The results of a national study on the effects of professional development and teachers' learning found the latter to be the major challenge.

The researchers' state that:

- Our results suggest a clear direction... in order to provide useful and effective professional development that has a meaningful effect on teacher learning and fosters improvements in classroom practice, funds should be focused on providing high quality professional development experiences.

The same is true for professional development for teaching librarians in the academic environment. If Levy's prediction comes to fruition, and information specialists define their professional identity primarily in terms of *educational* practice, then a new challenge presents itself to professional developers, educators and library and university administrators to develop programmes which meet their needs. They should stand on notice and rise to the challenge.

BEHAVIOURAL CHANGES

As Rader indicates, to develop information literate graduates, 'librarians will have to break out of their traditional reactive mode become leaders and innovators in their interaction with faculty, students and administrative leaders". They do, categorically, need the time, support and capacity to 'teach classes, design curricula, or sit in the seats of educational power and control".

If the teaching and learning of generic skills is a core goal of the parent institution, then so, too, should it be considered for the academic library, and the priorities of the librarians will necessarily shift accordingly.

Therefore, traditional organisational structures must be changed to allow librarians to focus on more specialised areas of librarianship such as teaching and learning. Vanreenan supports this view when he states that libraries must not only establish and support new jobs but also reprioritise, or abandon entirely, those duties and services which become unnecessary. Any alteration of the reference service status quo will demand as much of a cultural shift in attitudes as it will organisational change, particularly as librarians relinquish duties and tasks which have long been perceived to be core business.

As priorities shift, it may become necessary to further consider the role to be played by other professional and para-professional library personnel in managing many routine reference tasks to ensure that reference librarians have the time to 'teach, do research and practice the of information acquisition and dissemination". Perhaps, as Kohl postulates, 'instruction services need to be located in their own department, reporting as highly as possible within the library organisation", thereby acknowledging the importance of a library administration's support of information literacy and promulgation into the traditional teaching foundations of the university. The onus, ultimately, is on library administration to investigate and implement a range of systems and strategies which support and enhance information literacy and allow for growth and change to occur.

This action might include:

- The creation of specialist teaching roles and provision of para-professional assistance;
- Attention to workforce options such as personnel recruitment, selection and deployment;
- Active facilitation of professional development;
- Targeted strategic planning;
- Appropriate budget allocation and reallocation; and
- Organisational support at all levels of the organisation.

Key—Engagement in Non-traditional Areas

Academic institutions should now recognise antiquated opinions, such as those expressed by Cronin who believes that 'librarians... are professional employees whose role is to support, not define or negotiate, the academic mission of the university", as relics of a time past, and strive to build a new paradigm for all teaching staff within the institution. As Frank *et al* affirms, librarians need, and must now embrace, the opportunity to actively engage scholars with innovative and effective services that stretch beyond traditional boundaries.

Any examination of the role of the new librarian must take into consideration the extenuating needs and responsibilities of, and demands upon, the contemporary librarian-educator, and seek, therefore, to encourage and accommodate more complex involvement in non-traditional activities.

Broadly, this involvement demands that librarians be charged with the responsibility to proactively engage in discussions, debates and decision-making processes pertaining to the broad university teaching and learning agenda, nonspecific enquiry relating to student learning, and specific facultyrelated curriculum issues.

This engagement may take various institutionally-dependent forms but should include some, if not all, of the following options:

- Active membership on university, faculty and school-based teaching and learning committees;
- Participation on curriculum-related working parties, and course review and development teams;
- Contribution to activities related to the establishment and implementation of academic policy and programmes;
- Active engagement in issues relating to online and flexibly delivered teaching and learning;
- Consultative participation in all areas relating to the development of generic skills;
- Contribution to, and participation in, staff development programmes and seminar series within the university which relate to improving teaching and learning;
- Participation in discussions relating to facilities and technology planning and infrastructure; and
- Contribution to knowledge creation in the form of publication, research and representation in all educational forums across disciplines and beyond library boundaries.

RELATIONAL CHANGES

To transform higher education and move beyond the boundaries of information literacy as a libraryonly issue, librarians, educators and administrators must continue to develop tools of collaboration and communication about information literacy in the context of teaching, learning and research.

As Frank *et al.,* recognise, faculty and administrators are the primary agents in determining the library's overall impact on the campus community, and universities need to remove the political barriers between information literacy specialists and academics to foster an integrated educational culture.

Teaching and Learning

The key to establishing information literacy in the curriculum, Chiste notes, requires a change in focus from the way "teaching colleagues approach collaboration with librarians, to the way librarians approach collaboration with them". Any 'high political overheads' potentially wrought by librarians striving to ultimately embed information literacy into the curriculum by developing new collaborative models, will eventually be rendered null and void as practice and opinion changes, either by necessity or by sheer recognition of the advantages in doing do.

Both librarians and academic teaching staff need to move beyond the concepts of teaching 'library skills', librarians providing 'additional teaching support' and academics 'relinquishing' portions of their timetable to squeeze in sessions on information skills. As they collectively move towards creating information literacy-responsive curriculum and assessment, the notion of who teaches what should be seen as fluid, negotiable and subject to a range of individual contextual factors relating to skills, confidence and expertise of the academic, subject discipline, delivery mode and even the size of the student cohort.

This point of 'role convergence' will appear as valid and indisputable as those traditional practices appear today. In this new paradigm, the librarian will play a greater role in the design and evaluation of information literacy rich curricula, and the academic a greater part in the actual teaching of the information skills. For the students and their learning, this adaptation of roles can only result in improved outcomes.

Research

Research into information literacy and its impact on teaching and learning has the potential to reinvigorate librarianship, stimulate new growth and lay the foundation for a pedagogically reflective and responsive professional culture within academic libraries. Such research also has the potential to make a significant contribution to the broader body of educational knowledge and practice of both librarians and academics alike. Furthermore, if undertaken in collaboration with academic colleagues, information literacy research can strengthen current partnerships and forge new alliances based on a platform of mutual understanding and common goals and aspirations. Although information literacy is an authentic paradigm, it still has a somewhat fragmentary research base. Commentators, such as Todd, have highlighted the lack of academic scrutiny of its role, the need for more evidence of benefits to learners of a focus on information literacy education and the need for the strengthening of the information literacy research base.

Todd has also posed potential challenges for those involved regarding the theoretical foundations of information literacy, which include:

- Increased understanding of the importance of information literacy;
- Articulation of stronger theoretical roots of information literacy;
- Information on the complexities of how people engage with information and the barriers they face.

Research of this nature will allow practitioners to better understand, predict, accommodate and/or respond to:

- The processes and patterns of information behaviour,
- Connections between the generic processes and discipline-specific contexts;
- The persuasiveness of modelling by academics and librarians;
- The relationships between types of learning, skills taught and learning outcomes.

By working together, academics and librarians can potentially solve old problems and pose new questions in these areas.

It should be expected that the institutions in which they work will recognise the critical need for teaching librarians to conduct information literacy research on an ongoing basis, and that essential practical and philosophical support will be provided in response to their need.

There is ample scope for ongoing information literacy research, particularly in response to the influence of ongoing developments in the educational sector such as graduate attributes, generic skills, online learning and industry demands and the future of information literacy development depends on the vision and determination of the discipline's protagonists to conduct that research.

Research into areas such as evaluation and assessment of information literacy knowledge and skills, creation of active learning environments and the development of generically-responsive curricula would also inform current and ongoing practice within academic institution across all levels of engagement. Particularly significant at this point in time would be research that focuses on the potential use of information literacy standards, such as those developed by the ALA and CAUL in 2000 and 2001. The final word on research must surely belong to Bruce who predicts that 'the present character of information literacy research suggests that it will continue to be exciting and relevant, and that 'it will make contributions to many fields beyond those which served as its cradle". Academic librarians need only to step forward and accept the challenge.

Key—Collaborative, Cooperative Partnerships

There is an inherent understanding that librarianship is 'characterised by cooperative practice and joint scholarship, often carried out in the context of organisations". Hill no doubt echoes a wide belief that librarianship is an almost 'archetypically cooperative discipline which depends on cooperative development of, and adherence to, standards". Librarians recognise that embedding information literacy into the curriculum requires a collaborative, integrated approach to curriculum design and delivery based on close co-operation between academic, library and staff development colleagues. Frank *et al* draws an important distinction between cooperation and collaboration.

Rather than an atmosphere of 'cooperation' where each party has its own goals and cooperate for the purpose of achieving these goals, developing an atmosphere of 'collaboration', where each person brings his or her own goals to the partnership, enables educators together to define shared goals and work to achieve those shared goals. It is certainly true that alliances are usually entered into when each partner sees that they have something to gain.

With new alliances imminent between academics and librarians in the emerging information literacy 'industry', Blackall curiously suggests that librarians get a better deal but recognises, perhaps rightly, that it is unlikely that academics will welcome their expanding influence into their curriculum. He questions why academics would be likely to happily share control over curriculum design with those whom they consider to be 'outside' their profession and muses on what advantages are due to academics from collaborative alliances. If the benefits are ambiguous to some, then perhaps the answer should be plainly stated.

With librarians acting as partners in planning the syllabus, establishing learning objectives, implementing the curriculum and evaluating outcomes, academics benefit by acquiring guidance and support in generic skills development, an opportunity to improve their own pedagogical and information skills, and exposure to diversified teaching and assessment strategies.

Collaborative curriculum design also opens them up to alternative models of teaching and learning, improves communication and builds trust and understanding between the academic and the librarian. Although academics may be used to working with a high degree of autonomy changing expectations, increased accountability and pressing need will demand that this model changes sooner rather than later. However, surely the true question should be to ask *what would students get out of collaborative partnerships between librarians and academics?* The answer: a more cohesive, responsive curriculum, improved student learning outcomes and students who are extremely competent in the retrieval, use and evaluation of information—in a nutshell, high quality learning experiences.

SUMMARY OF OUTCOMES

In May 2001, the National Information Literacy Survey, developed by ACRL and supported by the *American Association of Higher Education* (AAHE), was issued to the vice-presidents of academic units at approximately 2700 institutions. The results provide a snapshot of information literacy programming in higher education and, from the responses, it was clear that the small proportion of those who have programmes are looking for ways in which to assess student learning and evaluate the impact of their efforts. The study concluded that institutions need, and want, guidance on how to successfully implement information literacy programmes and curricula.

Librarians must now undertake this new role. Although the educational role of librarians is a broadly accepted concept the pedagogical role of librarians remains a vexed question, yet to be understood, accepted and fully realised. While the ways and means to establish this new function as core business for academic librarians are simple to propose, there is no doubt that the complexities of the process will be difficult to execute. As the academic librarian moves along the sliding scale from bibliographic instructor to teaching and learning practitioner, course supporter to curriculum co-designer, and practitioner to knowledge creator the following issues need to be addressed, and questions answered.

Consider:

- *Accredited status*: Will general status remain relevant, will faculty status improve opportunities or is there another, more suitable, model for academic librarians?
- *Salary*: Does the new teaching librarian warrant parity of salary for equivalent work, and, if so, whose responsibility is it to pursue?
- *Skills*: What levels and types of professional development are available and is it sustainable?
- *Research*: Whose responsibility is it to conduct information literacy research and is the time,

expertise and support available for librarians to undertake this role?

- *Structural organisation*: What actual changes are required, what will be the costs, and to whom?
- Engagement in non-traditional areas—how can it be encouraged, facilitated and sustained?
- Collaborative teaching and learning partnerships—how can they be enabled, fostered and supported?
- Marketing and promotion—what role does it play in raising awareness, changing attitudes and behaviours, and highlighting alternative solutions?

To create a model for the new teaching librarian will require the support, action and leadership of everyone in academic institutions, with each key group responsible for taking a lead role in driving, enabling and/or facilitating the process.

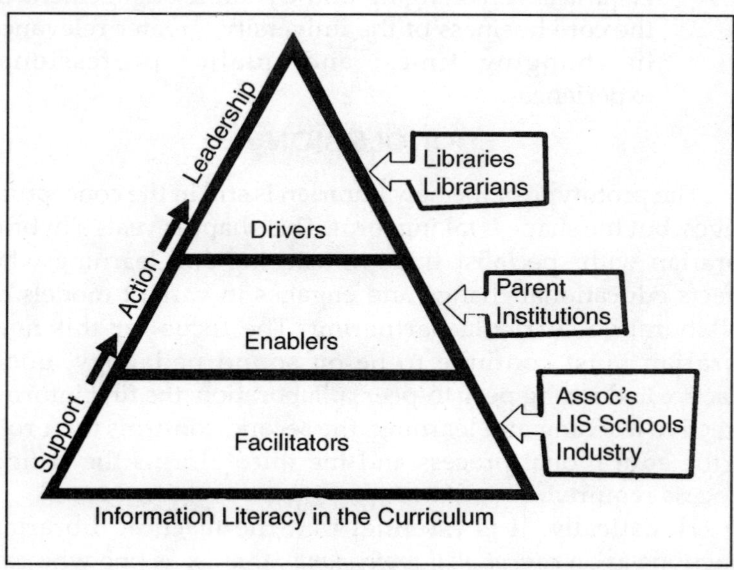

Fig 3.2 Levels of Responsibility

The new teaching librarian will be proactive rather than reactive, pioneering rather than traditional, inventive rather than cautious, and critical, rather than peripheral, to the learning process. The rewards for all staff in this evolving equation are predictably many but perhaps still somewhat indefinable at this stage - as time and experience of 'new ways of doing' allow for academics and librarians to develop and refine original models of teaching and learning, the rewards will begin to bubble to the surface in earnest.

However, the principal benefits for each group could be summarised as follows:

- *Students*: Contextualised embedded development of information literacy; cohesive blend between discipline content and generic processes; and meaningful learning experiences.
- *Academics*: Diversified professional support; shared and consistent pedagogical understandings; and quality teaching experiences.
- *Librarians*: Challenging and dynamic engagement in the core business of the university; greater relevance in changing times; and quality professional experiences.

CONCLUSION

The prototype of the new librarian is still in the conceptual stages, but the shape *is* taking form. This shape reveals a hybrid librarian with specialist skills in teaching and learning who affects educational change and engages in variant models of collaborative curricula partnering. The focus for this new librarian must continue to be on sound pedagogy, good practice and strong peer-to-peer collaboration; the first informs effective teaching and learning, the second confirms their role in the educational process and the third affirms the critical process required.

Holistically, it is essential that the teaching librarian functions as an *educational professional*; that is, as one who can 'engage in educational debate and decision-making processes, influence policy, forge strategic alliances and demonstrate diplomatic sensitivity". As the emphasis on generic skills increases, there will be greater opportunities for academic librarians to play a major role in the development of information and other generic skills by modelling curriculum approaches, providing and creating teaching and learning resources and, critically, by contributing expertise, advice and guidance in the area of information literacy. Although librarians may have to continue to argue the case for information literacy and their specific involvement in these areas for some time yet, the increased focus on reprofessionalising academic librarianship will only add credibility to their assertions and strengthen their arguments. As teaching and learning opportunities present themselves, it is essential that librarians and the organisations in which they work are receptive to, and prepared for, the change. Ultimately, it is the responsibility of individual librarians and academics, academic libraries and their administrators, institutions and their administrators, professional associations and librarianship educators "to develop a new paradigm not only for our libraries but also for our profession" which will serve to enrich higher education for students.

4

Accession

INTRODUCTION TO REGISTRATION

The professional museum goes beyond simply collecting objects., it must also collect information. Often the importance of careful registration and cataloguing are overlooked in the busy environment of local museums and small historical societies. The task of registrar may fall to a volunteer. PastPerfect Museum Software is designed to help address the needs of organisations with little or no training in collection management.

WHAT IS AN ACCESSION

An accession is one or more objects acquired at one time from one source, constituting a single transaction between the museum and a source.

WHAT IS REGISTRATION

Registration is the process of developing and maintaining an immediate, brief, and permanent means of identifying an object for which the institution has permanently or temporarily assumed responsibility. The registration system is the museum's memory. Some would argue that the records are as important as the objects themselves. Keeping good records is a primary function of a good museum. Your museum has placed its collections in your hands. Someday you will pass the collection on to its next caretaker. It is your fundamental responsibility to hand over the collection and its records in good condition.

The registration system ensures that:

- The museum's right of ownership of the object is established.
- Associations with a person, place, or event are preserved.
- Interpretation of the object is enhanced.
- Preservation of the object is aided.
- The museum can identify and account for every object in the collection.

What do you really need to know about each object:

- Accession number (Where did it come from?)
- Object ID or catalogue number (What is its unique identifying number?)
- Object name (What is it?)
- Location (Where is it kept?)
- Description (What does it look like?)
- Date (How old is it?)
- Dimensions (What features distinguish it from everything else?)

If your organisation is brand new, you have the unique opportunity to begin truly at the beginning. Your task is to implement a registration system that is easy to understand, flexible, and expandable. This can be accomplished by starting with a numbering system that is in keeping with professional standards throughout the museum community. You do not have to reinvent the wheel. The three-part numbering system is standard in the history museum field and is readily understood by museum professionals.

THE THREE-PART REGISTRATION NUMBER

The three-part registration system is both simple to apply and expandable. To begin, assign each accession to the year it was received. If the item or group of items was received by the museum in 2001, then 2001 is the first part of the three-part number. The second part of the number is derived from the chronological order in which the accession was received. The first group of items received in the year 2001 would be assigned the number 1. Now our number has two parts: 2001.1

is the accession number for the item or group of items. To further distinguish the items in the accession, simply add item numbers to the accession number to give each item in the accession a unique object ID number. The first item in the accession would be given the object ID number 1, the next would be 2, and so on.

Now our first item in the accession has the unique object ID number 2001.1.1. The second item would be 2001.1.2. Thus the system has given you three pieces of information: the year of the accession, the number of gifts in a given year, and the number of items in the gift. This system is simple to understand and unlimited in application. There are obvious advantages to the three-part numbering system. You do not have to worry about how many objects are in the accession. It is expandable to accommodate any number of items. The second advantage, and perhaps the most important, is that it identifies the source of the donation. The accession portion of the number can be related easily to the donor information. In PastPerfect, the source of the item can be viewed from any catalogue by clicking on the Accession button to the right of the source name and credit line. Some curators are tempted to use letters in their numbering system to save time. In sets of objects such as teacups, the temptation is to assign one object ID number and distinguish the various cups by letters: a, b, c, d, etc.

This is a common sight in collections:

- 2001.1.1a Teacup
- 2001.1.1b Teacup

Or, sometimes:

- 2001.1.1a–b Teacups

In sets of objects, such as identical teacups, you should number them individually. Think of them as a set of identical twins. You wouldn't name your children William—a and William-b. They have individual histories and may not always be together. In addition, the two cups will certainly have different condition reports, just as the children will have different medical histories. The two sets of information will be difficult to record on only one collection record. Don't be tempted to corrupt a perfectly good numbering system in this way. The relationship between the two objects can be recorded in PastPerfect through the Related Objects function. Don't ask your numbering system to work too hard. Some curators attempt to use the accession and object ID numbers to classify objects. Most of these systems break down as soon as they are implemented.

You may be tempted to use the prefix 'T' to indicate tools. Soon you realise that you have:

- Carpenter's tools (CTs)
- Shipwright's tools (STs)
- Next you identify seamstress's tools (ST2s)
- Blacksmith's tools (BTs)
- Dentist's tools (DTs)

Very soon you will need a scorecard to understand your own system. In addition, a numbering system that employs alphabetical prefixes will soon have items with identical numbers differing only in prefix. Museums with such numbering systems will find their recordkeeping complicated and confusing.

If you already have a registration system in place, PastPerfect can accommodate it as long as each item has a unique object ID or catalogue number. In the past, many museums simply assigned a chronological number to each accession. A group of items might be given the accession number 5000 because that is the next number in the sequence. The individual items in the accession would be assigned chronological numbers as well. Thus, the items in this system might be assigned the unique object ID numbers 5000.1, 5000.2, 5000.3, etc. The next accession would be 5001 and so on.

THE ACCESSION SCREEN

The PastPerfect Accession screen allows you to create Accession Forms, the Deed of Gift, and a Thank You Letter. The Accession screen can be used to add, edit, and print accession records. When adding a new accession record, you can import a donor's name and address from the Contacts file. The bottom of the Accession screen displays a list of catalogue records that are in the accession. The Deed of Gift command button allows you to edit or print a Deed of Gift form. Use the Thank You Letter button to display and print a letter to the donor.

The Deed of Gift form and Thank You Letter are prepared automatically from donor information entered when adding the accession record and from information contained on the Default Deed of Gift form and the Default Thank You Letter. These default forms are accessed from the Add command button in the Accession folder.

THE ACCESSION RECORD 'S RELATIONSHIP TO THE CATALOGUE SCREENS

In PastPerfect, the accession number refers to the unique number that defines an item or group of items in a museum collection from a single source at one point in time. Essentially, accession refers to the donor or source of the item or items rather than the items themselves. The object ID is the unique catalogue number assigned to each item in a collection. An accession can contain any number of unique object IDs.

THE ACCESSION PROCESS WITH PASTPERFECT

When objects come into the museum, they should be evaluated before being accessioned into the collection. Temporary Custody allows you to record important information about the source and print a receipt for the donor prior to the museum's decision to accession and number the items. Once the decision has been made to accession the objects, an accession record and number will be assigned to the collection. However, there may be occasions when items are accessioned immediately.

The basic steps to accession items into the collection are:

- Click on the Accession command button;
- Add a new accession record;
- Complete the form by entering data in each field;
- Click on the Save command to save the entry;
- Add catalogue records to the Accession;
- Complete the Deed of Gift and Thank You Letter.

STEP 1 : CLICK ACCESSION

To open the Accession screen, click on the Accession command button on the PastPerfect main menu. The accession record that was last viewed will display. If this is the very first accession record entered, the screen will display blank data fields.

STEP 2 : ADD A NEW ACCESSION RECORD

Click on the Add command button at the top of the Accession screen to display the New Accession screen.

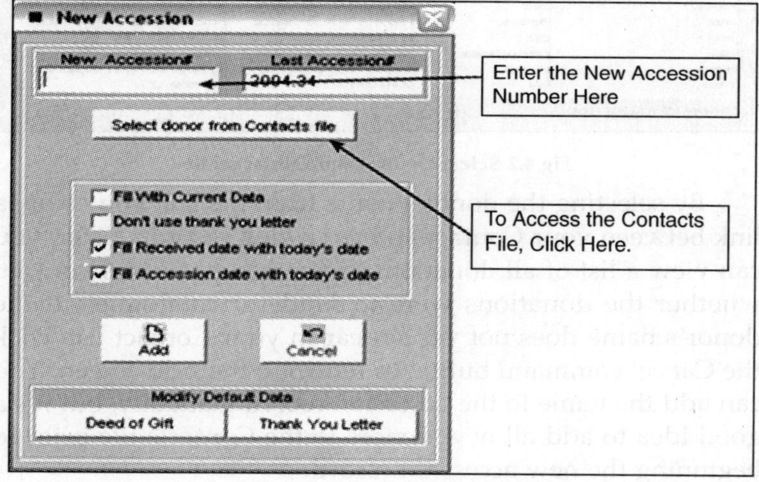

Fig 4.1 New Accession Screen

Type the accession number in the blank box. Accession numbers can be up to 15 characters long, including numbers and punctuation. PastPerfect recommends assigning two-part numbers, such as 2001.1, where the first four digits represent the year of accession and the next three digits identify the chronological order of the accession in the year. However, PastPerfect will support any numbering system that your museum may already have in place. The number that was last assigned is displayed for your reference. Press Select Donor from Contacts File to view a list of all names entered in your Contacts file. If the donor is already in your Contacts file, double-click on the name and the donor information will automatically be entered in the accession record.

■ Select donor from contacts file

Click on column heading to change sort order

Lastname	Firstname	Company	Name & Title
Baker	Kate	Picture Perfect Photo Studio	Kate Baker, Owner
Blaine	Fiona		Mr. and Mrs. Bernard Blaine
Carter	Rose		Rose Ellen Carter
Carter	Millicent	Perfect Shoe Company	Millie Carter
Danner	Karen		Karen E. Danner
Ekrom	Gary	Gotta Go Enterprises	Gary Ekrom
England	Bethany L.	Pastime Software Company, Inc	Bethany L. England
Feldstein	Leo	Incunabula & Ephemera Shoppe	Leo Feldstein
Fitzgibbon	Barbara	Cherry Hill Realty	Barbara E. Fitzgibbon
Gomez	Ginger	Pastime Software Company, Inc.	Ginger M. Gomez
Gomez	Brian	Pastime Software Co., Inc.	Brian L. Gomez
Griffin	Jennifer		Jennifer Griffin
Hanover	Henry	Caliber Software, Inc.	Henry T. Hanover
Harvey	Jason	Plumsteadville Historical Society	Jason Harvey, Director
Hilton	Richard L.	Pastime Software Company, Inc	Richard Hilton, Chief Software Archite
Hilton	Earl	Hilton Real Estate Company	Mr. & Mrs. Earl L. Hilton
Hilton	Ernestine McMillan	Earl Hilton Real Estate Company	Ernestine McMillan Hilton
Holmes	Margaret	The Better Girdle Company, Inc.	Ms. Margaret D. Holmes, Manager of M
Hosea	Paul	One to One.com	Paul Hosea, CEO

Double-Click on donor to select

Fig 4.2 Select Donor from Contacts File

By selecting the donor's name from the list, you create a link between your Contact and Accession records. Later, you can view a list of all donations given by a particular contact, whether the donations were to funds or catalogues. If the donor's name does not yet appear in your Contact list, click the Cancel command button to return to the Add screen. You can add the name to the accession record manually, but it's a good idea to add all new donors to the Contacts file prior to beginning the new accession record.

The check boxes in the middle of the Add New Accession screen provide you with some shortcuts. If Fill with Current Data is checked, PastPerfect will copy all information, including the donor's name and address, from the last viewed record.

Check this box *only* if you have not selected a new donor name from the Contacts file. If Don't Use Thank You Letter is checked, PastPerfect is prevented from creating a thank you letter for this donation. Check this box only if you do not wish to use PastPerfect to print a thank you letter for this accession. If Fill Received Date with Today's Date is checked, the programme will automatically insert the current date in the

Received Date field. Check this box if you would like to add the current date by default. If Fill Accession Date with Today's Date is checked, the programme will automatically insert the current date in the Accession Date field. The last two buttons under Modify Default Data—Deed of Gift and Thank You Letter—access the default data screens for those documents. Finally, click Add. PastPerfect will verify that the accession number you assigned is not a duplicate. If it is a duplicate, you will be notified and asked to enter a new, unique accession number.

STEP 3 : COMPLETE FOR M BY ENTERING DATA IN EACH FIELD

Another way to view the field descriptions while viewing the screen is to use 'What's this?' help. Using the mouse, click on the '?' in the upper right-hand corner of the screen. Then move the mouse over a field and click to display the description. To enter data in a field, move the cursor to the field and start typing. To advance the cursor to the next field, press the Tab key. To move the cursor to the previous field, press Shift-Tab. You may use the mouse to jump to any field on the screen by positioning the mouse arrow over the field and pressing the left mouse button. Enter the source or donor and contact if the donor is an organisation. In the Description box, enter a brief description of the objects received. The description will appear on the Thank you letter and Deed of Gift.

STEP 4 : PRESS THE SAVE COMMAND TO SAVE THE ENTRY

When you have finished entering information in the data fields, press the Save command at the top of the screen. If you do not want to save your entries, click the Cancel command. As it saves, the programme will prompt you to verify the donor's name as it will appear on the deed of gift form, the thank you letter address name, and the thank you letter dear name. To make any changes, just type in the box before pressing Done.

STEP 5: ADD CATALOGUE RECORDS TO THE ACCESSION

Once you have entered the data for the accession record, you will need to add the items to the catalogue record list. To add these items, click the Add catalogue records command button

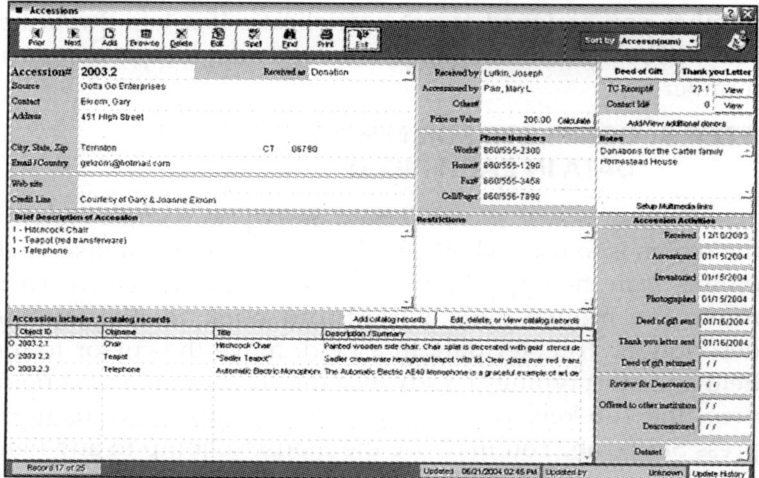

Fig 4.3 The Accession Screen

When you press the Add catalogue records command button. The following screen will appear.

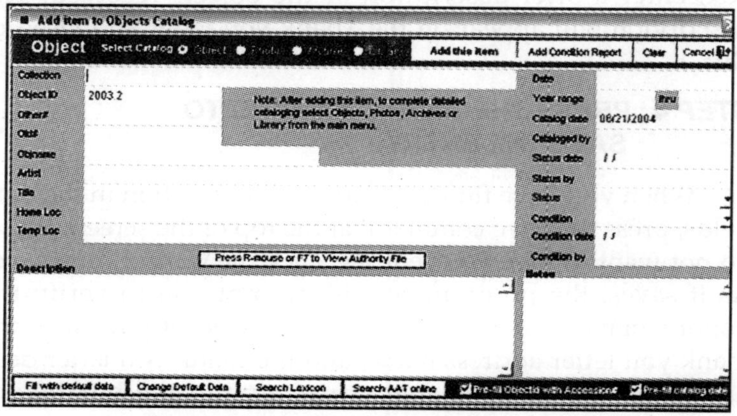

Fig 4.4 Add Catalogue Records to Accession

Select the correct catalogue for the new item by clicking Object, Photo, Archive, or Library at the top of the screen. Then enter data in the fields. Click Add This Item to complete the entry. The new item will appear in the list at the bottom of the Accession screen and a record will be created in the appropriate catalogue.

To fully catalogue the item, open the Objects, Photos, Archives or Library catalogue screen from the main menu and locate the new entry, and click Edit. From the Accession screen you may also click on the command Edit, delete, or view catalogue records to view details about the catalogue records contained in the Accession, edit the record, delete the record, or fill out a detailed condition report about the record.

STEP 6 : COMPLETE THE DEED OF GIFT AND THANK YOU LETTER

On the Accession screen, the Deed of Gift command button will allow you to edit or print a Deed of Gift form. Use the Thank You Letter command to display and print a letter to the donor. The Deed of Gift form and Thank You Letter are prepared automatically from donor information entered when adding the accession record and from information contained on the Default Deed of Gift form and the Default Thank You Letter. These default forms may be accessed from the Add command button in the Accession folder.

Modifying the Default Deed of Gift

To modify the Default Deed of Gift form, click Add on the Accession screen. At the bottom of the New Accession screen you will see the Modify Default Data box. Select either the Deed of Gift or Thank You Letter command button.

Click in the first box and enter the name and address of your institution. In the second box, type the default legal text of your deed of gift contract. The third box is for the Footer, which appears the last signature line. In this example, we used it for the statement confirming receipt of the gift. The Received As box allows you to enter a default value for this field. Click Save and Exit to complete your modifications.

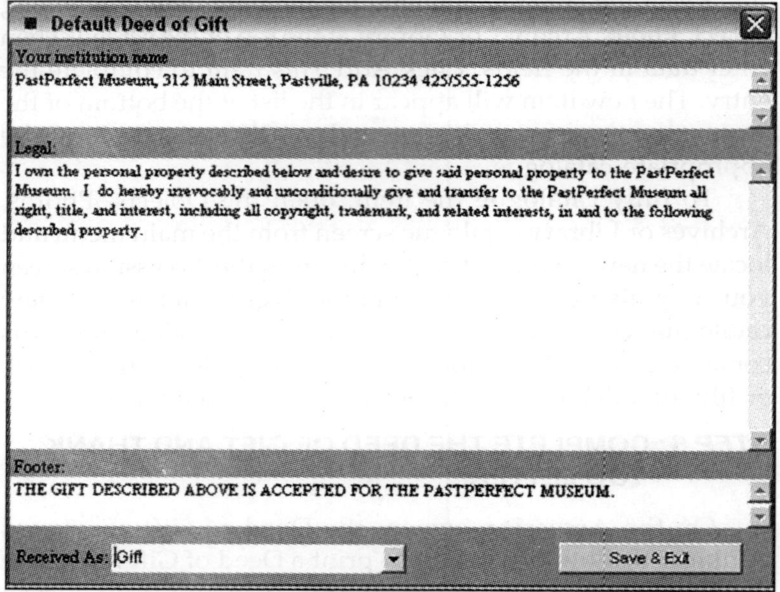

Fig 4.5 Default Deed of Gift

Print the Deed of Gift

To print the Deed of Gift, from the Accession screen, click on the Deed of Gift button and click Print. You may want to click Preview to view the document first. Proofread the document, and then press the Printer icon to print. If you need to make changes before printing, click on the Edit button. The text box at the bottom is for the In Memory Of information if the donor wishes to acknowledge someone in this way.

The text in the footer comes from the default form and cannot be modified here. There may be times when you'd like to change the legal text for one Deed of Gift without changing the default settings for all future Deeds of Gift. To do so, click the Custom Legal radio button, and click Edit. Type in the custom legal text and click Save. Your changes will affect this Deed of Gift form only.

Deed of Gift Edit | Preview | Print | Close

Status ☑ Deed of Gift sent date 01/16/2004 ☑ Deed of Gift returned date 02/10/2004

Name: Ekrom, Gary Date: 12/10/2003

Address: 451 High Street

City: Torrinton State CT Zip 06790

Phone H/W: 860/555-1290 860/555-2300 Fax: 860/555-3458

◉ Default Legal ○ Custom Legal

I own the personal property described below and desire to give said personal property to the PastPerfect Museum. I do hereby irrevocably and unconditionally give and transfer to the PastPerfect Museum all right, title, and interest, including all copyright, trademark, and related interests, in and to the following described property.

Description of Gift:

1 - Hitchcock Chair
1 - Teapot (red transferware)
1 - Telephone

By my signature below I accept the forgoing condition and acknowledge reading any attached information.

This gift is given in memory of: Sara Jean Ekrom

Dated: ________ ________ Donor/agent

________ Donor/agent

Date received: ________ Received by: ________

THE GIFT DESCRIBED ABOVE IS ACCEPTED FOR THE PASTPERFECT MUSEUM.

By: ________ name ________ title ________ date

Fig 4.6 Deed of Gift

To make changes to the default data, you must follow the procedure. Modify the Default Thank You Letter—The procedure to modify the default Thank You Letter is similar to changing the default Deed of Gift. Click the Thank You Letter button on the New Accession screen to open the Default Thank You Letter screen.

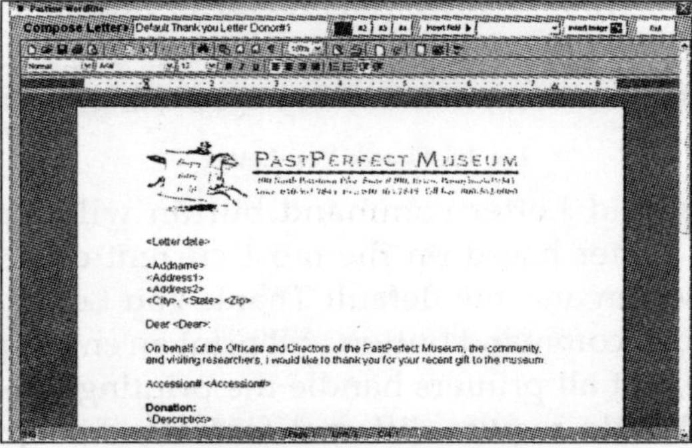
Compose Letters Default Thank you Letter Donor#1

PASTPERFECT MUSEUM

<Letter date>

<Addname>
<Address1>
<Address2>
<City>, <State> <Zip>

Dear <Dear>:

On behalf of the Officers and Directors of the PastPerfect Museum, the community, and visiting researchers, I would like to thank you for your recent gift to the museum.

Accession# <Accession#>

Donation:
<Description>

Fig 4.7 Default Thank You Letter

Four default letters can be composed, one for each donor. Click on the numbers #1-#4 at the top of the screen to select a letter. The letter that you see is a mail-merge letter which means that you can include fields that will be replaced by data from the accession record.

Print Thank You Letter

To print a Thank You Letter for a completed accession, click on Thank You Letter from the Accession screen. You should now see the mail-merge fields replaced with data from the accession record. Proofread the document, and then click the Printer icon to print. If you need to make changes before printing you can. Changes made here will not affect the Default Thank You Letter form.

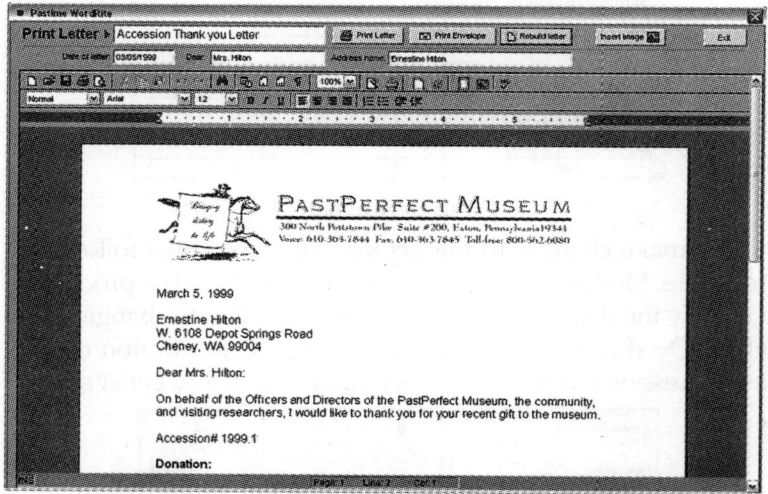

Fig 4.8 Thank You Letter

The Rebuild Letter command button will rebuild the Thank You Letter based on the most current data from the Accession screen and the default Thank You Letter text. The Print Envelope command button will print an envelope for the letter. Since, not all printers handle the printing of envelopes and those that do require different formats, this option may not always work with your printer. You may need to set up the envelope to print with your printer from the Reports menu by selecting Accessions | Thank you Letter Envelope | Modify Report Layout | Modify Custom Layout.

MULTIPLE DONORS

The Accession record will allow you to record information about three additional donors. A separate deed of gift and thank you letter may be printed for each donor. To add another donor, click on the Add/View Additional Donors command to open this screen.

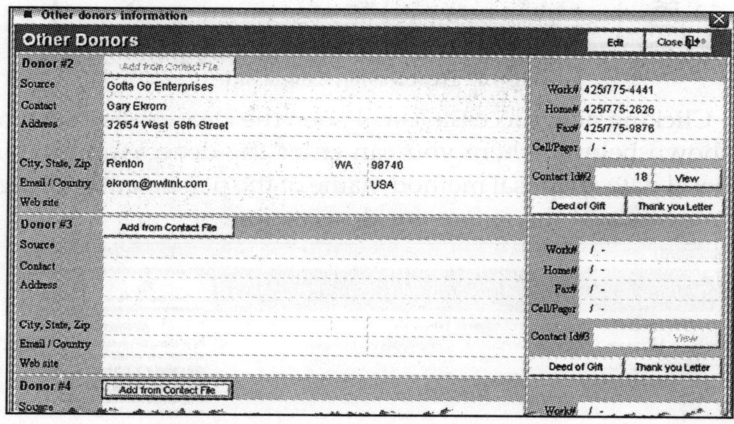

Fig 4.9 Multiple Donors

You can type in the donor information or press Add from Contact File to select a donor from your Contacts database.

THE DEACCESSION PROCESS

PastPerfect provides two methods of deaccessioning items. The first is simply to change the catalogue record's status to Deaccessioned.

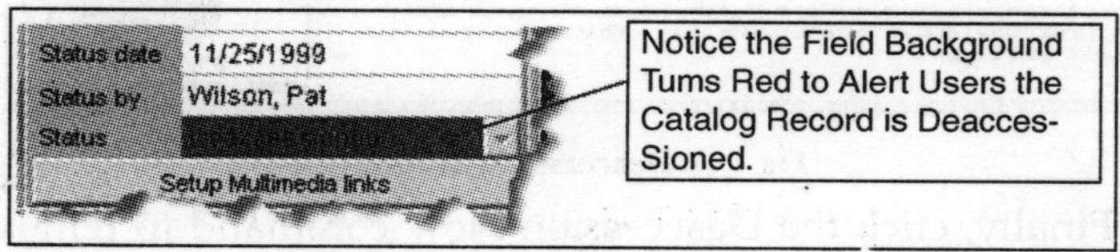

Fig 4.10 Status-Deaccessioned

If you prefer to remove deaccessioned items from the catalogue, you can use the Deaccession function. This function allows you to remove the items from the catalogue and place them in a special Deaccessioned file. To deaccession an item and move it to the Deaccessioned file, first locate the item in the, Objects, Photos, Archives, or Library catalogue. Then click on the Edit command button. This will reveal the Deaccession command button. The Deaccession command is only available in Edit mode.

Fig 4.11 Deaccession Command

Clicking on Deaccession will open the Deaccession screen as shown below, where you can enter the deaccession date, disposal date, disposal method, name of the person authorising the process and the reason for deaccession.

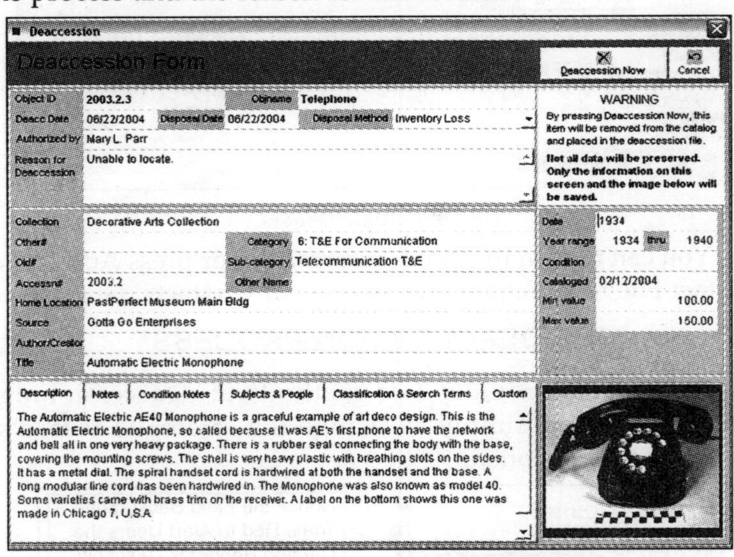

Fig 4.12 Deaccession Screen

Finally, click the Deaccession Now command to remove the item from the catalogue and move it to the Deaccessioned file.

Global Deaccession

On the Deaccession screen there is a Global Deaccession command. This option will allow you to move all catalogue records with status= Deaccessioned to the Deaccession file.

5

Online Computer Services

EVOLUTION OF TECHNOLOGY IN BRIEF
INTERNET TECHNOLOGY—IT'S USE IN ACADEMIC LIBRARIES

HISTORICAL BACKGROUND OF TECHNOLOGY

The middle of the 19th century and 20th century needs a special mention because the period marks the age of revolution with new modes of communication technology. Instead of 'paper' man invented use of terminals, computers printers and other types of data communication devices. 'The use of paper', has been completely superseded by the Super Highway Technology.

In this electronic age, academicians have come very close to non-book materials. During 1990s, we had more justification for this feeling than any other generation. In the history of mankind so many technologies have emerged and all of a sudden compelling us to change ways of thinking. People have started recognising the importance of Information Technology as an effective tool in satisfying the human needs. In efficient governance and in developing human resources, efforts are being directed towards improving the utilisation of the scarce academic resources, thereby integrating the society globally. Telecommunication and computerisation are being increasingly seen today as means to improve efficiency of operation. The quality of ' library service ' has vastly improved with the introduction of communication technology.

EVOLUTION OF COMMUNICATION TECHNOLOGY

Telecommunication plays an important role while designing an effective functioning of the on-line libraries. Digital technology, improved antennae systems and use of microcomputers have been instrumental in achieving a communication revolution. The recent trends in telecommunications are the use of Internet technology and e-mail technologies.

They accommodate a wide variety of multimedia communication services that are very popular in most developed countries and are now gaining importance in developing countries like India as well. Advances in both telecommunication and computer technologies have facilitated the designing of new software thereby making the delivery of information quicker, convenient and efficient than ever before. It is a fact that users feel increasingly comfortable with computers. The communication technology land line and satellite communication have made the world a 'global village'. In such a challenging situation academic libraries have to welcome not only e-mail, LAN and similar services but also Intranet and Internet services in their libraries.

OVERVIEW OF INTERNET

A world- wide communication system that links millions of computers has been developed. Such a network is called the Information Super Highway or Cyber Space most popularly known as the Internet. The Internet permits two way speech which allows millions of people to communicate by either sending messages through their computers or receiving messages from other computers all over the world.Internet in normal usage is a network of computers. In other words we can say that it is a network of networks. Internet made a humble beginning way back in the 1970s in the United States under the Department of Defence-Sponsoring a collection of computer network known as ARPANET. It connected about 64 computers providing admissions to researchers and commercial sectors. Within a span of thirty years, the system has considerably advanced in research and technology. It connects millions of people and shares information in different fields like agriculture, defence, transport, economics, sports, medicine, education and libraries. Although its popularity is spread over the developed countries, Internet has been only a recent development in India.

INDIAN EXPERIENCE

Just a few years ago that the public sector organisation VSNL introduced Internet to the Indian community. At present approximately 4,00,000 commercial users have access through VSNL whereas from education and research communities 5,00,000 users have access through ERNET. So, around 10,00,000 Indian people are directly connected to the NET which is a small fraction of the total population of India. VSNL has been channelising the information particularly from the four International Gateways at Mumbai, Delhi, Calcutta, and Chennai. To give more access to e-mail and Internet, VSNL has installed new Gateways at Ahmedabad, Kanpur, Ernakulam, Jullandar, Bangalore and Hyderabad.

INFRASTRUCTURE NEEDED

To have admission to the Internet, specific equipment is required. Primarily the computer forms the backbone of the network. A personal Computer, a commonly used machine that is easily available can perform the task. Telephone lines form an important part with information passing through these lines and this facility can be availed of through additional payment to the telephone department. A device which is necessary to use the Internet is called Modem. The Modem sends/passes the information across phone from one computer to another computer.

Now-a-days computer has become part of the Internet. One has to subscribe to an *Internet Service Provider* (ISP) which gives the user admission to the Internet. In India, the VSNL is the service provider that is connected to the webs of many popular countries including USA. VSNL has its main Internet admission node in Mumbai. It also has various other remote admission nodes at Pune, Calcutta, Delhi, Bangalore and Chennai that link to the US Web through the main node in Mumbai.

INTERNET APPLICATION IN LIBRARY MANAGEMENT

For instance, when the Librarian in Sri Sathya Sai Institute of Higher Learning wishes admission to the Internet, the modem connected to the Library's computer establishes the link to the VSNL which automatically connects the Librarian to the main Web through the Internet admission node in Mumbai. The VSNL offers admission to the Internet for a reasonable fee. Once it gets connected to the service, a list of areas that he/she can use appears on his/her computer screen in the Central Library.

For instance, topics like Sciences, Social Sciences, Humanities and Engineering subjects also will appear on the screen. Using the mouse the Library staff can click on any item of their interest and information on the particular subject will automatically appear on the screen. Penguin India, Foundation Books, Allied Publishers, Springer, Kluwer and other publishers are tied up in the web to help book lovers while placing orders for books and subscribing journals through on-line. Internet application—Technical section: A subscriber/ teacher/library staff can use the on-line catalogues for selecting recent editions of books. The Librarian can send an order via Internet whether to Penguin India or Informatics or any other related publisher and avail discounts too. It also provides instant information for library executives regarding the subscription of journals; sending reminders for missing issues and informing payment clearances.

Internet Application—Reference Section

The Academic library especially at the University level associates with outstanding scholars who expect ready made information like SDI. To satisfy them every librarian should maintain close contact with professional and non-professional bodies like INSDOC and INFLIBNET—INFONET etc., The staff should refer various types of information sources available on Internet. They may be commercial databases, open access databases, and licensed databases.

ADVANTAGES IN BRIEF

Internet can be convenient and efficient in the context of desktop automation; Internet is purely a paperless tool in the communication chain; Internet as network medium disposes of transmission delays imposed by geographical distance. Internet does not cost much;Internet can shrink social as well as geographical distance; Internet can support and sustain academic interests of the research community.

INFORMATION COMMUNICATION TECHNOLOGY AND DIGITAL STORAGE IN LIBRARIES

The relatively recent change from the term *Information Technology* (IT) to *Information and Communication Technology* (ICT) due to the convergence of IT and ICT has open up new challenges for libraries. Information Technology is the collective name for a group of technologies that are concerned with the storage, retrieval, manipulation, analysis, and transmission of information. Since, the fabrication of the first modern computer in the mid 1940's, computer technology has developed at a tremendous pace to the point where it has penetrated almost all occupations and has spread to the far concerns of the world. Similarly, communication technology has made rapid progress in the post World War II period. But it is the development of this technology in the last 15 years that has made IT so important. The development in this area have been brining about a revolutionary change in the way humans work, and in the way they interact with each others. The spread of telecommunications has brought into limelight the Internet, the global intercommunication of computer networks. This has made available a large store information to all concerns of the world.

Information Technology provides the following services for information:

- Storage of large amounts of information in a cost effective manner;

- Structuring of information to enable quick retrieval of what is required;
- Analysis of stored information to help in decision making;
- Sharing of information among people geographically dispersed;
- Quick transmission of information over large distances.

IT consists of five components, *i.e.*, electronic science, computer science, tele-communication science, artificial language and human interface.

INFORMATION COMMUNICATIONS TECHNOLOGY—CREATING NETWORKS WITH GROWING REACH

It involves rapid advances in two technologies—digital storage and processing of information and satellite and optical fibre transmission of information– are creating new and faster ways of storing, handling, distributing and accessing information. These innovations enable the processing and storage of enormous amount of information, along with rapid distribution information through communication networks. In 2001 more information can be sent over a single cable in a second than in 1997 was sent over the entire internet in a month. Linking computing devices and allowing them to communicate with each other creates networked information systems based on a common protocol. Individuals, households and institutions are linked in processing and executing a huge number of instructions in imperceptible time spans. This radically alters access to information and the structure of communication extending the networked reach to all corners of the world.

TECHNOLOGICAL TRANSFORMATIONS

Today's technological transformations are intertwined with another transformation, globalisation and together they are creating a new paradigm—the network age. These transformations expand opportunities and increase the social and economic rewards of creating and using technology. They are also altering how and by whom technology is created and owned, and how it is made accessible and used. Technology is not inherently good or bad the outcome depends on how it is used.

SOME INITIATIVES IN IT SECTOR

The Department of Information Technology has setup Community Centre (CICs) at 487 blocks in the seven North Eastern States 9 Arunachal Pradesh, Assam, manipur, Meghalaya, Mizoram, Nagaland, Tripura) and Sikkim to provide connectivity at the block level and thus promote application of Information Technology for accelerating socio-economic development of the region.

INFORMATION TECHNOLOGY ACT

The Government of India has created the necessary legal and administrative framework through the enactment of the Information Technology Act, 2000. While on the one hand it seeks to create the public key infrastructure for electronic authentication through digital signatures.

DIGITAL LIBRARY

Digital Libraries are a form of information Technology in which social impact matters as much as technological advancements. Future knowledge networks will rely on scalable semantics, to automatically indexing the community collections so that users can effectively search of billion repositories.

NATIONAL INFORMATION CENTRE (NIC)

It provides informatics services for decision support to government offices/bodies at national, state, district and block levels. It offers network services. NIC also provides video conferencing facilities.

INFORMATION TECHNOLOGY USE IN LIBRARY MANAGEMENT SYSTEM

The IT revolution has also embraud the library system. A massive and rapid computerisation process throughout the levels of the library system has made IT an integral part of the library management scene in many countries all over the world. The incorporation of IT into the day-to-day activity of libraries has a strong impact on virtually every aspect of their management processes. Although there is no agreed definition of IT, the term 'IT' includes three main components—*management information system* (MIS) or *decision support system* (DSS), hardware, and human factors. A management information system is the set of structure and procedures that govern the collection, processing, analysis, presentation and use of information within an organisation.

IMPACT OF ICTS IN LIBRARIES

Technology is changing the nature of libraries and librarians, and it continues to exert a major influence on the strategic direction of libraries in society. Today the library services are transitioning from local traditional collections to global resources provided on demand via the most advanced networking technologies.

DIGITAL DATA STORAGE IN LIBRARIES

Digital data storage media for storing digital data are constantly being developed, improved or superseded, and any discussion of them here can only be taken as description of the current situation i. e., optical discs, magnetic media, other media for digital data storage. The concept of the 'digital library' evolved out of potential for digitisation of all forms of media: print, image, sound, complex data sets, and computer simulations of non-time-bound sequences, otherwise not demonstrable events, etc., and retrieving them in context of multiple networked information systems. The digital library often serves as a multidimensional catalogue or index to bring together the resource discovery information of every resource that was topically, creatively, or by reason of other connections generatively related. A digital library does not only consist of digitised and digitally born information resources, but also of electronic metadata on non-digital objects. Digital Data: Considerable attention is now being paid to the possibility of converting the intellectual content of items in library collection into digital data by electronic means and storing it on magnetic tapes or discs. Both textual and pictorial information can be converted. For example by using optical character recognition devices which convert texts into their digital code equivalent, or by using scanners to convert text or, more usually, pictures into an analogue form.

Text can also be input by keyboarding. In addition to information already in another format being converted to digital format, much information is now originated in digital form and may appear only in that form in the library. Digital data have considerable advantages. They can be rapidly duplicated and speedily transmitted without deterioration through electronic communications networks to whatever the user is working. Storage: It is a mainly technical requirement, although new media may complicate storage decisions and costing. Today's large digital repositories use multiple level of mass storage media and mechanical robots to locate and mount the media.

Phases of Digitisation: Undoubtedly, digital media will have to co-exit with print media. Different kinds of collection could be digitised at different times depending on the priorities of the library. To start with, any one type of collection, for example, important out of print publications could be made available in digital form. Feedback of its usage can be sengut and analysed. In the next phase, another type of data could be converted into digital form. Digitisation Process: Digitisation is a process of converting paper documents to electronic format. Scanning process does the conversion. Digital information can be transmitted and received anywhere in the world where the infrastructure to send and received is in place.

Due to the implementation of the IT, the librarian need to be well aware of the technical issues, potential problems involved, trained manpower available, the hardware required, document management systems, optical character recognisation (OCR) technology for implementing digitisation of the collection and services. As been know the concept of digital library is growing very fast globally. It is a welcome trained that various institutions and professional societies are involved to provide opportunities for the library and librarians to upgrade and enhance the professional knowledge about digital library.

Various important aspects like digital libraries issues, architecture, electronic publishing, collection building, storage, organisation, transmission of digital information, creation and use of hypertext and hypermedia system, networks and their implications, manpower development, etc. We are in the early stage of a transmition from a print-based to a digital society. The latest technologies offer cheap computer processing power, cheap mass storage, inexpensive and ubiquitous access to high speed networks and retrieval devices give us the ability to create, to manipulate, to storage and especially to transfer large quantities of information in digital form at low costs.

Digital information can be stored on any medium that is able to represent binary digits 0 and 1. Conversion from the conventional storage to digitised format required discrete analysis as the primary function, based on user electronic storage and retrieval system. Some of the common digitised storage media that are presently used world over are the Hyper books, CD-ROM, Multimedia. New media are constantly being developed. Some that are still in experimental stages or have been only very recently introduced are digital videotape, digital audiotape and digital paper.

INFRASTRUCTURE FOR DIGITAL MANAGEMENT A CASE STUDY OF J.N.N. COLLEGE OF ENGINEERING LIBRARY

We are living to-day in a world of change and the changes we see all around us due to availability of information quicker than before, faster communication through e-mail, voice mail and video conferencing and the great influence of the Internet and web pages. The use of computer-based system in the libraries and information units is now commonplace all over the world. Computers are used to assist in a variety of functions such as maintaining and providing access to the catalogue of items in the collection, managing the issuing and returning of items from the collection, the acquisition of new items for the collection, controlling the serial publications and allowing the retrieval of information from the databases relating to bibliographic data financial or numeric data or the full text of documents.

DIGITAL INITIATIVES AT J.N.N. COLLEGE OF ENGINEERING LIBRARY

It is experienced that Bar-coding has revolutioned the library activities globally. A Laser Barcode printer was purchased and Bar-coding software was also installed. The Bar-coding labels for each book were generated.

BAR-CODING OF BOOKS

Printing barcode labels and pasting in three places of each book, *viz*. Title page, Secrete page and due date slip were entrusted with a contractor. This generating of Bar-coding labels and pasting the labels for all 53,500 volumes were completed within five months.

Retrieving of information through barcode labels using barcode scanner was tested. The computer displayed the Accession Number and the relevant bibliographic information was retrieved from the book database. The bibliographic information includes Accession Number, Author, Title, Call Number, Publisher and Keywords.

BAR-CODED IDENTITY CARDS

The work of bar-coding of identity cards for all users J.N.N. College of Engineering. College was entrusted to the Frontier Information Technology, Secundarbad. The identity card contains the attributes: Class, Dept, Eligibility, Valid up to, Blood group, Residential address, residence phone number. A stamp size photo of each member was scanned and printed on each card.

Both Librarian and Principal are signed on this ID card. The identity cards looked good rather than the old traditional plastic card. Each user used to carry this card and produce the same in the issue counter along with the books and get it issued. Now user feels happy in handling this bar-coded identity card. They also feel proud in producing the same card wherever he visits either inside the college or outside the campus.

NETWORKING AND MANPOWER TRAINING

J. N. N. College of Engineering, Library is a member of the DELNET. The users of the library access the resources listed in this network through the net connectivity. The library staff had their sufficient training at Frontier Information Technology, Secundarbad on various divisions of the library such as Acquisition, Cataloguing, Circulation and Periodicals control.

They received special training with regard to preparation of Bar-coded identity card. Various processes include:

- Scanning of the User's Photo;
- Printing the photo in the special art paper using the colour printer;
- Composing various fields, *viz.*, name class, branch, valid up to, eligibility, blood group, residential address, residence phone;
- Laminating the above paper using laminating machine;
- Books issue through scanner;
- Books return through scanner.

Our Library staffs were sent to nearest libraries to have practical exposure towards developing of barcoded identity cards. J.N.N. College of Engineering Library staff underwent hands on training nearest libraries studied the system form all perspectives. The hands on training assisted the Library staff to develop the barcode identity cards.

For this purpose the following equipments have been identified:

- Digital camera
- Colour printer
- Scanner
- Laminating Machine

J. N. N. College of Engineering Library staff has also studied various operations in DRTC Library, Bangalore.

DIGITAL ASSETS

- *Floppies*: Certain Books are accompanying floppies; such floppies are assigned the concerned Book Accession Numbers. These floppies are arranged serially and kept in the floppy boxes. J.N.N. College of Engineering Library has 200 floppies. Users lend and read these floppies in OPAC systems.
- *CDs*: Some new books contain CDs also. Such CDs are assigned the Concerned accession Number and kept in CD container. There are about 1,400 CDs available in Library. Users refer these CDs through OPAC system.
- *Software used in J.N.N. College of Engineering*: There was one software, which was developed by one programmer of computer science Dept. It had some limitations. Now, 'LIBRIS SOFTWARE' has been purchased and installed. This software put into use.
- *LAN*: Local Area Network was established by connecting all 6 systems in Library with a Main Server. Each system was connected Ethernet and Win proxy Card through Co-Axial cables.
- *UPS*: An UPS was purchased and connected with all 6 terminals in the Library.
- *Computers*: There are 7 computers available in the Library. PC's Configuration:
  - Pentium III/650 MHZ and above, 512 KB internal and external.
  - Cache memory 815 E-Intel.
  - Chipset motherboard 128 MB SD RAM.
  - Minimum 17.1 GB/HDD IDE Drive.
  - 1.44 MB FDD, 32 Bit Graphic Card 52*CD Drive, 17 inch Colour.
  - Monitor with electronic turner and energy saving windows.
  - Keyboard, Logitech Mouse, ATX Cabinet with preloaded and O.S.Windows 95/98.

- *Printers*: There are one Dot Matrix and one Laser Printer available in the Library.
- *Bar-Code Printer*: One Bar-Code Printer is also printing in barcode labels in Laser Printer was purchased along with 2,500 Book Barcode sheets and 5000 ID Barcode Label Sticker Sheets.
- *Book Database*: A book database was created with 53,500 records. Bibliographic information about each Access No. Title, Author, Call Number, Keywords, Publisher, Price, etc.
- *Periodical Database*: A periodical database was created entering all current journal's bibliographic information. The data entry for receipt of periodicals is being entered into computer. Reminders for non-receipt of periodicals is taken as print out and sent to the periodical suppliers.

ADVANTAGES

Computerisation of Library operations saves much time of the Library Staff and users. Students and Staff members feel happy to handle Bar-coded Membership Card. Bar-coding facilities stock verification of books and journals.

DRAWBACKS

Since, we implement computerisation, our library staff does dual job entering all operations manually and through computer. Staff finds this as a job. In the beginning it may be do their, jobs through computer only. During power failure time, staff face problems to operate computer. These problems can be solved using UPS. An UPS* was purchased and connected to all systems in the library. This UPS solves power problem up to some extent.

HOW TO IMPLEMENT IN FUTURE

Our library staff will prepare bar-coded identity cards for fresh students in future using the barcode equipments. Similarly barcode labels will be generated and pasted in three places of each new book purchased in future. Stock verification will be done online using the barcode scanner in future.

PURCHASING CD CABINET

To preserve CDs it is proposed to purchase a CD Cabinet. All CDs will be serially arranged and kept in proper order. Whenever a user requires particular CD, Library Staff can provide the same for reference purpose.

ROLE OF OPEN SOURCE IN HIGHER EDUCATION

WHAT IS OPEN SOURCE

Traditionally, a programme is defined as a set of instructions which tells a computer what to do. The Windows operating system by Microsoft is a programme, or a set of instructions, which tells the user's computer how to send information to the disk drive, how to take information from the user, and how to communicate with pieces of hardware such as the modem or the network card. However, these programmes are compiled, which means that they are translated into the binary code which the computer understands.

The lines of instructions, which are translated into the binary code, are called the source code of the programme. If a user or a programmer has access to the source code behind the programme, then the user is able to alter the programme, changing the way that it works. For most proprietary, or closed source, programmes, the source code is not available for users or programmers to alter.

This means that if a user encounters a bug in the closed source programme, they will not be able to fix it themselves, but must rely on the software vendor to fix the error. As many frustrated users know, this can often take a very long time. Open source software, by contrast, is software for which the source code is freely available.

The web server Apache is a programme which runs as many as two-thirds of the web servers on the Internet. Apache is open source, which means that anyone can access the source code for Apache and make changes in how the programme works.

OPEN SOURCE PLAIN AND SIMPLE

Open Source Software (OSS) refers to software programmes that are distributed with the source codehence open source. The open source licence allows users the freedom to run the programme for any purpose, to study and modify the programme, and to freely redistribute copies of the original or modified programme.

Open Source is a Way of Building Software

Open source software is often constructed using the same time-tested methodologies and practices used to construct proprietary software.

However there are a number of interesting differences that result from the difference in rights conferred by the licence:

- The software evolves more rapidly and organically. Many individuals and teams working in parallel produce advances beyond the capacity of a single team. The improvements are managed into releases by a core team much like the proprietary alternative.
- Users' needs are rapidly met as the OSS model harnesses their collective expertise and contribution. Improvements to the software are often contributed by users who have fixed a problem or added new features.
- New versions are released very often and rely on the community of users and developers to test it, resulting in superior quality software tested on more platforms, and in more environments than most commercial software.
- The development 'team' is often largely volunteers, distributed, many in numbers, and diverse. Often, paid members of the development team will manage the project and organise the work of the volunteers.
- Security is enhanced because the code is exposed to the world. In proprietary packages, shortcuts and poor programming are more easily overlooked because only a select few see the code. Like peer

reviewed papers, open source code is subject to much greater scrutiny and thus produces a higher calibre result.

Open Source is a Way of Doing Business

Open source is often thought of as free software. In fact, one of the benefits is that anyone can use, modify, and redistribute the software without a licence fee. While the code is free, the benefits have much more to do with the freedoms than the cost.

On the surface it may appear that free software is in opposition to the 'business' of software and, while the open source model challenges the traditional models, open source represents great opportunity for customers and businesses alike. Without the restrictions of a proprietary software licence, any institution or company with the skills can use the software to solve their own needs or offer products and services of value to others.

Businesses based on open source software typically add value by:

- Offering services such as implementation, training, and support;
- Packaging and integrating open source software to make its installation and use easier for a wider market;
- Creating complementary, add-on, or enhanced software for sale. Open source affords institutions, as consumers of software, unparalleled control over the use of software to meet business demands and control over where they deploy their budget dollars. Taking into consideration its core competencies and available resources, an institution may use its own people and resources, hire external resources, or partner to share costs. The principles of open source software-freedom to run the programme for any purpose, to study and modify the programme, and to freely redistribute copies and modifications-are simple, yet have powerful and far reaching implications.

COMPARISON TO PROPRIETARY SOFTWARE

One of the great misconceptions about open source is that it is an alternative to commercial software. Rather, open source software is an alternative to proprietary software, but often acquired through or supported by a company—in other words commercial. Fundamentally, the difference between open source and proprietary software has to do with control. Where the open source licence imparts freedoms to use, modify, and redistribute the software, the proprietary licence restricts use, modification, distribution, and more. Vendors of proprietary software restrict access to and use of the source code because the source is knowledge-and knowledge is power.The open source licence corrects the balance of power between producers and consumers of software.

Access to the source code is about freedom and choice. After all, most of us aren't software engineers—we can't start adding features and fixing bugs just because we have access. Yet access to the source code is important to all of us because access is control. Open source clearly offers advantages for the consumer, but it also represents a significant competitive advantage to companies that adopt compatible strategies. IBM, HP, Sun Microsystems, Apple Computer, Red Hat, Novell, and many other companies attribute significant revenue from strategies built on commercialisation of open source software. Mainstream press coverage of open source has been accelerating all over the world, but the press coverage in higher education has been nothing short of explosive in recent months.

Vendors of proprietary software have been carefully crafting their powerful and influential messages about open source. Some attempt to categorise open source as something applicable to research and experimentation. Others cast open source as comparable to open standards. Still others warn about considering open source software for mission critical applications. Each of these messages uses generalisations that distort the truth. Let's examine some of the important attributes and how open source and proprietary approaches compare:

ATTRIBUTE OPEN SOURCE PROPRIETARY

Licence: Licensed to provide freedom to use for any purpose, modify, and redistribute.Licensed to restrict use to 'acceptable uses', protect against modification and redistribution.

Control Balanced: Consumers and providers of commercial offerings have equal access. Vendor is in control. Often large up-front investments in the software, training, and other implementation costs create a lock-in situation that strips the consumer of control.

Innovation Rapid and diverse: Leverages a very large community of users and developers working in parallel. Limited to vendor investments. Typically caters to the features sought by the largest audience. Low levels of innovation. Longevity/ Risk of abandonment Software will always be available as long as it serves a useful purpose. The larger the adoption the safer the investment. No single point of failure. Dependent on the success of the vendor. Single point of failure. Security and reliability As the great tradition of peer review produces high quality academic and scientific works, open source projects produce software that is generally more secure and reliable.

Like peer reviewed papers, open source software is subject to greater scrutiny and leverages a larger collective intelligence than proprietary software. Total Cost of Ownership (TCO) Acquisition cost Low or no initial licence cost. Licence costs on the rise in education. Implementation and support costs OS community support and competition for commercial support keeps costs low. Choice allows consumer to bear costs internally which may further decrease cost. Costs determined by and coupled to vendor.

Lack of choice: Alternative service organisations often lead to higher costs. Costs of scale No additional licence cost with additional users, servers, etc. Licence costs generally rise with increased use. Platform support Broader platform and server support increases leveraged investments in existing institutional infrastructure. Platform support limited to what the vendor offers. May not fit well with institutional infrastructure. As we can see from the comparison, open source promises some impressive advantages over proprietary software. While open source has a rich history in education, a recent convergence of powerful drivers and enablers are precipitating a strong movement towards open source in higher education.

ROLE OF OPEN SOURCE IN HIGHER EDUCATION

Open source is changing the nature of the software business in many settings, but the movement is particularly impressive in education. While open source has nearly a 20 year history of success producing leading software, it has mostly been in the infrastructure domain—the protocol implementations, servers, development frameworks, and utilities that enable the e-mail programmes, browsers, and other applications we all depend on. Open source has not been a significant model for producing application software—until recently. In the past few years colleges and universities have begun to produce enterprise open source applications like course management systems and electronic portfolios that compete directly with their proprietary counterparts. These e-learning applications are leading a movement in higher education from proprietary software towards open source.

A snapshot of the current proprietary software environment in education reveals some compelling drivers:

- Tight budgets have focused attention on software acquisition costs, and total cost of ownership;
- Growing resentment of vendor power, particularly in the wake of price increases and licensing changes that many institutions felt powerless to reject;
- Lack of innovation. Learning technology has not lived up to its potential to improve learning. and some enablers of a more effective model;
- Collaboration technology has made large-scale collaborative work across institutional, geographic, and cultural boundaries more effective;
- Software design patterns, development technologies, and standards have evolved in a way that facilitates modular, interoperable software components;

- Proven business models and education focused companies that embrace open source;
- Strong cultural appeal of open source in academia.

We observe many of these drivers and enablers beyond the context of higher education. Perhaps the cultural appeal in academia represents the 'tipping point' for a powerful movement unique to colleges and universities. At the heart of the cultural fit between academia and open source are common philosophy and values. Creating and sharing knowledge for public good is a key part of the mission of colleges and universities, and a core part of the philosophy driving open source software. Colleges and universities are also home to some of the best software engineers in the world. Yet most institutions don't have a plentiful supply of available talent to meet evolving needs-individually. The open source model provides colleges and universities a way to leverage cultural values of collaboration and sharing to gather resources and work together for the common good. Unlike contexts outside of education, working together doesn't blur institutional brand or threaten a school's income. As a result, higher education not only boasts some of the best software engineers, but also has a plentiful supply of willing talent- a critical success factor for open source.

A common challenge to developing software is understanding the needs of the users and turning that understanding into a suitable software design. While there are many different approaches and software methodologies, the open source model clearly has an advantage since, the individuals most involved in teaching and learning are deeply involved in the development of the software for teaching and learning. Another critical success factor for open source is the emergence of education-focused companies that embrace open source as the preferred model for business. Although colleges and universities are well suited to develop world class enterprise software, supporting that software for other institutions isn't an activity that helps fulfill their mission. A new ecology has emerged where commercial organisations, colleges, and universities play complimentary and collaborative roles. The Andrew W. Mellon foundation, the William and Flora Hewlett Foundation, and others have recognised the need and the potential and have made considerable financial resources available to seed open source projects and help create the new ecology. While there are literally thousands of active open source projects all over the world addressing most application domains, there are a number of notable projects particularly interesting for institutions of higher education.

ROLE OF STORAGE DEVICES IN DIGITAL LIBRARY ENVIRONMENT

Storing documents is one of the foremost jobs of present digital library and it's professional. In order to store a large number of digital collections and to retrieve them at any point of time, the necessity for having a computerised system in this regard was felt; digitalisation of printed material was the result. It is highly valuable for storing the information in an organised manner and retrieves the same quickly. Managing documents in the proper order is very much necessary in library to provide better services to the user community and some permanent solution to preserve the library material was needed. The permanent solution will be digitalising the printed materials, which can be transmitted and received anywhere in the world where the infrastructure to send and receive is in place. This new access of technology will help to preserve the information in digital form for future use for future generation.

WHAT IS DIGITAL LIBRARY

Although Metrics for traditional libraries such as precision and recall can be directly applicable to some aspects of a digital library and have been widely accepted, the digital library is much more complex and there is much more to be considered. Matrices are required to deal with issues such as the distributed nature of the digital library, the importance of user interfaces to the system, and the need for systems approaches to deal with heterogeneity among the various components and content of the digital library.

The main activities of users can be classified into five categories:

- Locating and selecting among relevant sources;
- Retrieving information from them;
- Interpreting what was retrieved;
- Managing the filtered-out information locally; and
- Sharing results with others.

Definition of Digital Library

Digital Library can be define as 'Computer-based information system for acquiring storing, organising, searching, distributing and displaying digital materials for end-user access; not necessarily network-based but designed and constructed so as to be capable of attaching or being attached to a network' It means it is clear that fundamental mission of libraries for the users are not changed, *i.e.*, easy access to knowledge and information but the processes tools, techniques are totally changed. Digital Libraries are viewed as systemic providing a community of users with coherent access to a large, organised repository of information and knowledge. This organisation of information is characterised by the absence of prior detailed knowledge of uses of the information. The ability of the use to access, recognise, and utilise this repository is enriched by the capabilities of digital technologies. More people are recognising that digital library is not a topic only computer and information science, but advances in digital library also depend on efforts from legal community. Digital libraries are libraries extended and enhanced through digital technology.

Important aspects of a library that may be extended and enhanced include:

- The collection of the library;
- The organisation and management of the collection;
- Access to library items and the processing of the information contained in the items;
- To communicate information.

The following tables shows some difference between Traditional Library environment and Digital Library environment.

Knowledge Transfer methods	In Traditional Library	In Digital Library
Between Users Conversation over	Personal meeting, 'Users meet and discussion, E-mail, Chat, Alerts, telephone, Fax, Letters, etc.	Message boards/ dicussion groups. Electronic Comments on Resource, etc.
Between Library Staff and Users	Library Orientation programmes, Seminars, Reference service, Latters, Notice, CAS and SDI services, Newsletters, Brochure, etc.	Online Messagae Board, E-mail Online Alerts, Online Announcements, Online News, Online Learning, etc.
Between Library Staff/ Administrative	Letters, Paper files, Memos, Notice, Meetings	E-mail, Alerts, Scheduler, Calendars, online address book, document clusters

PURPOSE AND FUNCTION OF DIGITAL LIBRARY

Purpose of Digital Library:

- To speed up the systematic development of the means to collect, store and organised information and knowledge in digital form, and of digital library collection;
- To promote the economical and efficient delivery of information to all parts of society;
- To encourage cooperative efforts which leverage the considerable investment in research resource, computing and communications network;
- To strengthen communication and collaboration between and among the research business, government and educational communities;
- To contribute to the life long learning opportunities of all people.

Function of Digital Library:

- Provide access to very large amount of information resources to the users wherever they are and whenever they need;

- Focus on providing access to primary information apart from the secondary sources;
- Support multimedia content along with the text makes the information more useful and understandable to the users;
- Network accessibility in an Internet and Intranet environment;
- Provide user-friendly interface to enable the users for access information comfortably;
- Provide hypertext links for navigation through the required reference;
- Support client server architecture;
- Support advanced search and retrieval for better output to the users;
- Integration with other digital libraries.

WHAT IS STORAGE TECHNOLOGY

Computer technology may conveniently be grouped into: processor technology, storage technology and software aspects. In storage technology considering advances in devices for digital information storage it may be stated that most of the primary storage in computers is now supplied by semi-conductor circuits. There have been significant developments in memory technology affecting three areas of performance spectrum; the high speed, high performance the midrange and the low speed bulk memory systems.

It is now possible that even a small computer system might have cache memory, a small associative memory retaining most recently referenced information and in a readily available place. In some cases, cache memory may be at the top of a hierarchy of memories having a wide variety of characteristics. Memory management, dynamic memory allocation, and virtual memory schemes, generally found in large computer systems, are now appearing on computers which are small and less costly. The development of Charge Coupled Devices (CCDs) and bubble memories have filled the gap which previously existed in the continuum of memory devices such as Fixed-head magnetic disk and these are slower than other semi-conductor memories. These memories have advantage over magnetic disk in that they contain no mechanical parts and could be used to store significant amount of information and can be treated as a structured file system. There has been continuous improvement in recording densities of magnetic media. Floppy disk and microfloppies provide a convenient media to store data. The development of video disk has added a new dimension to the information storage technology. Video disks could be used to store large volumes of information in digital form. These kinds of mass storage are believed to be very useful in the development of information storage and retrieval systems. It may be stated that all these innovations in storage technology provide us a variety of alternatives depending on the requirements of speed of operation.

TYPES OF COMPUTER STORAGE

Computers systems include two types of digital information storage: internal storage, within the CPU and the Backing storage on external devices such as disks or tapes. Different types of storage media differ according to a number of criteria such as speed of operation, capacity cost, reliabilities, the degree to which information is immediately accessible, etc. The various types of storage devices are available in computer market like Network Storage, Backup Storage, Internal Storage and PC Storage Products but we think the manufacture wise classification are different.

Internal Storage Devices: Internal storage is also known as main, primary or core storage, or memory. It is used to hold those instructions and data required at any moment while a programme is running, which must be available instantaneously. Silicon semiconductor chips are now invariably used for internal storage; these are categories as either RAM or ROM chips. ROMs are used for data which is never altered for example, a computer's operating system instructions, while RAM is used for data which is liable to change often, and instructions used in the execution of a programme Backup storage: Backup storage, also termed external storage, is used to hold programmes ad data which are read into internal storage when required. The most common form now, as for the last thirty years, is magnetic storage media, either tapes or disks. With both of these, data is recorded onto a plastic surface, coated with a varnish containing an oxide which can be magnetised in one or two directions; each magnetisation representing one bit of data. Data is written or read with the help of read/write heads. Small electromagnets, close to the surface. Magnetic Tapes are very commonly used for storing large quantum of data for which rapid access is not necessary; especially for archival data backup, etc.

Tapes are cheap means of storing data but access is generally slow. Small cassette tapes, of relatively low capacity are used with microcomputers. Magnetic Disks are most widely used form of baking storage, suitable for holding information required rapidly for example, data for running programme. In the type of disk drive in large computer system, data is recorded on the flat surfaces of circular disks revolving on a common spindle, with one read/write head for each disk. Access times typically 0.01 second, although much faster than tape, are rather slow by comparison with other computer operations and disk access times are one of the main limiting factors in the speed of operation of retrieval system with information stored on disk.

Disk capacities have increased greatly, from original values of about 10 MB to present units with 1 GB which is one thousand million bytes. Smaller computer systems use Winchester disks, with a single hard disk in a sealed unit, floppy disks, which are compact, cheap and convenient for transfer of programmes and data.

They are limited in storage capacity, with relatively slow access times, and less movement than a hard disk in day to day use. Floppy disks are available in two sizes, 1.44 MB and 1.2 MB but now-a-days 1.2 MB floppy are not used. So, we would mention only two types one is Internal Storage and External Storage. In Internal Storage device it may be Network Storage, Internet Storage, Hard Disk Storage, etc. and External Storage devices like Floppy, CD ROM, CD Writer, DVD, USB

Port, Pen drive and many more but we discuss only external storage drives.

Storage Device type	Size and Capacity	Features
Floppy	1.44 MB	Very cheap, easily available and small data transfer its very useful
CD Drive	700MB / 80Min 52x combo drive	CD Drive provide only reading facility
CD Writer (D+R+W)	52x internal and ext. writer	Back up and restore eight times faster than tape, drag-and-drop files
DVD	USB 2.0 interface built	Digital multimedia information, larger storage capacity for audiovisual content Buffer under runs eliminating
REV up	35 GB/90 GB drive 128 bits data encryption and password protection	1 Transfer speed up to 8x faster than tape and more than twice as fast as DVD for immediate full-system recovery 2 Proven hard disk technology for ultimate reliability 3 Professional backup software included
Pen Drive	Up to 1 GB or more	High quality
USB Memory Key	64MB to 256 MB capacity	Store and share loads of information with your choice of flexible, high-quality portable storage drive
AIT Drives	70 GB to 200 GB (compres)	Highest density in tape with a 3.5 inch form factor AIT one of the

(Contd...)

		fastest tape formats in terms of data retrieval and also more reliable and lower cost
DDS Data Cartri.	72 GB10 years archival life	High performance reliable back-up at a great value
Zip Drive	100 MB to 250 MB	More speedy and capacity wise best rather than internal and external drive floppy
Ultrim Cartridge	200 GB to 400 GB	Per tape is exhaustively qualified for better use

In the description of different types of readily available storage devices but the common and maximum uses of the only CD or CD Drive so we discussed how CD useful in digital library environment and also replacement of book in traditional library to digital library. The contents of a digital library get to the readers via direct physical transmission: one person talked to another. These kinds of transmission have so many disadvantages. The other transmission methods like physical objects computer network technologies can perform the duty in a better way.

The mainly used physical objects are books and CD ROMs. Books are the permanent version of information. The economics of scale in modern publishing are such that it is difficult to issue a book today in a small press run. Since, so many to the costs of printing a book are incurred before the first copy comes off the press, a small press run means high costs and thus high prices.

Scholarly journals are even more affected by the push by authors to see their names in print. Their prices have been raised to levels that no one could have imagined 30 years ago; today a journal subscription can cost as much as a new car. Since, the authors are not being paid for their contributions, and since, journals do not carry a retailer's mark-up, these prices reflect the very small number of libraries that are still willing to subscribe.

CD ROM

The first product in evolutionary optical storage of information is CD ROM. It is a permanent optical-based storage device that in conjunction with an associated drive becomes a powerful peripheral for the PC. The CD ROM puts multi megabytes permanently store data bases at user front end of a PC. Its only drawback is that the end users cannot put his own information on it. CD ROM stands for Compact Disc Read Only Memory. A compact disc is a 12cm diameter disc made from polycarbonate substrate and a reflective metalised layer. A disc weighs 16 grammas. A typical CD ROM can store about 650 MB data.

One would get a better idea of the size of the data that a CD ROM can hold if we say that a CD ROM can hold about 250000 pages of text of 5000 handling systems and services CD ROM can store full motion video, animation, graphics, text and high resolution audio. One should keep in mind that a floppy drive cannot run a CD ROM. For running a CD ROM one would require a CD ROM drive. The time taken by a CD drive to find and grab a piece of information is known access time. This is usually in milliseconds. The smaller the access time, the better the drive; the amount of data transferred form the CD ROM to the computer in unit time is known as transfer rate. The basic rate is 150 *kilo bytes per second* (kpbs) and '4x' drive transfers at the rate of 600 (4*50) kbpsz. Today '16 xs' become the normal CD drive.

However, in the market '24 xs' is also available. One would require more the 450 high density floppy diskettes to store an equivalent amount of information on CD compared to hard disc or floppy diskettes. Read Only Memory means that the information stored on a compact disc can only be read but it cannot be modified. As CD ROM stores text, graphic or still images audio and video or moving images, one would need to install a sound card and speaker to enjoy the world of multimedia that a CD ROM offers. The music CDs were followed by CD ROMs. CD ROM can hold a variety of multimedia information. At one point of time, it was called

CD-I or compact disc interactively to the user's instructions. Of course, today such terminology has become irrelevant as almost every CD ROM available in the market is interactive.

The benefits of storing data in the CD ROM are:

- High storage capacity
- No head crash
- Low error rate, correctable data
- Long life
- Random access
- Early transportable
- OS independent file system
- Low cost
- Reliable medium
- Less shelf space

This benefits that made CD ROM practically attractive in today's competing information environment are:

- *Multi-Media*: The ability to deliver unlimited end users access to over 600 MB information delivered using ordinary post means. It can be used for text, graphics, data, audio and video in one simple purchase.
- *Multiplatform*: It is the first truly system independent media with appropriate SWI, CD ROM allows equal access to information regardless of the computer HW or SW platforms used by the end users.
- *Multilingual*: Sophisticated CD ROM systems today allow the end users to select the operating language at choice and change it on-the-fly.

The technology which will most characterise the nineties is multimedia, Multimedia technology integrates text, images, graphics, video, animation, sound or music. It is interactive on the lines of technological barriers extra disk space required to store multimedia formats and broad bandwidth to transmit the text.

METADATA AT DIGITAL-INFORMATIVE ERA

Collection of Items are called Data. The additional Information's about the objects stored within our collections may be Traditional or e-format is represented in the form of Metadata, which is nothing but data about data. In General, metadata is machine understandable information. In Library environment, metadata is commonly used for any formal scheme of resource description, applying to any type of object, digital or non-digital. From Computing Point of View, the content management system contains digital objects. Thus, Metadata is also one of the components of Digital Library. Both Digital objects and Metadata are components of Digital Library.

Digital objects are described, structured, summarised, managed and otherwise manipulated in surrogate form through the use of 'metadata', which literally means data about data. Metadata is usually produced through a process called 'cataloguing' that is often carried out by trained librarians. Collections of such information are commonly stored in 'catalogues'. In computerised environments, metadata may be automatically or semi-automatically extracted or derived from the original content or the 'full text' may simply be indexed and searched.

WHAT IS METADATA

Metadata is 'DATA ABOUT DATA' or 'INFORMATION ABOUT INFORMATION' Metadata is structured Information that describes retrieval for managing Information Resource. Which states that most data is waste without Metadata. Metadata describes data elements and their attributes such as name, size, data type and also Data Structures like length, field, columns, etc. It also has information about the location of data, how it is associated ownership, etc. Also, metadata describes specific characteristics about spatial data, which provides guidelines with a Standard Format.

The Information may includes Name, Ownership, Description, Currency, Status, Access, Quality, Contact Details, etc. It helps us to know where exactly Information locates, Information requirement, relevant Information where exactly locates, even with in another part of your Organisation, etc., are the special features of Metadata. Metadata can be encoded in MARC in 'keyword=value' pairs or in any other definable syntax. Many current meta data schemes use SGML or XML. XML is an extended form of HTML which allows for locally defined tag sets and the easy exchange of structured information. SGML is a superset of both HTML and XML and allows for the richest mark-up of a document.

PURPOSE OF METADATA

The purpose of metadata according to Haynes the Purpose may be expressed as information retrieval, management of information services, documenting ownership and authenticity, interoperability.

- Information retrieval is a dynamic process which involves the user, the system and the librarian. The system indicates the usage of the computers, but can also be the manual catalogue. To obtain proper retrieval of relevant documents, the metadata representation is most important and should satisfy the users.
- Metadata also helps in management of various information services like OPAC, SDI, etc.

  It is a vehicle for documenting ownership and authenticity of the information.
- It also focuses importance towards the interoperability of information across continents.

Also, the Purpose extends to:

- Resource Description.
- Administration and Management of Resources.
- Record of Intellectual Property Rights.
- Documenting Software and Hardware Environments
- Resource Discovery.
- Preservation Management of Digital Resources.
- Providing Information on context and Authenticity.

TYPES OF METADATA

Metadata is divided into different types:

- Descriptive Metadata
- Administrative Metadata
- Structural Metadata
- Subject Metadata

Descriptive Metadata

Descriptive Metadata are used in the Discovery, Indexing and Identification of Digital Resources by semanting means. It is visible to the User of a system. Descriptive Metadata refers to the author, title content, etc. Preservation information refers to the best way of preserving documents like air conditioning or preserving books in the form of files at Systems, which requires meta fields to maintain with.

Administrative Metadata

To maintain Collections, this Administrative Metadata is used. Administrative Metadata is Managing metadata. Rights management metadata is a form of administrative metadata dealing with intellectual property rights. This Administrative metadata pertains to acquisition, vendor, location, etc. Also, it encompass a variety of data related to viewing, interpretation; use and management of digital objects over time. It includes technical data on creation and quality control, which has rights management, access control and user requirements.

- *Management Information*: Managing Information according to User requirements and reflects the output.
- *Technical Information*: Technical Information expresses the Technical details such as Name of the file, its Type, Hardware, Software, Resolution of the Images scanned, Colour space, Pixel dimensions, File relationships, Compressions etc. Using related Information provides User Tracing Information.
- *Structural Metadata*: Structural Metadata is nothing but interface which complies individual digital object into more meaningful units for the users. Structural metadata indicates how compound objects are put together. Structural Metadata is used for representing Physical Entity through Navigation, Information Display and Display. Searching Contents among them or with in them. Structural metadata has information about Physical forms of the resources.

- *Subject Metadata:* To have effective Searching this Subject Metadata is used. For Browsing structure this Subject Metadata is used, with Keywords, Classification Codes, Classification System, Terms from Thesauri and Subject Heading.

HOW METADATA IS USED IN TRADITIONAL LIBRARY CATALOGUING

Traditional Library Cataloguing is a form of metadata, and MARC 21 and the rules sets in AACR2 are metadata standards. Other metadata schemes have been developed to describe various types of textual and non-textual objects such as archival materials, visual materials, geographic information, and science and social science datasets. In mid 1990's Schwartz mentions the term metadata, which is used with database management, began to appear in the LIS literature. However, within a short period the topic became very popular in the area of research concentration, giving rise to several hundred publications. Lange and Winkler traced the history of the term metadata back to the 1960s, but noted that it began to appear more frequently in the DBMS literature in the 1980s. Vellucci notes that the term metadata transcends boundaries among various stakeholders in the development of the internet and provides a common vocabulary to describe a variety of data structures.

XML (EXTENSIBLE MARKUP LANGUAGE)

XML is a Markup Language in the world of Web Designing and Programming. The markup text is a methodology for encoding data with information about it itself. Examples of markup are universal in the real world. The systematic arrangement of data elements for machine processing contains metadata multiple applications. The Resource Description Framework (RDF) is developed under World Wide Web Consortium (W3C), which enables encoding exchange and reuse of structured Metadata. RDF is a language for representing information about resources of World Wide Web, which is particularly representing Metadata with Web Resources. RDF utilises XML as a common syntax for processing of Metadata. XML is a simple and very flexible Markup Language with a great technology also runs in any platform with any Environment. The XML syntax is a subset of the International text processing Standard Generalised Markup Language (SGML) which is meant for Web. The XML syntax provides vendor independence, flexible framework, instant push technologies with Channel Definition Format (CDF), Electronic Commerce uses the Open Trading Protocol (OTP) and Mathematical Markup Language (MML), Pre-defined Tags, User Extensibility, Validation, Human Readability, etc., to indicate complex structures. By exploiting the features of XML, RDF focuses the structure of expression of semantics with machine processing standard Metadata.

WHAT DOES METADATA DO

An important reason for creating descriptive metadata is to facilitate discovery of relevant information. In addition to resource discovery, metadata can help organise electronic resources, facilitate interoperability and legacy resource integration, support digital identification and support archiving and preservation.

HOW TO CREATE METADATA

To encode Information the Data should be expressed in proper way. Create a Single disk file for each metadata record, that is, one disk file describes one data set. Then use some tool to enter Information into this disk file so that the metadata confirm to the standard.

The procedure is:

- Assemble Information about the data set.
- Create a Digital file containing the metadata, properly arranged.
- Check the Syntactical Structure of the file. Modify the arrangement of Information and repeat until the syntactical structure is correct.
- Review the content of the metadata, verifying that the information describes the subject data completely and correctly.

DIGITAL IDENTIFICATION

Most metadata schemes include elements such as standard numbers to uniquely identify the work or object to which the metadata refers. The location of a digital object may also be given using a file name, URL, or some more persistent identifier such as a Persistent URL (PURL) or the Digital Object Identified (DOI).

Persistent identifiers are preferred because file locations change frequently, making the URL invalid. In addition to the actual elements that point to the object, the metadata can be combined to act as a set of identifying data, differentiating one object from another for validation purposes.

ARCHIVING AND PRESERVATION

Recently created resources are the current metadata. However, there is a growing concern that digital resources will not survive in usable form into the future. Digital information is fragile; it can be corrupted or altered according to the requirement. It may become unusable as storage media and hardware and software technologies change. Format migration and perhaps emulation of current hardware and software behaviour in future hardware and software platforms are strategies for overcoming these challenges. Metadata is key to ensuring that resources will survive and continue to be accessible into the future. Archiving and preservation require special elements to track the lineage of a digital object to details its physical characteristics and to document its behaviour in order to emulate it on future technologies.

RESOURCE DISCOVERY

Metadata serves same functions in resource discovery as good cataloguing does by:

- Allowing resources to be found by relevant criteria;
- Identifying resources;
- Bringing similar resources together;
- Distinguishing dissimilar resources; and
- Giving location information;

DUBLIN CORE

The Dublin Core Metadata Element Set arose from discussions at a 1995 workshop sponsored by OCLC and the National Centre for Supercomputing Applications (NCSA), which brought together Librarians, Digital Library Research Scholars, content experts and text-markup experts to develop discovery standards for electronic resources. As the workshop was held in Dublin. Ohio gave rise to a meta format called in the name of Dublin Core.

The continuing development of the Dublin Core and related specifications is managed by the Dublin Core Metadata Initiative (DCMI).

Table 5.1 Dublin Core Data Elements

Group	Element	Description
Content	Title	Name of the resource
	Subject	Topic describing the content of the resource
	Description	About the content of the resource
	Type	The nature of the content of the resource
	Source	A reference to a resource from which the present resource is derived
	Relation	A reference to a related resource
	Coverage	The extent or scope of the content of the resource
Intellectual Property	Creator	Who is primarily responsible for creating the content of the resource
	Publisher	Who is responsible for making the resource available
	Contributor	Who makes contributions

(*Contd...*)

		to the content of the resource
	Rights	Information about rights held in and over
the		resource
Instantiation	Date	Date the resource was first manifested Format The
physical or digital manifestation of the		resource
	Identifier	A unique reference to the resource within a given context
	Language	A language of the intellectual content of the resource

The elements fall into three groups, which roughly indicate the class or scope of information stores in them: elements related mainly to the content of the resource, elements related mainly to the resource when viewed as intellectual property and elements related mainly to the instantiation of the resource. The Dublin Core Metadata Editor is a service that retrieves a given web page and automatically generates Dublin Core metadata suitable for embedding in the section of the page.

- <head>....................</head>

In addition to generating instantly the Dublin Core tags for a given web page, the DCDot service also provides an editor for users to edit the tags or add or edit contents, which can then be resubmitted to create metadata.

ROLE OF METADATA IN INFORMATION MANAGEMENT SYSTEM (IMS)

The role of Metadata in Content Management is something Interesting and worth interrogating. Metadata is used in variety of Situations and applications with widespread web applications. For 'Searching' techniques, the metadata role is very very important. If the user started searching in the name of 'Isolation and Purification' one can get number of references for the above said Topic. The associated keywords are analysed and the related topics may also appear to satisfy the user needs. The terms can be grouped into associative and hierarchically subordinate or super-ordinate terms. This can be represented with the concept of Isolation and Purification. Dr. Ranganathan classification, the Personality, Energy, Matter may be defined. The subordinate terms can be incorporated into the classification schedule and used in assigning subject headings or keywords.

This will serve the purpose of the user and the classificationist. However, change of keyword into subject heading is a different procedure. These are all metadata contents. Also, it serves as a good example for Information Retrieval. Finally, the most important fact is that there should be facility in the software for upgradation of the metadata when required. The elements holds related detailed border schema for description, which is enumerated from narrower schema, to increase both recall and precision. This type of Principle is applicable to any type of Information Management System.

METADATA INTEROPERABILITY FOR CATALOGUING OF E-JOURNALS

The content of digital libraries includes data and metadata that describe various aspects of the digital record that consist of links or relationships to other data or metadata, whether internal or external to the digital library. Interoperability, as defined by the IEEE is 'The ability of two or more systems or components to exchange information and use the information that has been exchanged. This makes it necessary that every library has to examine the issue of data and metadata required for accessing their documents. Metadata is provided in order to provide richer searching than would be possible using standard free-text indexing. In particular it was desirable to allow users to search on a number of fields including Author, Title and Discription. In addition it was felt desirable to allow users to restrict searches by issues by article type. In this chapter, we compare the metadata elements chosen by Libsys, Marc, and conser programme for e-journals and to see whether they are interoperable

METADATA

Metadata Expand the use of data embedded in the digital object or text, and find ways of integrating different kinds of metadata. Metadata has been defined as 'data about data'. It is information about an electronic resource which may be embedded in the resource. Currently work is being done to define a metadata record which adequately describes a wide range of electronic objects.

The aim is to give the authors or information providers associated with electronic resources the means to describe the resource themselves, to a defined standard. The idea is that in describing the resource you need something which is more informative than an index entry, but less complete then a formal cataloguing record. Gilliland-Swetland metadata is more than description; a more inclusive conceptualisation of metadata is needed as information professionals consider the range of their activities that may end up in incorporating it into digital information systems. Repositories also create metadata relating to the administration, accessioning, preservation and use of collections. Acquisition records, exhibition catalogues, and use data are all examples of these, even though they are largely still created in paper form.'

There are three main types of metadata:

- *Descriptive metadata*: Describes a resource for purposes such as discovery and identification. It can include elements such as title, abstract, author and keywords
- *Structural metadata*: Indicates how compound objects are put together, for example how pages are ordered to form chapters
- *Administrative metadata*: Provides information to help manage a resource, such as when and how it was created, file type and other technical information and

who can accesses it. There are several subsets of cataloguers decisions about whether a catalogue record should be created for a whole set of volumes or for each particular volumes in the set, so that the metadata creator makes similar decisions

Metadata is structured information that describes, explains locates or otherwise makes it easier to retrieve, use or manage an information resource. Traditional library cataloguing is a form of metadata and MARC21 and the rule sets used with it such as AACR2 are metadata standards. Metadata can be embedded in a digital object or it can be stored separately. Metadata will not be lost and obviates problems of linking between data and metadata, and helps to ensure that the metadata and object will be updated together. In this chapter, we intend to compare the interoperability of Libsys metadata with Marc 21 and Conser.

HOW TO CATALOGUE E-JOURNALS USING METADATA

Metadata is used to improve the utility of data by providing a structure of framework for describing that data. Metadata elements are in effect fields of information that can be stored and manipulated in catalogue. Metadata is particularly useful for large collections of documents or other materials, it can be used for managing the resource and for finding specific items.

A Catalogue becomes an found by some libraaries is an essential tool for retrieval. Libraries made a commitment to provide users with online access to full-text journals, found in publisher packages and aggregator databases, via Web lists and OPAC with details such as holdings coverage, embargo, source, open access, and local subject headings. The metadata of e-journals were first tracked on spreadsheets in EXCEL for Web lists and were also cataloged in the OPAC, a dual-maintenance system which later proved to be needing improvement as library electronic journal collection expanded. Libraries thus developed an interim solution and a long-term solution for managing e-journals access. The interim solution is to replace EXCEL with Microsoft ACCESS in processing e-journal metadata, still a dual-maintenance system but with greatly reduced maintenance work and enhanced timeliness of ejournal metadata in the OPAC and on the Web lists. The long-term solution is to generate e-journal Web lists from the OPAC with streamlined e-journal metadata batch-loading process using Innovative's Electronic Resources Management Module.

The OCLC / NCSA Meta Data workshop in Dubin, Ohio held in 1995 proposed the following core set of elements to appear in Uniform Resource Characteristics (URC):

- Title
- Creator
- Subject and Keywords
- Description
- Publisher
- Contributor
- Date
- Resource Type
- Format
- Resource Identifier
- Source
- Language
- Relation
- Coverage
- Rights Management

Increasing size and complexity of the digital information available on the web demands for methods of its organisation. Uniform and structured meta information which can effectively be employed to achieve this goal. Metadata support efficient and effective organisation, access and retrieval of information contents in a digital library. Meta information is used in effective designing of browsing and search interfaces of a digital library. Describing a resource with metadata allows it to be understood by both human and machines in ways that promote interoperability. Most metadata schemes include elements such as standard numbers to uniquely identify the work or object to which the metadata refers. Metadata is key to ensuring that resources will survive and continue to be accessible into the future. Metadata elements are in effect field information that can be stored and manipulated in a database or a stylesheet.

Alternatively the data elements may be embedded in a document, delimited by tags. The marked up metadata tags may also include details of the metadata schema used and the encoding system that has been adopted. Information retrieval is through a combination of key words, menus, and graphic map interfaces. Descriptions include the data custodian, custodian location, data cost, data quality, confidentiality constraints, spatial coverage, time period and a short description of the data set.

E-JOURNALS ON THE INTERNET

Using the Web, publishers can easily distribute hypertext documents with multimedia components to a global audience, and they have been actively experimenting with Web versions of new or existing electronic serials.

The Journal of Internet Cataloguing also looks at:

- Uniform resource identifiers and link-resolve services.
- Usability testing.
- Interoperability, crosswalks, and mappings among metadata schema.
- Learning object metadata.
- Using classification and automated assists for organising Web resources.
- Software and hardware for retrieving, reviewing, and describing Internet resources.
- Managing the catalogueing process of Internet resources
- The problems of maintaining catalogue records for remote electronic resources.
- Descriptive and subject catalogueing applied to Internet resources.
- Education and training.
- International issues in organising/catalogueing Internet resources.

The Journal of Internet Cataloguing is an essential resource for practising librarians and information specialists, library and information science educators and students, and systems administrators.

LIBSYS

'LibSys for library automation' is the prime mission of New Delhi based software company - Info-Tek Consultants Pvt. Ltd., engaged in providing software solutions for General Insurance and ERP/CRM since, 1984. Its continuous growth for the last 12 years, has made LibSys a defacto standard for libraries in India. Its acceptance in global market further strengthens its popularity across the country as the most field proven library system in a wide spectrum of libraries with unmatchable depth in functionality and features. The following is the libsys metadata structure for serials record

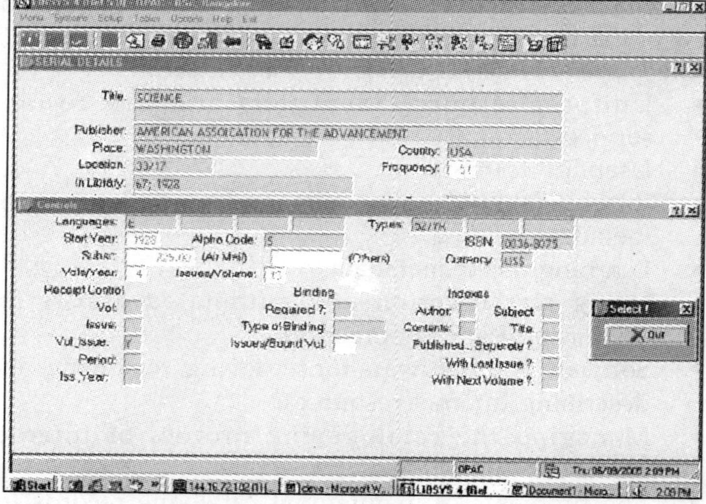

The Libsys metadata facilitates ordering receiving loose issues, recording bound volumes of journals in print medium this can be easily converted to e- Journal recording by changing the item receiving data into e-journal release data. The location metadata in libsys can be easily converted to url.. Bound volumes can give the link to Url.

MARC 21

The Library of Congress' Network Development and MARC Standards Office is developing a framework for working with MARC data in a XML environment. This framework is intended to be flexible and extensible to allow users to work with MARC data in ways specific to their needs. The framework itself includes many components such as schemas, stylesheets, and software tools. Library of Congress ' Network Development and MARC Standards Office has developed a schema for a bibliographic element set that may be used for a variety of purposes, and particularly for library applicationsa. An XML schema, the 'Metadata Object Description Schema' (MODS) is intended to be able to carry selected data from existing MARC 21 records as well as to enable the creation of original resource description records. It includes a subset of MARC fields and uses language-based tags rather than numeric ones, in some cases regrouping elements from the MARC 21 bibliographic format. MODS is expressed using the XML schema language of the World Wide Web Consortium. Marc also provides url linking facility in its tag. Metadata recorded for Journal of the American Chemical Society.

LC Control Number:	sn 96038212
000	01590cas 2200361 a 450
001	11784983
005	20000511061112.0
007	heubmb024bucu
008	950508c19959999dcuwr pbb 0 0eng d
010	__ |a sn 96038212
035	__ |a (OCoLC)ocm32438440
040	__ |a FTS |c FTS |d MCM |d DLC |d RPB |d CU-S
012	__ |a -3-7-0005100385-p-9608
042	__ |a lc
050	00 |a Microfilm (0) 99/8014
050	14 |a QD1 |b.A4 Suppl.
245	00 |a Journal of the American Chemical Society. |p Supporting information |h [microform].

(*Contd...*)

<table>
<tr><td>246</td><td>30 |a Supporting information, journal of the American Chemical Society</td></tr>
<tr><td>246</td><td>1_ |i Vol. 117, no. 6 has title: |a Journal of the American Chemical Society. |p Supplementary material</td></tr>
<tr><td>260</td><td>__ |a [Washington, D.C.]: |b American Chemical Society, |c c1995-</td></tr>
<tr><td>300</td><td>__ |a microfiches: |b negative</td></tr>
<tr><td>310</td><td>__ |a Weekly</td></tr>
<tr><td>362</td><td>0_ |a Vol. 117, no. 5 (Feb. 8, 1995)-</td></tr>
<tr><td>500</td><td>__ |a Title from eye-readable header.</td></tr>
<tr><td>515</td><td>__ |a Assumes vol. numbering of parent journal.</td></tr>
<tr><td>530</td><td>__ |a Online version available to subscribers with a site licence; files in HTML and PDF format.</td></tr>
<tr><td>650</td><td>_0 |a Chemistry |v Periodicals.</td></tr>
<tr><td>710</td><td>2_ |a American Chemical Society.</td></tr>
<tr><td>772</td><td>0_ |t Journal of the American Chemical Society |x 0002-7863 |w (DLC) 16003159 |w (OCoLC)1226990</td></tr>
<tr><td>780</td><td>00 |t Journal of the American Chemical Society. Supplementary material |w (DLC)sn 96038213 |w (OCoLC)4764975</td></tr>
<tr><td>787</td><td>1_ |t ACS electronic supporting information. Journal of the American Chemical Society |w (DLC) 00242806 |w (OCoLC)42258873</td></tr>
<tr><td>850</td><td>__ |a DLC |a MCM</td></tr>
<tr><td>936</td><td>__ |a Vol. 120, no. 7 (Feb. 25, 1998) LIC\</td></tr>
</table>

CONSER PROGRAMME

CONSER is:

- A cooperative online serials cataloguing programme.
- A source of high quality bibliographic records for serials.
- A source of high quality documentation and training

materials for the cataloguing of serials and the input of serial records.

- A group of serial experts who work together in an atmosphere of collegiality and trust.
- A promulgator of standards related to serials.
- A voice for serials in the library community.
- A component of the Programme for Cooperative Cataloguing.

CONSER began in the early 1970s as a project to convert manual serial cataloguing into machinereadable records and has evolved into an ongoing programme to create and maintain high quality bibliographic records for serials. In keeping with its evolution, the name was changed in 1986 from the CONSER Project to the CONSER Programme. In October 1997, CONSER became a bibliographic component of the Programme for Cooperative Cataloguing. now in process, serials catalogers will soon be in position to utilise all the computer file bibliographic record elements.

CONSER has taken a major step in developing policies for these new elements with the publication. Describing electronic access information is another challenge for the cataloguer due to the different areas of the record involved, including the new electronic location and access field. *AACR2* requires cataloguers to 'always specify the mode of access' for electronic serials in a note. The CONSER 'mode of access' note now includes more general information to limit redundancy with the 856 field, which contains the detailed information needed to locate and access documents. Serials cataloguers now use the note field 538 for the more general information as the field is newly available through format integration.

1	010	sn95-7042
2	040	NSD $c NSD $d OCL $d DLC
3	012	$l 1
4	022	01080-6059
5	037	$b Centres for Disease Control and Prevention, 1600 Clifton Rd., Mailstop C-12, Atlanta, GA 30333

(*Contd...*)

6	042	nsdp $a lcd
7	069	1 SR0083699
8	08210	616 $2 12
9	090	$b
10	049	DLCC
11	1300	Emerging infectious diseases (Online)
12	2100	Emerg. infect. dis. $b (Online)
13	2220	Emerging infectious diseases $b (Online)
14	24500	Emerging infectious diseases $h [computer file]:$b EID.
15	24630	EID
16	260	Atlanta, GA: $b National Centre for Infectious Diseases: $b Centers for Disease Control and Prevention, $c[1995-
17	310	Four times per year
18	3620	Vol. 1, no. 1 (Jan.-Mar. 1995)-
19	538	Mode of access: Internet e-mail, FTP, and World Wide Web.
20	500	Description based on: hypertext/World Wide Web version; title from EID home page.
21	5168	ASCII, Acrobat, and PostScript file formats
22	530	Online version of: Emerging infectious diseases (Print).
23	7102	National Centre for Infectious Diseases (U.S.,)
24	7761	$t Emerging infectious diseases (Print) $x 1080-6040 $w (DLC)sn 95007041 $w (OCoLC)31848353
25	8560	$u mailto:lists@list.cdc.gov $i subscribe $f EID-* $z Include desired file format following the hyphen in the filename: IED-ASCII, EID-PDF, or EID-PS
26	8561	ftp.cdc.gov $d pub/EID $l anonymous $z Each issue is in a separate subdirectory (*e.g.*, vol1no1). There are additional subdirectories for each file format
27	8567	$

METADATA INTEROPERABILITY

Metadata as a tool to facilitate exchange of information between interoperating systems and interoperability of metadata schemas themselves which can help to facilitate systems interoperability.

There are three different types of interoperability:

- *Semantic interioperability*: Achieved through agreements about content description standards;
- *Structural interoperbility*: A data model that is used for specifying semantic schemas; and
- *Syntactic introperbility*: Which provides a syntax for expressing metadata: an example is XML.

Metadata Crosswalks

A crosswalk allows metadata created by one community to be used by another group that employs a different metadata standards. Crosswalks are important for virtual libraries where resources are being collected from a variety of sources and are expected to act as a whole, perhaps with a single search engine applied. While these cross walks are key they are also labour intensive to develop and maintain. Reconciling metadata created in different environments is a major challenge and some effort has been devoted to mapping equivalent metadata elements between different metadata schemas. These mappings can be displayed as tables and are known as crosswalks. They can be used within systems to effect transformations between metadata objects. Crosswalks are a starting point for assessing the suitability of data sources for import. Table provide a comparative statement of interoperability between LIBSYS, MARC 21 and CONSER Programme.

	LIBSYS	CONSER	MARC21
Title	Title	Title	245: Title
Publishers	Pub	Pub	260: Pub
Place	Place pub	Combined with with	Combined pub
Country	Country	Country used	257can be

(*Contd...*)

Location/URL	Manual:Yes	Yes (Electronic)	856 (Electronic location)
Frequency	Frequency	Frequency	310
Starting Date	Starting Date:Manual	Yes (Electronic)	362 (Starting electronic pub)
Language	Language	Language	041
Alphe code	Alphe code	Not available	030
Control Number	Control Number	Control Number	010
ISSN	ISSN	ISSN	022
Vol.Year, Holding data	Available in separate file	Available in separate file	841
Subject	Subject	Subject	650
Supplement	Supplement recorded as an issue	NA	050
Note	Yes	Yes	500

The library participates in a metadata harvesting protocol to provide extracts of local metadata in a common format to a service provider so that information about the collection is automatically included in a number of relevant tools such as catalogues and portals.

The Web page is linked to the library's web site dedicated to resources. Where it is available to researchers in context with archival and visual materials, digitised secondary sources, etc. Administrative, structural, and descriptive metadata for web site also has been created to hold all of its pieces together to allow them to be managed and allow them to be accessed.

SCIENTISTS VIEWS ON TRENDS IN DIGITAL LIBRARY IN BANGLADESH AND INDIA

Over With the knowledge revolution came into the scene, there has been a sea change in the concept of library also. The beginning of the new millenium itself is the beginning of the new digital information era. The digital library, electronic library and virtual library have become most oftenly-spoken words today among the library and information scientists. The same has been in existence since, last decade, even though not in full swing.

India, becoming one of the pioneer countries in the software engineering in the world, has also introduced Digital Library (DL) in different institutional set-ups. INFLIBNET Centre, Ahmedabad is also playing a crucial role in this regard. Our neighbouring sister country Bangladesh has also started DL in various educational institutions.

METHODOLOGY

The Second International Convention, PLANNER—2004 was held during 4-5 November,2004 in Manipur University, Imphal in which about 200 delegates from Bangladesh and India were attended. During the convention jointly organised by the INFLIBNET Centre, Ahmedabad and Manipur University, Imphal, views of the delegates were collected through a questionnaire to understand the present scenario of DL in the two countries.

Most of the delegates were Library and Information Professionals, Scientists, Computer Specialists, Executives of high ranks in the field of Library and Information Activities. The delegates who have returned the questionnaires are being considered here as Library and Information Scientists.

ANALYSIS OF DATA

Sample Characteristics

Altogether 50 questionnaires were distributed randomly among the scientists and received 38 filled in questionnaires. Three of the returned questionnaires were found incomplete which have summarily been rejected making the response to 35 (70.00 per cent) only.

Of the 35 returned questionnaires 06, (17.14 %) are from Bangladesh and remaining 29 (82.86 %) are from India. The personal identification of the scientists is shown in table.

Table 5.2 Personal Identification

Scientists	Sex		Total	Qualification		Total
				(%)		(%)
	Male	Female		P G	Ph.D.	
	(%)		(%)	(%)		(%)
Bangladesh	05 (83.3)	01 (16.67)	06 (100.00)	04 (66.67)	02 (33.33)	06 (100.00)
India	17 (58.62)	12 (41.38)	29 (100.00)	20 (68.97)	09 (31.03)	29 (100.00)
Total	**23 (65.71)**	**12 (35.29)**	**35 (100.00)**	**24 (68.57)**	**11 (31.43)**	**35 (100.00)**

Male representation is higher than their female counterparts as seen and all the scientists under the sample study possess minimum Post Graduate Degree, 31.43 per cent of them being Ph.D. holders. They are found to be associated with technical and academic institutions holding responsible posts and involved in the matters concerning digital information.

Existence of DL

The existence of DL in the institutions where the scientists are engaged is understood from table. As responded only 40.00 per cent of the institutions of the two countries exists DL, while it is 50.00 per cent in case of Bangladesh it is only 37.93 per cent in case of India.

Table also highlights that there exists no DL is full swing, 42.86 per cent are in initial stage and 57.14 per cent are in planning stage. Most of those DLs are also found to be launched since, late nineties and beginning of the new century.

Table 5.3 Existence of DL and Its Stage

Scientists	Existence of DL		Total (per cent)	Stage of DL			
	Yes	No		Initial	Full	Planning	Other
	(%)	(%)		(%)	(%)	(%)	(%)
Bangladesh	03 (50.00)	03 (50.00)	06 (100.00)	02 (66.67)	–	01 (33.33)	–
India	11 (37.93)	18 (62.07)	29 (100.00)	04 (36.36)	–	07 (63.34)	–
Total	**14 (40.00)**	**21 (60.00)**	**35 (100.00)**	**06 (42.86)**	–	**08 (57.14)**	–

The major problems behind the non-existence of DL in both the countries include:

- Lack of funds and interest

- No interest in planning
- Lack of manpower, resources, infrastructure
- Lack of coordination

Planning to Introduce DL

Considering the essentiality of the DL, all those scientists engaged in the institutions where there is no existence of DL presently expressed that their parent organisations are planning to introduce DL, even though, it a matter of time only, as recorded in table.

Table 5.4 Planning to Introduce DL

Scientists	Yes	No
Bangladesh	03 (100.00)	Nil (0.00)
India	18 (100.00)	Nil (0.00)
Total	21 (100.00)	Nil (0.00)

Objectives of DL

As opined by the scientists, the major objectives of the DLs, which are in existence in their respective institutions, include:

- To serve the users at door point
- To automate the library operations
- To create databases of resources
- To provide bibliographical services and indices
- To make network among the academic libraries
- To provide browsing facilities
- To provide services quickly and economically
- To share resources effectively
- To render services efficiently

Technological Requirements

The availability and readiness of technical requirements for the development of DL are understood from the table. Most of the requirements are found to be developed relatively in the two countries. The table is self-explanatory.

Table 5.5 Technological Requirements: Readiness for DL

Requirements	Scientists			
	Bangladesh (06)		India (29)	
	Yes (%)	NO (%)	Yes (%)	NO (%)
Locally Developed Database	05 (83.33)	01 (16.67)	21 (72.41)	08 (27.59)
Sufficient Number of Computers	05 (83.33)	01 (16.67)	27 (93.10)	02 (6.90)
Software and Its accessories	06 (100.00)	00 (0.00)	23 (79.31)	06 (20.69)
LAN facility	06 (100.00)	00 (0.00)	27 (93.10)	02 (6.90)
Network Connectivity	04 (66.67)	02 (33.33)	25 (96.20)	04 (13.80)
Internet Connectivity	02 (33.33)	04 (66.67)	25 (96.20)	04 (13.80)
Multimedia Kits	03 (50.00)	03 (50.00)	19 (65.51)	10 (34.49)
Well trained manpower	03 (50.00)	03 (50.00)	22 (75.87)	07 (24.13)
Computer hardware	06 (100.00)	00 (0.00)	26 (89.65)	03 (10.35)
Facilities to coordinate, manage the entry, search and retrieve	05 (83.33)	01 (16.67)	24 (82.75)	05 (17.25)
CD-ROMs, Floppies etc.	03 (50.00)	03 (50.00)	22 (75.87)	07 (24.13)
Digital Information resources	02 (33.33)	04 (66.67)	27 (93.10)	02 (6.90)
VSAT facilities	02 (33.33)	04 (66.67)	28 (96.55)	01 (3.45)
Digital Storage Media	03 (50.00)	03 (50.00)	22 (75.87)	07 (24.13)

DL Services

The various DL services as experienced by the scientists are recorded in table.

Table 5.6 DL Services

Services	Scientists			
	Bangladesh (06)		India (29)	
	Yes (%)	NO (%)	Yes (%)	NO (%)
Shared Cataloguing	01 (16.67)	05 (83.33	20 (68.97)	09 (31.03)
Union Cataloguing	02 (33.33)	04 (66.67)	16 (55.18)	13 (44.82)
Access to Bibliographic	04 (66.67)	02 (33.33)	17 (58.62)	12 (41.38)

(Contd...)

Database				
Online Catalogue	03 (50.00)	03 (50.00)	16 (55.18)	13 (44.82)
Access to subject gateways in specific disciplines	02 (33.33)	04 (66.67)	10 (34.49)	19 (65.51)
Subscribing to e-journals	03 (50.00)	03 (50.00)	27 (93.10)	02 (6.90)
Reference services provided by librarians and experts on the web	01 (16.67)	05 (83.33)	21 (72.41)	08 (27.59)
Links to web sites	01 (16.67)	05 (83.33)	23 (79.31)	06 (20.69)
Procuring e- reference sources	01 (16.67)	05 (83.33)	17 (58.62)	12 (41.38)
Documents Delivery Services	02 (33.33)	04 (66.67)	15 (51.72)	14 (48.28)
Online CAS	02 (33.33)	04 (66.67)	21 (72.41)	08 (27.59)
Digitisation of library resources	04 (66.67)	02 (33.33)	27 (93.10)	02 (6.90)
Bulletin Board	04 (66.67)	02 (33.33)	20 (68.97)	09 (31.03)
Referral service	03 (50.00)	03 (50.00)	20 (68.97)	09 (31.03)
E-mail service	06 (100.00)	00 (0.00)	26 (89.66)	03 (10.34)
Consortia subscription	01 (16.67)	05 (83.33)	22 (75.87)	07 (24.13)
Web based OPAC	01 (16.67)	05 (83.33)	19 (65.51)	10 (34.49)

Feedback from the User

The feedback from the users of DL & its services in both the countries are listed here below:

- Users want to have their facility to use DL service;
- Users provide helps to selection process;
- Some users are not acquainted with DL services;
- More digital services are required by them;
- Some users are still ignorant about DL;
- To the users mostly in NE India the concept of DL is very new and they are digital phobia; and
- There is question of non-satisfaction to the services.

Problems and Prospects

The scientists of the two countries are found to be encountered with the management of DL & providing its services.

Some of the specified problems are:

- Financial constraints
- Shortage of skilled professional manpower
- Lack of infrastructure
- Non-awareness of DL by majority
- Absence of Internet connectivity and VSAT facility
- Poor IT knowledge
- Disturbance of power supply
- Lack of networking facility to share resources

Inspite of all these constraints, there are also prospects and benefits from DL as listed below as felt by the scientists:

- DL enables to provide services quickly and economically
- It can fulfill the interests and demands of the users
- It opens scope for resource sharing
- More users are attracted
- Through DL services geographical gap can be bridged
- It improves the quality of services
- It saves the space problems also

As Suggested by them, the following points may be taken into account for the successful implementation of the DL in both the countries:

- Campaign for developing and growing interest among the planners
- Making fund available to start with
- Training of professionals for the purpose
- Development and adaptation of a uniform system for sharing its resources
- Education and training for the users community
- Team work is required for their cooperative venture
- Work culture on the part of library and information professionals requires to be developed

- Convention like PLANNER should be organised continuously
- A national policy on the matter requires to be chalked out
- Compilation of union catalogues requires urgently

MULTILINGUAL ACCESS TO INFORMATION IN A NETWORKED ENVIRONMENT CHARACTER ENCODING AND UNICODE STANDARD

One of the great benefits of digital libraries is the ability to make information available to a wide audience without geographic constraints. As large-scale digital libraries contribute to the dismantling of the geographic barriers to information access, however, the barrier raised by language considerations becomes apparent. In order to make information available to the widest possible audience, this language barrier must also be tackled.

Ideally, a global digital library would provide access to information in all the languages of the world, to all people, all the time. Anyone anywhere could create information in their native language, yet others, wherever they are, could discover that information and have it translated into their favoured languages and formats. Such an ideal situation may well be beyond our reach at the present moment, but it raises issues worthy of investigation.

No single collection, user interface, or set of system capabilities will serve young and old, novice and expert, artist and physicist, in New Delhi and New York. Nor will any single system provide adequate access to books, music, movies, and numeric data, much less serve applications as diverse as ecommerce, weather modelling, census tracking, library catalogues, and virtual classrooms.

Yet people with varying backgrounds and skills, speaking in different tongues, have similar information needs. Content of interest may exist in a wide variety of forms and languages, and the same content and collections may be of interest to a wide range of people, for many different reasons.

The prospect of a global digital library presents several opportunities like:

- Making information resources accessible to particular user communities while at the same time making those same resources accessible to a broader, improperly-defined, and perhaps unknown audience.
- Enabling users to bridge the many formats, representations, and languages of individual digital libraries in their quest for information resources.

The issue of multilingual access to information is an example of the tradeoffs between tailoring to local communities and generalising to a global audience.

This particular issue is:

- Urgent in view of the rate at which new text is being created.
- Long-term—in view of the relative stability of languages compared to the ephemeral nature of new media formats.
- Broad-reaching—in view of the fact that some form of textual content is involved in most forms of electronic communication, whether alone or as descriptions of other media.

This chapter addresses issues related to multilingual access to digital information repositories in general, and the problems associated with character encoding of multilingual text in particular with special emphasis to the practices followed by library community in this regard.

FROM MONOLINGUAL TO MULTILINGUAL DIGITAL LIBRARIES

Language is one of the most critical factors in access to information. Information is usable and useful only if it is in a language that can be read or otherwise understood. Communication between people speaking a common language, whether English, French, Mandarin, or Hindi, is influenced by factors such as subtleties of phrasing, vocabulary, regional accents, and knowledge of the subject matter being discussed.

In monolingual information retrieval, some of these difficulties are ameliorated through:

- Standardising forms
- Controlled vocabulary
- Algorithms that employ knowledge of grammatical structure and word frequency in the language

People often need information that exists in languages other than those they read or speak, however. Human translators can bridge language in oral and written communication. They can translate between spoken languages in real time, and they can translate texts. Translation is a challenging intellectual task, as no two languages map precisely onto one another.

A word in one language may have several meanings in the other, and the interpreter must determine which is most appropriate. Conversely, one word may incorporate multiple meanings in another language and the appropriate subset must be identified. Often, a narrative explanation is needed in place of a single word. Meaning depends on context as well as on choice of words. Metaphors and idioms are particularly difficult to convey in other languages.

Translators are really interpreters of meaning; that is why automatic translation is so limited. Computers can provide approximate translations, particularly of scientific texts, but are far from a reliable substitute for expert human language interpreters. Providing access to information in multiple languages is a challenge inherent in constructing a global information infrastructure. It is also fundamental to tailoring and interoperability trade-offs. Given a choice, people generally prefer to communicate in their native language, both online and offline. Communication in international environments frequently involves multiple languages, however, and people often need information written in unfamiliar languages.

The problem of multilingual access to information affects not only users in countries in which several languages are spoken but also all those who search material in information sources or databases containing material in more than one language. This is the case in the majority of scientific or research databases. In addition, the growth of networks means that we can easily access information/databases outside our own immediate circle—in another country, another continent. In doing so, we encounter problems concerning not only search interfaces, but also concerning search keys like, subject or even author in another language.

Multilingual information access is a pervasive problem in automation, and it is of great concern for anyone exchanging information over computer networks. Multilingual access issues affect e-commerce, information institutions such as libraries, archives, museums, academic institutions at all levels, and those who produce hardware and software for network applications. However, it is important to understand the connotation of the term 'multilingual access.' Multilingual access is frequently used to cover a variety of topics, and it is necessary to define the use of the term 'multilingual' in the context of this chapter. We frequently hear talk of multilingual systems in reference to search environments, whereas the actual access points themselves are in fact monolingual. Multilingual user environments are now standard in the majority of systems.

MULTILINGUAL ACCESS TO INFORMATION

Multilingual digital libraries are being created by countries with more than one national language, by the European Union, and by international research consortia and international businesses. Major scientific, technical and medical databases, such as INSPEC and Medline, long have contained metadata in English to represent materials in other languages.

Monolingual digital libraries also are being created in many different languages. Many of these digital libraries are of interest well beyond the borders of the countries creating them, and to users who are native speakers of other languages. A fundamental challenge of constructing a global information infrastructure and a global digital library is to provide access to these collections, regardless of the language of the content and the language of the information seeker. The World Wide Web offers access to information resources in many languages. Certain developments facilitate multilingual exploitation of these resources.

Some search engines allow the user to restrict retrieved sites to those in particular languages; some also provide the searcher with an interface in a chosen language. Many Web sites also offer their information in several languages, one of which typically is English. Systran, a machine translation system available from the AltaVista search engine, can even translate a search statement or a retrieved page from one language to another. Despite these features, however, language also creates obstacles to full exploitation of Web resources. Not all languages are catered for by these multilingual tools. Machine translation output typically is but a rough and ready version of a human translation. The varieties of scripts in which the written forms of the world's languages appear also create major problems in searching, inputting, displaying and printing text in non-Roman scripts. Multilingual access to information is a complex problem.

Peters and Picchi have divided it into two basic parts:

- Multiple-language recognition, manipulation, and display—involving matters such as encoding character sets and symbols so that they can be manipulated; and
- Multilingual or cross-lingual search and retrieval—referring to search for content in other languages, otherwise known as 'cross-language information retrieval.'

The first point addresses the problem of allowing digital library users to access the system, no matter where they are located, and no matter in what language the information is stored; it is a question of providing the enabling technology. The second point implies permitting the users of a digital library containing documents in different languages to specify their information needs in their preferred language while retrieving documents matching their query in whatever language the document is stored; this is an area in which much research is now under way. Let us first have an outline of this second point

Cross-Language Information Retrieval

The interface of a multilingual digital library must include features to support all the languages that will be maintained by the system and to permit easy access to all the documents contained. However, it must also include functionalities for multilingual or cross-language search and retrieval. This implies the development of tools that allow users to interact with the system, formulating the queries in one language and retrieving documents in others. The problem is to find methods which successfully match queries against documents over languages. This involves a relatively new discipline, generally known as *Cross-Language Information Retrieval* (CLIR), in which methodologies and tools developed for *Natural Language Processing* (NLP) are being integrated with techniques and results coming from the *Information Retrieval* (IR) field.

Peters and Picchi have identified three approaches that are being studied for solution of the CLIR problem:

- Text translation by machine
- Knowledge-based techniques
- Corpus-based techniques

Text translation can be divided further:

- Translating the full content of the digital library into another language
- Translating only the query

Translating the full content is rarely feasible except in very small and specific applications. In the area of meteorological reports automatic translation is reasonably successful. For most applications, translating queries appears to be more promising. Queries in English can be translated into Japanese and searched in Japanese databases, and vice versa. Knowledge-based approaches involve multilingual dictionaries, thesauri, or ontologies. In these approaches, searchers can construct a query using terms in their own language. The multilingual thesaurus is then used to translate the terms into the target language; they are then submitted to databases in that language. Thesauri can be translated pair wise or among a larger number of languages. In the latter case, a common core of terms would be established, and then the linguistic equivalents in each language would be determined. Corpus-based techniques involve linguistic characteristics of a language and the distribution of terms in a collection of documents.

Information retrieval techniques developed for monolingual retrieval, such as vector-space models and probabilistic methods can be employed for multiple languages. Usually some test databases in each language are required to 'train' the algorithms about the relationships between corpora in each language. Each of these methods is both promising and problematic. None are complete solutions, and all are under active study. For any of the cross-language techniques to be effective, however, underlying technical issues in managing multilingual text must be resolved.

Multilingual Recognition and Representation

Despite its name, until recently the World Wide Web had not addressed one of the basic challenges to global communication: the multiplicity of languages. Standards for protocols and document formats originally paid little attention to issues such as character encoding, multilingual documents, or the specific requirements of particular languages and scripts. Consequently, the vast majority of WWW browsers still do not support multilingual data representation and recognition. Ad-hoc local solutions currently abound which, if left unchecked, could lead to groups of users working in incompatible isolation.

The main requirements of a multilingual application are to:

- Support the character sets and encodings used to represent the information being manipulated.
- Present the data meaningfully.
- Manipulate multilingual data internally.

CHARACTER ENCODING

Character encoding is at the heart of the data-recognition, data-manipulation, and display components of multilingual information access. The creation of characters in electronic form involves hardware and software to support input, storage, processing, sorting, displaying, and printing. Each character—or ideograph in languages such as Chinese, Japanese, and Korean—needs a unique code to ensure that it sorts, displays, prints, and is matched properly upon searching.

Additional codes are required for punctuation, direction of text, carriage returns, and line feeds. The internal representation of each character determines how it is treated by the hardware and the application software. To the dismay of those whose languages have far larger character sets, typewriter keyboards were initially designed for the English language; thus, they contain only 26 letters, 10 numbers, basic punctuation, and a few special symbols. Only a few more symbols and function keys were added when the typewriter keyboard was adapted to become a computer keyboard. Many versions of the QWERTY keyboard are now in use worldwide, varying the location of letters. Special characters, such as letters with diacritics, can be generated by programming individual keys or by programming key sequences, often using escape key.

The same key sequences on two different keyboards may produce two different characters, depending on the encoding system employed. Conversely, key sequences required to generate a character vary by keyboard and encoding system. Effective data exchange is heavily dependent on character encoding.

Characters produced from different applications may appear the same on a screen or a printout but have different internal representations. Merging or transferring data between applications requires a common character-encoding standard or software to map variant encoding formats. Searchers need to have the appropriate keyboards and software to generate characters in the encoding standard in which the contents of a digital library are stored, whether locally resident or available through mapping software located at the digital library site or elsewhere. Local printers and displays must have the appropriate software to interpret and produce characters accurately. These factors are not specific to digital libraries; rather, they are issues for all distributed applications on a global information infrastructure.

MONOLINGUAL, MULTILINGUAL, AND UNIVERSAL CHARACTER SETS

For character encoding many standards and practices exist, viz.:

- Those that are language specific
- Those that are script specific
- The remaining are universal standards that support most of the world's written languages

Digital libraries employ many different character-encoding formats, and this often leads to problems in exchanging data. After many years of international discussion on the topic, it became evident that adopting a universal character set offered the greatest hope for exchanging text in digital form. If data in all written languages were encoded in a common format, then data could be exchanged between monolingual and multilingual applications, whether e-mail, e-commerce, or digital libraries.

Which common format to accept was a matter of long debate, however. In 1991, the Unicode Consortium and the International Organisation for Standardisation (ISO) finally reached an agreement to merge the 16-bit Unicode Standard and the 32-bit ISO standard into a common 16-bit Unicode Standard. Version 1.1 was first published in 1993; version 4.0 is currently the accepted Unicode Standard and the latest revision is numbered as 4.1.0. Unicode can support more than 96,000 distinct characters. Version 4.0 of the standard provides about 96,382 characters from the world's alphabets, ideograph sets, and symbol collections. Version 4.1.0 of the standard has included a further 1273 new characters. A growing number of world's major hardware and software vendors are supporting it and it is being incorporated into popular operating systems and programming languages. A list of such Unicode enabled products can be found from the Unicode Consortium's homepage. As software for e-commerce, digital libraries, automated library management systems, and other applications begin to support Unicode, it will become more widely adopted. Unicode Standard represents a tremendous advance for multilingual computing, but more work is needed in order to achieve a truly multilingual Web.

The impact will be manifold: it will help in the publication and preservation of materials in ancient and historic scripts, facilitate the online teaching of languages using such scripts, and provide universal access to our cultural and literary heritage. As storage costs continue to decline, the storage requirements of Unicode will be an insignificant issue, particularly for new applications. In the meantime, substantial amount of text continue to be produced not only in language-specific and script-specific encoding standards but also in local and proprietary formats. Any of this text maintained in digital libraries may become legacy data that has to be mapped to Unicode or some other universal standard in the future. For the present, digital library designers face difficult trade-offs between the character-set standards in use by current exchange partners and the standard likely to be in world wide use in the future for a broader range of applications.

TRANSLITERATION AND OTHER FORMS OF DATA LOSS

A long-established intermediate approach to character encoding for languages that cannot be typed on a standard computer keyboard is transliteration, which matches characters or sounds from one language to another but does not translate meaning. Languages written in non-Roman scripts, such as Japanese, Arabic, Chinese, Korean, Persian, Hebrew, and Yiddish, Russian, and Devanagari, are transliterated into Roman characters in many applications. Transliteration is necessary when mechanical devices such as typewriters and computers do not support the necessary scripts. It also is helpful for people without full proficiency in the scripts of the language. The transliteration process may be irreversible, and thus some data loss takes place. Despite the existence of an international standardisation body, multiple transliteration systems exist for Cyrillic, Asian, and other character sets. Thus transliteration can be inconsistent, which is why the same Russian name may appear as 'Tchaikovsky' or as 'Chaikovoskii' depending on which system is used to transliterate Cyrillic characters. Data also are lost when languages written in extensions of the Roman character set, such as French, Spanish, German, Hungarian, Czech, and Polish, are stored without the diacritics that for additional characters, all of which are collapsed into o if the diacritics are omitted). Data loss is not exclusive to text, however; it is widespread in visual and aural media.

Image compression is essential for efficient transmission of either still or moving pictures, and application-specific image compression standards exist for such applications as facsimile transmission, pictures, moving images, and high-definition television. Compression algorithms are made more efficient by discarding some of the data to reduce the granularity of the image.

Images subjected to 'lossy' compression are legible and suitable for many applications, but the original image cannot be reconstructed. 'Lossless' compression retains the full content but requires more storage and more transmission time. Similarly, for music, a popular compression algorithm known as MP3 is used to squeeze digital audio by a ratio of 12:1. MP3 compresses music sufficiently that audio files can be sent via the Internet or stored on a hard disk. Music compressed in MP3 can be expanded and played by an MP3 player with a near-CD-quality sound, yet the files are small enough to be attached to an e-mail message.

The music industry is promoting another standard, and Microsoft is promoting yet a third standard named Windows Media Audio for music compression and distribution. The acceptance of technical standards for music and other audio may be determined as much by the availability of playback devices as by the quality of reproduction. The amount of data loss that is tolerable varies by application. Far more data loss is tolerable in e-mail and in teleconferencing than in financial, legal, or bibliographic records. Textual data that have been transliterated or stripped of diacritics are likely to contain variant forms of words that will not match and sort properly, incomplete words that will not exchange properly with digital libraries using complete forms, and incomplete forms that are not adequate for authoritative or archival purposes.. In digital libraries, any kind of data loss can result in information retrieval errors.

PRACTICES OF THE LIBRARY COMMUNITY

An essential component of any library application is an encoding methodology that allows computers to process characters and symbols used to represent language information in written form. For years the encoding mechanism was not developed under a unified umbrella nor did it reach various languages equally. Without a standard unified character code, users have to use different software and terminals to display or enter data in different languages, especially when dealing with more than a few scripts.

The international library community began developing large multilingual digital libraries in the 1990s. Language representation is a particular concern for major research libraries, whose collections may include materials in as many as 400 written languages. Standards for record structure and character sets were established long before either Unicode or the Internet was created. Hundreds of millions of bibliographic records exist around the world in variations of the MARC format, although in multiple character-set-encoding formats and multiple forms of transliteration.

USMARC was implemented with the *American Library Association* (ALA) character set, which extends the English language keyboard to include diacritics from major Roman-script languages. The ALA character set is used by *Online Computer Library Centre* (OCLC), the largest bibliographic utility in the world, and by most American library applications; languages not included in the ALA character set tend to be transliterated. The increasing interest in adapting USMARC and other forms of MARC to Unicode reflects the fact that other systems will have to accommodate the huge quantity of MARC records that already exist in other character-set formats. The Library of Congress–which contributes its records in digital form to OCLC, to RLG and to other cooperatives in Europe and elsewhere–has done original-script cataloguing for the JACKPHY languages since, the early 1980s. RLG pioneered the ability to encode the JACKPHY languages in their original-script form for bibliographic records, using available script specific standards.

The Library of Congress, OCLC, RLG, and other bibliographic utilities around the world exchange records encoded in full-script form. Libraries took a long-term view of their data, capturing and representing non-Roman characters in their fullest form many years before search and display technologies were widely available. Full vernacular script in these records can be printed on catalogue cards, but until very recently scripts could only be displayed on computers with special equipment. Even though JACKPHY records from OCLC, RLG, and other sources are loaded into the online catalogues of individual libraries, most applications only support searching the transliterated forms. Integrated library automation software that supports Unicode is becoming more widely available, thus allowing records in non-Roman scripts to be displayed on most terminals and computers.

The Library of Congress has implemented a new integrated library system that incorporates Unicode, enabling them to display their JACKPHY records on public terminals in full form. These records were viewable only through other systems outside the Library of Congress. The international library community is more and more concerned about multilingual, multi-script data exchange as new regions of the world come online. The European Union is promoting Unicode and is funding projects to support Unicode implementation in library automation. In the mid 1990s, Borgman conducted a study of six countries in Central and Eastern Europe each with its own national language and character set, found that a variety of coding systems were in use. More than half of the research libraries in the study used Latin2, one used Unicode, and the rest used a national or a system-specific format to encode data; none used the ALA character set.

VIRTUAL REFERENCE PRACTICES IN LIBRARIES OF INDIA

The world has grown increasingly visual as the boundaries for television, graphics, videos, movies, computer games and educational multimedia blur, and the proliferation of wireless networks, intelligent agents, and handheld devices drives the need for anytime, anywhere access to multimedia information.

Images in this millennium have the potential to become an even more dominant means of cultural communication and education as they provide more immediate, global, easily understood, and powerful ways for communicating than ever before. For many people, however, online tools and resources for locating images and other non-textual materials may be unfamiliar, difficult to learn, or insufficient to answer their image information needs. As well as the difficulty that users have in expressing information needs in general and image needs specifically.

Until automated systems can resolve these issues, expert human intermediation is necessary. Visual reference professionals from educational institutions and libraries are well positioned to mediate between patrons and Web-based multimedia resources, but they may require additional tools and training to handle questions and provide solutions to users with non-textual information needs. The question faced by libraries, research institutions, educational institution and other cultural heritage institutions in this world of visual information is how to respond to a growing public demand for 'roundthe-clock' networked accessibility to digital information and virtual information collections.

Moreover, how can they provide access to resources that cross institutional boundaries and disciplines? It is impractical to assume that a single institution will have resources for all needs, or to expect that one expert would be knowledgeable about all collections. It is also impractical to assume that the public will necessarily know how to locate appropriate image collections or how to search for digital information. Having a very large number of readers, Indian educational institutes, and research institutes really require the virtual information providing to its users. One approach to answering these problems can be found in an emerging Digital Reference Practice/Virtual Reference Practice. The Virtual reference Practice has spearheaded a project to provide media mediation within the framework of a collaborative network of experts from a diverse range of libraries of India. The conceptual framework for this network is built upon a successful digital reference model that has been widely embraced by the digital library community.

DEFINITION OF VIRTUAL REFERENCE PRACTICES

Virtual Reference Practices can be defined as the provision of real-time personal assistance to patrons via web-based interactive software. To meet the user at his or her 'point of need' and to satisfy the patron's information need, the librarian can use e-mail to answer a fairly specific or simple question. The 'point of need' may happen when the library is closed, or when the user is unable to get to the library. This way, users can still be in contact with experienced reference libraries.

Although most librarians have an idea about what digital reference practice is, they are less sure what to call it. There are various terms in use: online reference; digital reference; electronic reference; virtual reference; live reference. Generally speaking, virtual or live reference refers to transactions in real-time, using chat and video-conferencing. Online, digital, electronic reference includes e-mail and web form transactions. However, these distinctions are quite often blurred and overlap. 'Digital reference practice' is used to include two broad components: 'it is Internet-based and designed to connect users with experts'. More importantly, Virtual reference refers to a network of expertise, intermediation and resources placed at the disposal of someone seeking answers in an online environment. Virtual reference service can provide support for users who find online tools and resources unfamiliar, difficult to learn, or insufficient to answer their information needs. It can also provide valuable user feedback to collection builders so that they may better tailor their resources and maximize their investment in content creation.

VISUAL REFERENCE PRACTICES IN LIBRARIES

Visual resource collections have been around for hundreds of years, and the practice of providing visual reference practice in these collections is at least as old as documented library reference practice—perhaps older. The first academic slide libraries date back to the late 1800 B. C. at about the same time that librarianship and general reference practice began to emerge as areas of professional practice and study. The *reference interview* is a central focus of this work and consists of the librarian interacting with the patron to clarify an information need, determining appropriate resources and collections to search, crafting appropriate search strategies, and assisting the user in assessing the relevance of the search results. There is a large body of literature pertaining to the reference interview, but little that addresses the unique aspects of conducting the reference interview for an image information need.

THE VIRTUAL REFERENCE MODEL

Virtual Reference Model is a general process model developed through an empirical study of high capacity digital reference services.

The model consists of 5 steps:

- *Question Acquisition* is a means of taking a patron's questions from e-mail, web forms, or embedded applications. This area of the model concerns best practice in 'online reference interviews' and user interface issues;
- *Triage* is the assignment of a question to a process or topic expert. This step may be automated or conducted via human decision support. Triage also includes the filtering of repeat questions or out of scope questions;
- *Answer Formulation* details factors for creating 'good' answers such as age and cultural appropriateness. Answers are also sent to the patron at this point;
- *Tracking* is the quantitative and qualitative monitoring

of questions for trends. Tracking allows the creation of 'hot topics', and may indicate where gaps exist in the collection; and

- *Resource Creation* concerns the use of tracking data to build or expand collections and better meet patron information needs.

Every text-based virtual reference practice should use this simple model in India. However, the important question is whether the model can be extended to enable digital libraries to provide reference assistance in the retrieval of information and other visual resources. Experts who provide visual resource reference assistance within digital library environments may require additional tools and training to handle questions and provide solutions to users with non-textual information needs.

PROJECT DESIGN

The Virtual Reference Practice project goal is to extend the digital reference model to the digital library community in order to support integration, interoperability, and seamless access to shared visual resources. Therefore, a central focus of this research is to explore how human expertise mediates between image needs and image resources in the digital library environments. As a first step in this research, it is important to develop a model and some metrics for examining users' image needs, the sufficiency of image resource description on the web, the role of collaboration and triage, and the work of human intermediatores.

A number of issues are currently being explored during Phase One of this project including:

- How is digital library triage affected by expanding the existing model to include museum reference services?
- What does 'out of scope' mean in this environment?
- What types of functionality do patrons need to assist them in asking for information?
- What tools do experts need in providing image answers?

CURRENT RESEARCH TASKS

- Survey digital libraries with existing virtual reference services to examine how they perform routing of, and collaboration in, answering image queries.
- Interview visual resource professionals who provide reference assistance to investigate how they conduct digital reference interviews and question negotiation.
- Analyse information requests to model information-seeking behaviour on the Web. Analyse the content of reference requests to create taxonomy of information needs.
- Analyse reference responses to create a refined model of digital reference for information retrieval. Perform content analysis of answers to information -related enquiries from multiple perspectives.
- Analyse disconnects between the language patrons employ to describe information needs, and libraries use to describe images in their collections. Identify opportunities to create metadata automatically.
- Build iterative models. Create a model that incorporates findings, including unanticipated but required elements unique to supporting information intermediation in the virtual reference environment.

The second phase of this project will be to incorporate the results from Phase One into an operational system and software that will support the performance of reference tasks for the virtual reference practicing community.

EVALUATING THE SYSTEM

Evaluations of the effectiveness of the virtual information system will be conducted in a multi-method, iterative approach utilising both qualitative methods and quantitative metrics.

The four primary methods of evaluation will be:

- Unobtrusive log analysis.
- Tracking of question assignment patterns.
- Survey of patrons at the point of access.

- Survey and interviews with virtual information professionals.

Data will present a picture of how patrons seek help in retrieving information in the virtual information environment and will drive iterative improvement to the virtual information reference desk software.

Results will also demonstrate:

- General benefits of collaboration among museums and libraries in providing digital reference.
- Benefits for the virtual information Reference Desk participants in answering image questions.
- Benefits to patrons seeking help with their information needs.

MULTIPLE INTELLIGENCES: A NEED OF THE DAY IN DIGITAL ENVIRONMENTAL ERA

The concept of intelligence, a very old one, has been employed in the most varied ways over the centuries. This century, primarily ordinary individuals have used the word 'intelligence' in an effort to describe their own mental powers as well as those of other persons. Consistent with ordinary language usage, 'intelligence' has been deployed in anything but a precise manner. Forgetting about homonyms, which denote the gathering of information; individuals living in the West were called 'intelligent' if they were quick or eloquent or scientifically astute or wise. In other cultures, the individual who was obedient, or well behaved, or quiet, or equipped with magical powers, may well have been referred to by terms, which have been translated as 'intelligent'. This chapter has been made an attempt to know the intelligence among the younger professionals in the filed of Library and Information Science. For which very few intelligence concepts were taken into study and presented.

DEFINITIONS

There are three different definitions for Intelligence as follows:

- Intelligence is the ability to solve problems. This is the core feature involved in IQ tests—problem solving and logical reasoning to determine the one right answer;

- Intelligence, however, is not limited to the capacity for rapid, logical problem-solving and convergent thinking. Intelligence includes the abilities to create products and to provide valuable services. This expands our understanding of intelligence to include divergent thinking and interpersonal expertise. Original thinking outside the conventional, academic realms can be easily overlooked, disparaged, and neglected in school, at home, and in the workplace; and
- Intelligence isn't something that only happens 'in the mind' but it also includes the materials and the values of the situation where and how the thinking occurs. The availability of appropriate materials and the values of any particular context or culture will thus have a significant impact on the degree to which specific abilities will be activated, developed, or discouraged. This is sometimes referred to as situated or distributed intelligence or contextual thinking.

The unitary concept of general intelligence symbolised as embodied in the IQ score has been with us for nearly 100 years as a recognised theoretical and scientific verity. Construct of a single overarching general ability is widely accepted. Corno report that there are approximately 120 different measures of general ability.

Yet they also acknowledge that not all scholars are in agreement, with this concept. Both Gardner and Sternberg2 advocate that intelligence should not be reduced to a single overarching construct. In 1983 Gardner3 first identified seven distinct intelligences. Further Gardner, in 1999 identifies an eight intelligence.

Sternberg argues that that people posses three independent abilities:

- Analytic;
- Creative; and
- Practical.

PRESENT SCENARIO

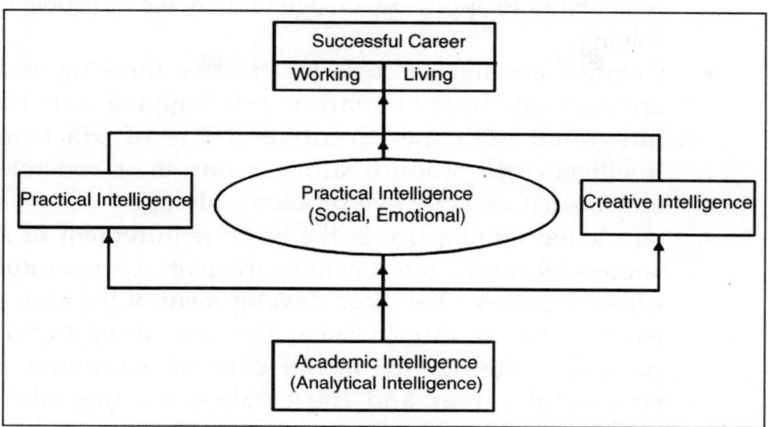

Fig 5.1 Successful Career and Successful Intelligence

The relationship between a successful career and a successful intelligence, in which personal intelligence is the core component Figure illustrates the following:

- There are four types of intelligence that lead to a successful career, the traditional intelligence and the other three non-academic intelligence–personal intelligence, practical intelligence, and creative intelligence. A balanced development among these four types of intelligence can make a successful career and fulfillment of life.
- There is a close relationship between academic intelligence and achievement in different academic subjects. Different kinds of academic intelligence can influence achievement in different subjects, such as linguistic intelligence for literature, logical-mathematical intelligence for math and science, musical intelligence for music, spatial intelligence for fine arts, and bodily-kinesthetic for sports, dancing, and drama.
- Personal intelligence could be referred to as social intelligence or emotional intelligence, which involves intrapersonal intelligence and interpersonal intelligence.

- Practical intelligence belongs to the field of cognition. It is an ability to apply knowledge to daily life or problem solving.
- Creative intelligence includes creative thinking and creative attitude. Creative intelligence can be integrated with the executive ability of practical intelligence to produce stronger power or concrete effect, such as a creative problem solving.
- Academic intelligence is the basic requirement of a successful career, but it is not sufficient. A successful career requires a balanced development of the above four types of intelligence. On the other hand, personal intelligence is the core of achieving a successful career and the catalyst for the other constructs of intelligence.

During the past century, there has been considerable movement on the 'intelligence front,' and this trend shows no sign of abating. In this study attempt has been made to briefly describe three historical steps, or phases, in the development of thinking about intelligence, focusing in particular on work inspired by the Theory of Multiple Intelligence.

MULTIPLE INTELLIGENCES

Verbal/Linguistic—Word Smart

The ability is to think in words and use language to express ideas. This intelligence includes the ability to manipulate the syntax or structure of language, the phonology or sounds of language, the semantics or meanings of language and the pragmatic dimensions or practical uses of language.

Interpersonal—People Smart

The ability is to understand and interact with other people in a variety of ways. This intelligence involves sensitivity to facial expressions, voice, and gestures; the capacity for discriminating among many different kinds of interpersonal cues; and the ability to respond effectively to those cues in some pragmatic way.

Intrapersonal—Self Smart

The ability is to understand your feelings and who you are in the world. This intelligence includes having an accurate picture of one's strengths and limitations; awareness of inner moods, intentions, motivations, temperaments, and desires; and the capacity for self-discipline, self understanding, and self-esteem. Further it is also studied the availability of this intelligence among the Library and Information students.

OBJECTIVES

- To identify the multiple intelligence among the library Science students.
- To identify the MI among Post Graduate students.
- To identify the MI among the between Male and Female students.

HYPOTHESES

- All the library and Information Science students are having equal amount of Multiple Intelligence.
- Post Graduate students in Library and Information Science are having more MI than UG students.
- Female Library and Information Science students are having more MI than male students.

DATA ANALYSIS

Sample Size

A total of 255 have responded out of 300 Library Science students considered for the study in Correspondence Education, University of Madras The students were grouped into two categories and representing those students grouped and same is shown in table, among the respondents 52.2 per cent drawn from BLIS students, 47.8 per cent from MLIS students.

Table 5.7 Course Studying of Respondents

S.No	Course Studying	Frequency	Per cent
1	BLIS	133	52.2
2	MLIS	122	47.8
	Total	255	**100.0**

Classification of Respondents by Age

The age of the respondents were grouped into three categories as shown in table. From the *Table,* it is seen that 61.6 per cent belongs to the age group of between 25-29 years; followed by 32.2 per cent fall in the age group 20-24. The analysis reveals that 25-29 age group students higher under study

Table 5.8 Respondents by Age Wise

S.No	Age Group	Frequency	Per cent
1	20-24	82	32.2
2	25-29	157	61.6
3	30-34	16	6.3
	Total	**255**	**100.0**

Classification of Respondents by Sex

The sample students have been classified by sex and the analysis is presented in the table. In the *Table,* it is observed that 54.1 per cent of Female. It is interesting to note that 45.9 per cent of students by male. However the women participation is considerably equal to male.

Table 5.9 Respondents by Sexwise

S.No	Sex	Frequency	Per cent
1	Male	117	45.9
2	Female	138	54.1
	Total	**255**	**100.0**

Classification of Respondents by Basic Qualifications

The respondents' basic qualifications were grouped in three categories as shown in *Table.*

Table 5.10 Basic Degree Qualifications of Respondents.

S.No	Qualifications	Frequency	Per cent
1	B.A	156	61.2
2	B.Sc	76	29.8
3	B.Com	23	9.0
	Total	**255**	**100.0**

It is seen from the *Table,* that more than fifty per cent of the respondents 61.2 per cent were BA, followed by 29.8 per cent are B.Sc qualified students and B.Com is 9 per cent.

Classification of Respondents by Post Graduate Qualifications

The respondents' PG degrees were grouped in three categories as shown in *Table.* It is seen from the *Table,* which more than fifty per cent of the respondents 62.5 per cent were MA, followed by 28.2 per cent are M.Sc qualified students and No PG degree is 9.4 per cent.

Table 5.11 PG Degree Qualifications of Respondents

S.No	Qualifications	Frequency	Per cent
1	MA	159	62.4
2	M.Sc	72	28.2
3	UG	24	9.4
	Total	**255**	**100.0**

FINDINGS IN RELATION TO HYPOTHESES

The study undertaken indicates that the hypotheses:

- All the library and Information Science students are having equal amount of Multiple Intelligence.
- Post Graduate students in Library and Information Science are having more MI than UG students
- Female Library and Information Science students are having more MI than male students.

NEEDS FOR DIGITISATION OF LIBRARY: TECHNOLOGY AND SUPPORTING FORMAT

The Dr A P J Abdul Kalam, President of India, International Conference on Digital Libraries: Knowledge creation, preservation, access, and management on 24-27 February 2004 keynote address conclusion, said that Digital Library is a national mission. We should see that all the schools, colleges, and universities digitise their libraries in their own native languages and connect to the outside world within 4 years. We have to ensure availability of fibre optic cables, satellite communication and wireless infrastructure especially in remote areas. It is also essential to realise high bandwidth technology like Multiple 10 Giga Bits connectivity across the country.

The topic of 'Digital Libraries' is currently the subject of world wide debate and research. To some simply suggests 'Computerisation of traditional libraries' to others, who have studied library science it calls for carrying out the function of libraries in a new way encompassing new types of information resources, new approaches to acquisition, new methods of storage and preservation, new approaches to classification and cataloguing, new modes of interaction with and for patrons more reliance on electronic system and networks and dramatic shifts in intellectual organisational and economic practices. The handling and use of rare books, fragile books and non-book materials are not new problems to libraries.

In recent years libraries are acquiring non-book materials and have been developing special collections at an accelerated rate. As a result of this many university libraries have established a separate unit of special collection. This collection covers rare-books, maps, manuscripts, pamphlets, posters, broadsides, newspapers, musics, non-musical recordings, micro facsimile, microfilms, university archives, slides and films, book plates, pictures, painting, graphic materials, coins and currency, stamps, little magazines, clipping files. etc.

NEEDS FOR DIGITISATION

Most of India's ancient manuscripts were written on bhurj patras. Ancient India was well developed in the subjects like Astronomy, Mathematics, Space Science, Medicine, Defiance, Political System, Economics, etc. Unfortunately many of these valuable manuscripts were lost due to improper care. Some of them were destroyed due to water, fungus, fire and som were purposely destroyed by foreign invaders. Book is one of the medium which deal with comprehensive knowledge and information.

Preserving the books and other reading materials is a burning question which the librarians of past and present are facing. Therefore, it is urgently needed to find out some permanent solutions to preserve the library materials.

OBJECTIVES

The main objectives of the digital library are:

- To capture, store, manipulate and distribute information.
- To introduce and provide new services.
- To provide need-based and retrospective search services to the user.
- To have large number of database in CDs'
- To avoid routine and redundant activities.
- To provide facility for networking and resource sharing.
- To access national and international journals which are being published only in machinereadable form.
- To digitise the documents for preservation and for space saving.
- To support library functions such as circulation, serial control, acquisition control, stock maintenance and other routine office works and developing in house database.
- To improve the cost effectiveness of library operations.

COMPONENTS

Digital libraries require well-tested and proven information technologies including the multimedia kit. Much of the work in digital libraries is achieved through E-mail service, by participating in Usernet, by accessing the database or servers through network, little Internet. Locally developed databases will contribute a lot to develop digital libraries.

In other words, the components of digital libraries are:

- *Data-Technical Data*: This consist of books and journals stored in digital form in a computer disk store. These are two ways to storing this information. One way is to photograph a page and Scan the image with a scanner. This form of storage is called a bit mapped form. It is practical way of storing old manuscripts, texts and journals. The practical way of storing old manuscripts, texts and journals. The image of the page may be retrieved and displayed on the video screen of the computer. The other way of storing a text is to present each character by its ASCII Code.

- *Numeric Data*: Consist of tables of various types such as physical property data of various materials from experiments, astronomical table's, etc. Such numeric data stored digitally may be used by curve setting programmer spreadsheet programmes, etc.
- *Graphic Data*: May be photographs, maps, drawings, etc. The simple way of storing such data is to scan the image and store it as a bit patterns. Data should in this form eases retrieval.
- *Photographs*: Colour and Monochrome are stored in bit mapped form using compression algorithms to reduce storage space.
- *Audio-Data*: Autio-data is digitised compressed using a commonly accepted standard comprehension algorithms and stored. A musical scores may also be coded and stored with Audiodata.
- *Video Data*: Audio-data is digitised compressed using a commonly accepted standard comprehension algorithms and stored. A musical scores may also be coded and stored with Audio-data.
- *Indexing*: Indexing and *inter*-linking multimedia data is extremely import and for ease of retrieval. Keywords in textual documents are selected and linked to related words with logical links by appropriate software. This is called hypertext. For materials on other media also related elements are selected and linked in what is known as hypermedia.
- *Linking*: The information collection of the digital library will normally not be stored in one computer. It will be distributed in may computers known as servers. All these servers will be linked by highspeed

communication links. The fact that the information in the digital library is distributed need not to be known to a user as it is not relevant from his/her point of view. A user gets easy access to the information based on his/her request regardless of its geographical location.

- *User*: Access the library from anywhere using a terminal or a computer connected to the network to which the information servers of the library are connected.

TECHNOLOGY

Until recently, not many people were happy to read from a computer screen. Quality of display was one of the factors behind it. Recent advances in the field of Information technology have improved not only the quality of computer display but also the font displayed on them. Besides, a variety of software are now available which are capable of manipulating and rendering information. Personal computers are getting cheaper and cheaper not only in the developed countries, out are also available at an affordable cost in the developing countries. With the availability of computers, capable of computing at a very high speed and having large disc storage space, it is feasible to digitise and store information in the form of high quality graphics, colour images, voice signals and video clips at a low cost.

HARDWARE OF DIGITISATION

In the early years of computing, computers were so expensive that it was difficult to purchase by libraries. Today, computers are cheap and middle-sized libraries in India are having computers. Apart from this, in the past, lack of hardware and absence of proper technology was also a hindrance in creating a digital library. In the present time, however, we have many hardware equipments available for digitisation process.

Some of these are mentioned below:

- *Flatbed Scanner*: Till today, the flatbed scanner is probably the most common piece of equipment available having compatibility with any personal computer. The scanner has a glass plate onto which the source document is laid face-down. The Charged Coupled Device (CCD), which allows to convert analog to digital, moves beneath the surface of glass and records the reflected light as an array of pixels. Flatbed scanners are both quick and economical to use. In the past their speed is increased and only single pass is required under the document. These flatbed scanners are often bundled with their own scanning software and sometime with *Optical* Character Recognition (OCR) software. The cost of these flatbed scanners have come down dramatically and now available at the rate as low as five thousand rupees. However, the main disadvantage of the flatbed is that it relies on contact scanning, and is thus unsuitable for rare or fragile material. It also requires the document to be placed flat on the glass, so any curvature of the source material will distort the image.

- *Sheet feeders*: Sheet feeders are very useful in case a library is having loose leaf documents for processing. The benefit of this type of scanner is its remarkable speed and one can leave it churning through the documents unattended. However, one can not load more than 100 pages into the feeder at one time. Yet one more demerit of the sheet feeder is that it is unable to deal with fragile or brittle items. Furthermore, these are not suitable for oversised documents, though various models of these scanner are available in the market.
- *Drum Scanners*: These are called as drum-scanner because the source document is actually attached to a glass drum. Though these scanners offer the highest resolutions but rarely found outside a dedicated scanning agency because of their high cost. Several other kind of scanners are also available such as slide scanners and Microfilm

scanners. Some of these are extremely cheap. Quality of scanning is normally in resolution, measured in dots per inch. For the textual material 300 dpi is a minimum quality of scanning, and 600 dpi is considered a good-quality resolution.

- *Digital Camera*: The digital camera is particularly useful in case of fragile or brittle items as these items can not bear the pressure of flatbed scanners. Many vendors have launched their products in the market over the past few years, Kodak, DC215, Kontran Progress 3012, Minolta, etc. Some of these are in use in libraries in India and overseas. For instance, the central library of University of Hyderabad (UOH) is using a model of Minolta for digitisation project of theses and dissertations. Large projects such as those running at the National Library of Scotland, the Arnamagnean Institute in Iceland, British Library, etc also uses high level cameras which are capable of giving an effective resolutions. However, there are some inherent problems with the digital camera in general. The scan time can be quite long meaning there by lighting conditions have to be maintained throughout potentially damaging procedure particularly when using warm lighting on documents. Also the are cumbersome pieces of equipments, which most of the time require some form of stand or cradle. Furthermore, these are not effective in the digitisation of books that could not be opened beyond 45 degrees because of delicate binding.

DIGITISATION SOFTWARE

Software for digital imaging covers three main area:

- Capturing the image;
- Processing the image; and
- Delivering the image

Initially, as suggested, need a piece of software having interfaced with the peripheral device used for scanning such as the camera or scanner. Important point to take into consideration when choosing the capturing software is the type of output file formats. This can be extremely significant particularly when it comes to create master image. TIFF is perhaps the most important image format available at the moment.

It is widely used as the cross-platform and archiving format in most digitisation projects, particularly as it allows for high-quality images to be saved without any loss in the original capture. Moreover, it is not tied to any particular scanner or display. Conversion from TIFF to other formats is relatively straight forward. Furthermore, images in TIFF are the best suited for universal accessibility and high resolution archival storage. However, the software should also be capable to produce Joint Photographic Experts Group (JPEG) derivatives for display on the World Wide Web. The JPEG and the Graphical Interchange Format (GIF) are the most popular image files delivered via the web and are ideally suited for displaying in all browsers.

Many digitisation projects create JPEG or GIF files format from their TIFF masters for subsequent delivery via the web. This is what know as processing the image and making it suitable for the end-purpose. Once the actual conversion process over, the most important issue is the eventual delivery of the digital collection.

In this step, primary emphasis should be given on what does the user want to see? The catalogues should be searchable and browsable. Facility for simple and complex searches should made available. Navigation aids should be both intuitive and apparent, and consistency maintained throughout. Additionally, there should be online help. On the one hand, the interface should be aesthetically pleasing while on the other hand, it should be open to accommodate the latest developments in technology.

FUNCTIONS

The primary function of digital libraries is to enable searching of electronic collections distributed across networks, rather than merely electronic repositories from digitised physical materials.

A digital library should have the following five integrated functions:

- *Creation and capture of content process of turning*: Integrating and importing multimedia objects into digital information–digital library content from many diverse sources different type to format;
- *Storage and Management*: Process of organising and managing digital content to ensure that it is available to users whenever they want access to it. Providing stable, reliable storage and management of data in an open environment across a broad spectrum of platform;
- *Search and Access*: To be able what the user need quickly;
- *Distribution*: To enable information owners to distribute their material in numerous ways: through existing networks, clients/server business solutions or the Internet; and
- *Right Management*: Providing extensive access control capabilities enabling content owners to capitalise on their protected assets.

DIGITISATION FILE EXTENSION AND USE

You see a file somewhere on the 'net with a name like "library.*xyz*" and you would like to download it and use it on your computer. Will it work? What does the file extension *xyz* mean, anyway? This paper provide answers to these questions. It is not meant to be read straight through; rather, it is meant to be a reference.

An extension may be looked up either with the 'find in page' option of your browser or by appending a '*#xyz*' to the 'go to' or 'URL' field on your browser. There is also a Search Interface that will return not only the specific extension sought but also other entries that reference it. Be aware though that it assumes familiarity with the computer basics discussed in the topic. You may notice that most extensions are three letters long. This is due to a historical limitation of the operating system called CP/M. In fact, the whole concept of file extensions comes from CP/M. Most modern operating systems do not attribute any special meaning to the '.' character. Be aware though that there is no standardisation to filename extension usage, and many different people have used extensions to apply to many different things.

XML AND ITS APPLICATION IN INFORMATION SYSTEM

Internet is a global information system, consisting of billions of web pages from which we can get information. The major activity on the Internet, that is electronic publishing and information uploading, are being done in quiet an unorganised way. The lack of proper organising huge quantities of information has not retrieve from the Internet. In any information system, we have followed certain tools and techniques to tell us which document contains what information.

These tools and techniques can be classification, cataloguing, indexing, etc. in the case of traditional information systems. As Internet is a distributed information system with disjoint information sources spread across the globe, we cannot bring the related documents together in the retrieval process. Hence, the tools and techniques meant for pinpointing information on the Internet need to be more accurate. XML is significant because it makes it much easier to share and search resources that are in different formats. Until fairly recently, this wasn't much of an issue for libraries.

Historically, libraries have served as centralised repositories of information. They purchased books, journals, films, and other information resources on physical media, and patrons found what the library owned by consulting a catalogue that listed holdings. Most catalogues are designed with the assumption that once a library records some descriptive information about each resource it has purchased, this information won't have to be radically altered. For physical resources, this works pretty well, since, the authors, titles, subjects, and physical characteristics of a book don't change. Once access to the Internet became widespread, it became clear that providing access to remote electronic resources could be very problematic. Catalogues are designed to provide access to physical resources that are under direct control of the library. However, people want to read journal articles, books, and useful Web pages stored in dynamically updated databases that are maintained and owned by other organisations that might be thousands of miles away. Online library catalogues are poorly suited for providing access to these works; so many libraries do not include these types of resources in the catalogue. As a result, it is often very difficult for patrons to know what electronic resources they can get t1hrough their libraries. This is where XML comes into the picture. It is impossible to search or display information unless it is structured in a meaningful way.

In plain English, this means that information providers need to agree on standards for encoding electronic documents so they can be retrieved in a uniform way. Libraries have encoded bibliographic records in MARC for many years, and that has allowed them to easily share catalogue records, which reduces costs while improving services. For a variety of reasons, it is not feasible to encode the new types of resources patrons want access to in MARC. However, when the information is stored in XML, it is possible to share and combine that data in ways that would not otherwise be possible.

INTERNET AND ITS' SEARCH ENGINES, SEARCH DIRECTORY AND META SEARCH ENGINES

There are many 'search engines'; 'meta search engines' and 'search directory' are available in the Internet. Example of a search engines is http://www.google.co.in, meta search engines is http:// www.mumma.com and search directory is http://www.yahoo.com. All of theses claim to be the information pin-pointer on the Internet. But the approaches of the existing search tools are ill planned and inefficient to say the least.

This is obvious from the two following important observations:

- The result of aparticular search is so high in recall and low in precision; and
- The output of the search result has no standard of any kind.

The search tools on the Internet use robots to collect information about the documents to generate keyword indexes. Generally, these tools use different algorithms to assign keywords to the document. Some of the robots collect keywords from the title whereas some collect from the first few lines of the document. But the very pre-assumption of the search robots, that the titles are expressive and the beginning few lines of a document focuses the content, do not hold good for maximum documents.

To give an example, if we search the Internet for term 'data', we should be sure to get results at least regarding 'database', 'data center', 'data warehouse', etc. Certainly the recall will be very high. The retrieval of irrelevant result can be reduced by subject gateway approach, but cannot be eliminated. The main cause of the problem in Hyper Text Markup Language (HTML), the standard for web publication is system-defined tag. This '*tag set*' is mainly for display of the content and HTML provides no tag to address the content precisely. eXtensible Markup Language (XML) designed by World Wide Web Consortium (W3C) promises a possible solution to this problem. The major advantage of XML over HTML is its extensibility, *i.e.*, provision of user defined tags and attributes to identify the structural elements of a document. XML also provides structural complexity to define document structure that can be nested at any level of complexity.

WHAT IS XML

XML is a extensible markup language for documents containing structured information. Structured information contains both content and some indication of what role that content plays. Almost all documents have some structure. A markup language is a mechanism to identify structures in a document. The XML specification defines a standard way to add markup to documents.

XML IS JUST LIKE HTML

No. In HTML, both the tag semantics and the tag set are fixed. An <h1> is always a first level heading and the tag <ati.product.code> is meaningless. The W^{3}C, in conjunction with browser vendors and the WWW community, is constantly working to extend the definition of HTML to allow new tags to keep pace with changing technology and to bring variations in presentation to the Web. However, these changes are always rigidly confined by what the browser vendors have implemented and by the fact that backward compatibility is paramount. And for people who want to disseminate information widely, features supported by only the latest releases of Netscape and Internet Explorer are not useful.

XML IS JUST LIKE SGML

No. Well, yes, sort of. XML is defined as an application profile of SGML. SGML is the Standard Generalised Markup Language defined by ISO 8879. SGML has been the standard, vendor-independent way to maintain repositories of structured documentation for more than a decade, but it is not well suited to serving documents over the web. Defining XML as an application profile of SGML means that any fully conformant SGML system will be able to read XML documents. However, using and understanding XML documents *does not* require a system that is capable of understanding the full generality of SGML. XML is, roughly speaking, a restricted form of SGML.

WHY XML

It is important to understand why it was created. XML was created so that richly structured documents could be used over the web. The only viable alternatives, HTML and SGML, are not practical for this purpose. HTML comes bound with a set of semantics and does not provide arbitrary structure. SGML provides arbitrary structure, but is too difficult to implement just for a web browser. Full SGML systems solve large, complex problems that justify their expense. Viewing structured documents sent over the web rarely carries such justification. This is not to say that XML can be expected to completely replace SGML. While XML is being designed to deliver structured content over the web, some of the very features it lacks to make this practical, make SGML a more satisfactory solution for the creation and long-time storage of complex documents. In many organisations, filtering SGML to XML will be the standard procedure for web delivery.

ORIGIN AND GOALS

XML was developed by an XML Working Group formed under the auspices of the World Wide Web Consortium (W^3C) in 1996. It was chaired by Jon Bosak of Sun Microsystems with the active participation of an XML Special Interest Group also organised by the W^3C. The membership of the XML Working Group is given in an appendix. Dan Connolly served as the Working Group's contact with the W^3C.

The design goals for XML are:

- XML shall be straightforwardly usable over the Internet.
- XML shall support a wide variety of applications.
- XML shall be compatible with SGML.
- It shall be easy to write programmes which process XML documents.
- The number of optional features in XML is to be kept to the absolute minimum, ideally zero.
- XML documents should be human-legible and reasonably clear.
- The XML design should be prepared quickly.
- The design of XML shall be formal and concise.
- XML documents shall be easy to create.
- Terseness in XML markup is of minimal importance.

HOW XML WORKS

In XML, Document Type Definitions (DTDs) may accompany a document, essentially defining the rules of the document, such as which elements are present and the structural relationship between the elements. DTDs help to validate the data when the receiving application does not have a built-in description of the incoming data. With XML, however, DTDs are optional. Data sent along with a DTD is known as 'valid' XML. In this case, an XML parser could check incoming data against the rules defined in the DTD to make sure data was structured correctly.

Data sent without a DTD is known as 'well-formed ' XML. With both valid and well-formed XML, XML encoded data is self-describing. The open and flexible format used by XML allows it to be employed anywhere a need exists for the exchange and transfer of information. This makes it powerful. For instance, XML can be used to describe information about HTML pages, or it can be used to describe data contained in business rules or objects in an electronic—commerce transaction, such as invoices, purchase orders and order forms. XML is separate from HTML, but XML could also be added inside HTML documents.

By embedding XML data inside an HTML page, multiple views could be generated from the delivered data, using the semantic information contained in the XML. Moreover, XML can be used for such compelling applications as distributed printing, database searches, and others. When most people think of the things that can be done with XML, they are actually thinking about a family of related technologies rather than a single markup language. On a related note, it is better to think of XML as a grammar than as a language. XML establishes rules for defining new formats. In regular markup languages such as the HyperText Markup Language (HTML), authors must use certain tags that make the text bold, create clickable links, draw tables, apply style sheets, etc. With XML, authors are free to make up their own tags and attributes if they don't feel that those that have been created by others meet their needs.

XML AND LIBRARIES

For years, libraries have been quietly using XML to perform functions such as improving access to archival materials, simplifying interlibrary loan processing, and enhancing digital collections, but increased reliance on the Internet for delivering information resources has brought XML into the mainstream, where its impact is starting to be felt by libraries of all sizes. As early as 1993, the library at the University of California- Berkeley started developing a method for encoding archival materials in XML. The outcome of this project was the development of the *Encoded Archival Description* (EAD) standard, which is now maintained by the Library of Congress.

Use of EAD has been increasing steadily over the years as a growing number of archival finding aids have been moved to the Web. For the past several years, individual libraries have been improving their services and saving money by developing their own XML applications. Since, 1998, Oregon State University has been using an application called *InterLibrary Loan Automated Search And Print* (ILL ASAP) to automatically search interlibrary loan requests and print request forms sorted by location and call number, complete with availability information, scannable Ariel addresses, shipping labels and billing data customised to the borrowing library or consortium involved.

This free application has been adopted by dozens of libraries around the country. More-ambitious XML projects have also been successfully implemented. The Washington Research Library Consortium uses XML to provide access to subscription databases, digital collections, materials requested via interlibrary loan, and library catalogues that run on a combination of commercial, open source, and locally developed platforms.

This system, known as *Access to Library And Database Information Network* (ALADIN) not only delivers content to seven academic research libraries, but also performs critical related tasks such as patron authentication using XML messages transmitted between applications over the Web. In the spring of 2002, the Library of Congress announced an official specification for representing MARC data in an XML environment, MARC XML. Even though sharing data between catalogues is relatively easy because of widespread support for the MARC format, the ability to express MARC data in

XML is useful for any library trying to develop tools or access mechanisms that combine MARC data with non-MARC resources. Now that a standard has emerged for representing MARC, it is reasonable to assume that vendors and others will develop tools that take advantage of the huge amount of data already stored in MARC format.

As a matter of fact, within a few weeks of the announcement of LC's specification, well-known tools used for manipulating MARC records such as *Java MARC Events* (JAMES) and MarcEdit already contained support for the new standard. As more libraries use XML, they are finding more uses for it. The eScholarship initiative at the California Digital Library not only uses XML to store books in a standardised format, but it also uses XML technologies to allow users to define their own displays. The Open Archives Initiative (OAI), an effort supported by OCLC, has developed a protocol that makes it easy to send a query to a database over the Web and receive the results in XML. OAI effectively makes it possible to perform searches of multiple databases simultaneously without the need for proprietary hooks into local databases. While this functionality is very similar to what was promised with Z39.50, OAI is much easier to implement, so the hope is that it will be widely used for many kinds of databases.

PLAN AND MANAGEMENT FOR LIBRARY AUTOMATION AND USE OF NEW INFORMATION TECHNOLOGY IN SPECIAL LIBRARIES

Planning for library automation has been defined as planning for 'integrated Library management systems' that computerise an array of traditional library functions using a common database. As physical, spatial and temporal barriers to acquiring information continue to crumble, libraries must plan for a broader and more comprehensive approach to providing automated services. Currently, libraries find themselves confronted with a second computerisation wave. The first wave took place during the seventies and turned manual back-room activities, such as acquiring, distribution and cataloguing, into computer-controlled activities. Essential in the computerisation wave of the 90s is the deployment of computer networks: campus-wide networks at universities as well as national and international networks. These networks provide access to remote electronic information by means of library information systems.

Furthermore, available electronic information is no longer limited to socalled secondary information. Also primary information has now become electronically available. Presently, we can refer to the electronic full-text versions of scientific journals. Electronic textbooks and readers enable us to consult information outside the library, *i.e.*, at the professional and private work site of the library's traditional customer. We must realise that all traditional library activities are being affected by this innovation: the character of all library tasks is about to change as a consequence of technological developments.

Within this context, we can observe a number of trends. One very important trend is the fact that the physical collection is becoming less important. Of course, in the humanities books will keep playing an important role in the next decades, but the number of electronic sources will gradually increase. The library is shifting its focus from concentrating on supply towards centering on what is asked for by its customers. In correspondence with this trend, information reference is becoming more and more significant.

The library acquires a gateway function, referring to information, irrespective of the location where it has been physically stored. Growing emphasis will be put on navigation. By and large, users will prefer to find their own way across the large amount of available information. To an increasing extent, service will be provided from a distance: the users will choose to consult their sources sitting at their own desk, at their own computer. This, in turn, implies that the library needs to increase the accessible electronic collection, which is accomplished by disclosing sources elsewhere, but also by electronically providing material that has already been available on paper. Of course, this development entails new problems related to the storage of electronic information.

IMPORTANCE OF LIBRARY FOR ORGANISATION/R & D CENTRES IN IT ERA

Special library have been in existence from the beginning of this centuries, whereas information centre engaged from the fifties and have now developed into major group of information institutions. Although special libraries and information centers has over lapping functional characteristics. Special libraries disseminate information and matter acquired by them answers, research questions, and direct users needs details on research information to appropriate some and handle towards periodicals to keep their user informed current development in this field. Parent organisation special libraries after serves a widely distributed group of users who only link being the common subject interest. The concepts of special libraries have been change in all aspects and librarians are known as cyberians.

NEED OF LIBRARY AUTOMATION IN SPECIAL LIBRARIES

In the changing scenario of information storage and retrieval, we have no option but to automate our information and library systems due to various reasons. Consequently, there is urgent need to reply following questions before /and after automation planning.

Questions you might ask are basic but important:

- What are the information needs of the organisation?
- Who will access the database?
- What will the content be?
- What is our computing environment or can it be changed?
- Who will maintain the data?
- Who will determine the process and procedural controls and standards?

We have to discuss the said questions with library staff, library committee and with users for better planning for library automation and use of new information technology in library.

STEPS FOR PERFECT LIBRARY AUTOMATION

Redefining and Planning for Library Automation

Library automation is a very complete process and needs exhaustive planning looking to the present and future needs of the users. This includes hardware, software, *moony manpower, materials and mechanics* (4M's), obsoleteness, updating, adoptability and very fast changing IT environment.

Selection of Hardware and others Required Equipment

- *System Purchase*: Purchase of the System if not available latest configuration of hardware and software, as well as the cost of preparing a site for the computer system. As having following latest configuration as follow:
  - *Processor*: Intel Pentium 4 processors up to 530J with Hyper threading.
  - *Operating system*: Windows XP Professional.
  - *Memory speed*: DDR2 PC2-4200 SDRAM.
  - *Memory expansion*: Four DIMM slots for expansion to 3GB memory.
  - *Graphics*: Integrated Intel Graphics Media Accelerator 900.
  - Hard Disk Drive: Up to 200GB 7200rpm Serial ATA.
- Networking of Computers (LAN) in library: Think and complete the library networking if not already available, etc. as Telecommunications dedicate at least one standard phone line that the vendor can use to dial up to your system. Internet accessibility is become more common for vendor troubleshooting, but you may still need that extra phone line.
- Retrospective data conversion costs are those associated with the creation of machine-readable bibliographic and, for circulation systems, patron records.
- Site Preparation—updating power supply, updating electrical wiring, cable for networking, furniture,

remodeling that may need to be done, adequate HVAC system

- Conversion Costs—This includes the costs of converting the catalogue and patron records. However, also consider the cost of staff time dedicated to the project. Bar-coding costs also fall into this category.
- Operating Costs—This category is often forgotten in automating a library. Typical costs in this category include on-going utility and telecommunications costs, software licence renewals, software updates, system maintenance fees, and miscellaneous supplies

Selection of Library Software and others Required Software

Following criteria might help the librarians to select the right software for other housekeeping operations:

- Who are the developers, whether an institution, or reputed company or few individuals? The preference is for institution and second preference is for the reputed company. One has to be skeptical about the software developed by individuals as there will be no continuity.
- How many times the software has been revised since, the time of its first launch?
- How many parameters are available for each module? More the parameters better will be the flexibility and needs no or minimum customisation.
- Whether the software has facility to import bibliographic data available in MARC 21 format and similarly export of data in this format.
- Training and guidance after installation.
- Whether available on major operating systems.
- Whether it is web interfaceble.
- Whether it can be interfaced with the e-mail system of the campus network.
- How many installations it has got in the country, since, when and major clients?

- Whether it can offer OPAC and different rights to different logins.
- Database architecture, Database migration, maintenance, database security, etc.

The Following are Latest Trends to be Considered Library Automation Software

- *Integrated library Management system*: An automation system in which the various applications share one bibliographic database. Each system comes with a set of core modules as well as additional modules, which can be added on, if necessary.
- *Core modules as*: Circulation, cataloguing and online public access catalogue are necessary minimums. Additional modules often cost extra and are therefore not always used by as many of the system's clients which can lead to less responsive development. Additional modules include acquisitions, community information, course reserves, imaging, Inter-library Loan (ILL), materials booking and serials. Acquisitions and serials are sometimes part of the same module and are often part of the core package, content management, e-learning, etc.
- *Client-server architecture*: Turnkey systems are quickly becoming a thing of the past. A client/server system is identified by a more powerful server machine that handles database manipulation and retrieval while leaving the user interface to the desktop client software. This shares the computational load between the client and server machines and gives the user a better experience through a faster interface.
- Z39.50: This is a protocol for computer-to-computer information retrieval. It allows users to access dissimilar library catalogues from the host institution's catalogue while using a familiar interface. Both a Z39.50 client and server are needed if you want to visit others and have others visit your catalogue. A Z39.50 client allows access to others'

catalogues. A Z39.50 server allows others to access your catalogue. Ideally access works both ways.

- *GUI interface for all modules*: Graphical and menu-driven interfaces have or are replacing commanddriven interfaces in systems.
- *MARC 21 and non-MARC compliance*: First, library systems developed to use MARC records. Now systems must allow for cataloguing formats, such as Internet resources, for which no MARC formats yet exist alongside MARC records.
- *Web-based patron catalogue*: Patron access is greatly increased when catalogues can be accessed remotely via the World Wide Web. Better systems contain password-protection to allow patrons to access portions of their own records remotely.
- *UNICODE*: This protocol expands the character set allowed and is essential for collections with materials in non-Roman languages. UNICODE encodes 65,000 different characters compared to the extended ASCII character set of 256 characters. Not all vendors have fully implemented this yet, but most are working on it.
- *RFID (Radio Frequency Identification Technology)*: RFID is the latest technology to be used in library theft detection systems. Unlike Electro-Mechanical (EM) and Radio Frequency (RF) systems, which have been used in libraries for decades, RFID-based systems move beyond security to become tracking systems that combine security with more efficient tracking of materials throughout the library, including easier and faster charge and discharge, inventorying, and materials handling? Following are the advantages of RFID systems, *i.e.* Rapid charging/discharging, Simplified patron self-charging/discharging, high reliability, High-speed inventorying, automated materials handling, long tag life, etc.

Today's integrated system must not only provide access to the traditional cataloguing, circulation, public catalogue (OPAC) and acquisitions modules, but must be capable of connecting through the local system into the systems of other vendors, remote bibliographic databases, CD-ROM drives on a local area network (LAN), and the Internet.

Users are expecting that their library systems be capable of, among other things:

- Providing seamless integration between online gateway and OPAC modules.
- Providing access for external users on the Internet to the library's OPAC.
- Monitoring the usage of remote databases that have been accessed through the gateway.
- Accessing the Internet using a variety of online database.

Essentially, what this means is that libraries must plan to use a library automation management system as a gateway for achieving access to resources outside campus. Stimulated by the Internet, which has created universal connectivity to information resources heretofore public/society/respected community and by Z39.50 interoperability standards and 'gateways,' users of individual are expecting to access the resources of other systems— anywhere and anytime. Moreover, the traditional definition of 'publishing' has been stretched by the creation and CDROMS, e-books, online databases, informational home pages and Web sites worldwide.

Finance Matter

Finance is an important aspect of any planning and automation is no exception to it, these are: Hardware, Software, Training, Staff, Networking (LAN, WAN, MAN & Internet). Speaking of funding, planners need to be aware that there are certain cost elements involved in the installation and operation of any automated system. These may be summarised as follows: Planning and consulting costs include direct, out-of pocket costs and indirect costs associated with getting started, etc.

Developing a Library 'Profile'

One of the most important planning tools involves collecting basic statistical information on the library collection, library in-house activities, user services, users' education, etc.

The following are examples of commonly needed data of:

- Number of titles and volumes in the collection, current and projected.
- Number of borrowers, current and projected.
- Number of materials circulated current and projected.
- Number of new materials acquired current and projected.
- Interlibrary loans lent to and borrowed from other libraries.
- Description of any cooperative arrangements involving the library.
- Library in-house activities and hours of operation.

In addition, it is important to take stock of any existing automation in the library by compiling the following data:

- Percentage of collection that has catalogue records in machine-readable form.
- Description of collection without machine-readable records, by category.
- Description of currently-automated library functions;
- Estimates of the location and number of workstations.
- Specifications for any existing equipment to be re-used with any future system.

At the same time that this data is being assembled, it is important to assess user needs and set service priorities. This can be accomplished by undertaking a focused, strategic planning process designed to involve the library's 'stakeholders.'

Developing a Strategic Plan

A library planning to automate should undertake a process by which representative staff and users can identify service needs and objectives.

The purpose of such an effort is to allow participants to articulate their interests and concerns share perspectives and learn about possibilities in a collaborative setting. Group interaction is an important contributing factor in the success of the goal, which is to develop and sustain library automation in the years ahead.

Here are the basic steps involved in this process:

- Ask participants to identify strengths, weaknesses, opportunities and threats in the library's environment.
- Group these factors into critical issue areas that are likely to have an impact on the libraries' future in developing and sustaining automation.
- Ask participants to explore their ideas and perceptions in relation to the question: 'How do you see the library providing user-friendly, cost-effective automated services as Current Awareness Services (CAS), Selective Dissemination of Information (SDI), online database, online journals, etc.
- Through a method of your own devising, ask participants to prioritise all of the ideas that come out of the above two 'brainstorming' exercises.
- Ask participants to shape these priorities into the draft of a strategic 'vision' for automation development consisting of a statement of purpose, goals and objectives for the library.

Setting Service Priorities

Your strategic vision must now provide the framework or context for the next step in the automation process, which is to determine which library functions should be automated and in what order of priority. Processes that are repetitive, occupy large amounts of staff time, require retrieving information from large, unwieldy files, or are high-profile functions of the library are prime candidates for automation.

Developing a Formal Specifications Document

It is very difficult to compare systems sensibly and pragmatically solely by randomly looking at systems, talking to sales representatives, reading literature or comparing broad cost quotations. For this reason, libraries use a formal document—often known as a 'Request for Proposal,' or RFP —that organises and standardises the information provided to and requested from the various system vendors. Utilising an RFP to solicit written responses from vendors makes it possible for you to systematically compare functionality, cost, maintenance, support, and all the other issues that are involved in system procurements. The process can save you money and will result in a wiser decision.

An 'Request For Proposal' Document

The following points should include these essential elements, among others:

- Library Background Information.
- Libraries Service Plan, Mission Statement, Technology Plan, other supporting information.
- Technical Inventory-Inventory of your existing hardware/software, and infrastructure.
- Size of your collection.
- Number of terminals.
- Number of patrons.
- Network operating system.
- number of servers.
- Type of wiring.
- Existing database that may need to be migrated into the new system—People soft, access database, etc.
- Specifications-Detailed listing of requirements the system should provide.
- *Module Requirements*: Circulation, Bibliographic Maintenance, Acquisitions, Serials, General System, and Report Generator, etc.
- System Technical Requirements.
- Network, System Design, Database Management System, Data conversion requirements, Hardware requirements.
- System Performance and Testing Requirements.

Be Ready for the Following upon the Receipt of Vender Proposals against Our Floated RFP

- A description of how the proposals should be arranged and submitted.

- Instructions on receiving vendor business and financial information.
- Criteria the library will use to evaluate vendor proposals.
- Questions regarding vendor training and documentation.
- Your functional and technical specifications.
- Also, vendors should be asked to describe:
- How they will create bibliographic, item and borrower databases.
- Their system maintenance programmes and services.
- Their site preparation requirements.
- Their delivery and installation methodologies.
- Their system performance guarantees.
- Their pricing and cost strategies, in detail.

Criteria for Vendor (for Hardware and Software) Selection

Upon the receipt of vendor proposals, it will be time to begin the process of system evaluation and selection.

This process involves a number of key steps:

- If possible, form a project team of persons to assist with the evaluations and the selection who have some knowledge of automation or who work in the area(s) being automated. People involved in the strategic planning process would be a good choice.
- Try to weed out proposals that are 'fatally flawed,' *e.g.*, where the vendor fails to reply to any of the functional specifications or the system is missing a module for a high-priority function.
- Begin in-depth reading of the 'surviving' proposals, carefully noting both deviations from the requirements as defined by the RFP and any aspect that is handled unusually well. Make a list of any parts of the response that are not clear and require further clarification.
- *Schedule system demonstrations*: They are an important component of the evaluation process. Allow the vendors to show off the vendor's system in the most attractive light; however, be prepared with a list of what you want to see along with questions you

would like answered. Use the same list with each vendor. This permits more effective cross-comparisons.

- Consider using computerised spreadsheet software in order to compare and evaluate vendor cost proposals. Costs may not be what they seem at first glance.
- Contact some of each vendor's current clients—sites of the same library type, and of similar size, where the hardware and software modules that have been proposed to you are currently in use.
- Assign point values to the criteria listed in the RFP and assign scores to the different proposals. The system with the highest score becomes the number one finalist, the system with the second highest score number two and so on. To maintain a negotiating edge, it is better to cut to two vendors rather than one. If that is impossible, maintain the illusion anyway. Remember: The selection process is not over until the contract is signed. Until that point, never let any vendors know that they have been eliminated, including those with fatal flaws.
- *Compare studies*: Do compare study of all received proposal from venders with theirs features, etc.

Putting Your System into Place

After the system selection process is complete, there are several important steps which must occur. You and your vendor will have to negotiate and sign a contract. You will want to test the system and make sure it suits your needs. You will want to make provisions for system maintenance. Finally, you will want to train both your staff and your users as much as possible to prepare them for when the system is up and running. With regard to training, the following must be considered: In thinking of automation planning, there is often a tendency to focus on the hardware and software aspects of planning, and to ignore the human aspects of automation—training and public relations. Without these, however, even the most carefully designed system may not be accepted by library staff or library users. To assure the success of your hard planning work, training and public relations plan should be part of any automation project. Fortunately, training can begin long before the system is installed. By involving staff at all levels in the analysis of operations, the identification of needs, the setting of priorities, the development of specifications, and the evaluation of systems, staff will gain much of the knowledge they need as the planning progresses. User acceptance and enthusiasm for your new automated system is certainly an important ingredient in a successful planning effort. If you are implementing a public access catalogue, it is probably the most important measure of success.

Public relations can allow you to accomplish three things:

- Make users aware of your new system and services;
- Motivate them to use the system; and
- Train them in using the new system and services effectively.

About the Database

In the rush to acquire hardware and software, librarians often forget that their most valuable product is the library's database. The creation of a high-quality machine-readable database provides the cornerstone upon which all present and future automation efforts rest. Vendors will come and go, hardware will become obsolete, software will be replaced, but a well-constructed, well-maintained database, with its accompanying local holdings, will be the library's transportable and viable link from system to system. Moreover, as library users begin to access not only their local system but systems in other libraries as well, the quality of respective databases will influence both the outcome of search strategies and the availability of materials.

Database readiness has several important facets:

- Catalogue records must be carefully converted from manual to machine-readable formats;
- Collections must be prepared for conversion through effective and ongoing weeding and inventory programmes;

- Once converted, collections must be properly maintained as titles are added, withdrawn, transferred and re cataloged; and
- Standards—for bibliographic, item and patron records as well—must be adhered to. In particular, adherence to well-established and accepted standards of description for bibliographic information in a machine-readable database is critical; because
- Without standards, files cannot easily be transferred from one automated system to another; and
- It is essential for libraries wishing to participate in resource sharing arrangements with other libraries, which will require such adherence as a condition of participation.

Results of Your Good Planning

- Confidence that you have selected the best possible system available, give technological and financial constraints.
- Confidence that you have addressed the priority needs of your library.
- Confidence that you have established a firm basis of understanding and a methodology for future planning.
- Confidence that automation activities are being implemented as part of a clearly articulated, overall plan for the development of library services.
- Confidence that you have the ability to respond quickly and effectively to unexpected opportunities and challenges, with a clear understanding of how these unexpected developments may be used to support the library's long range goals.

Feasibility Study of Your Plan

Immediately after the analysis and design for the system has been completed, a feasibility study must be conducted. The aim of a feasibility study is to determine if the project is achievable, if the benefits outweigh the disadvantages and to examine alternative solutions. It is designed to answer these questions: Is the proposed system realistic? Is it necessary? What other options is available? Is it affordable? The final output of a feasibility study is a report to be presented to the management.

DIGITAL REFERENCE SERVICE
LIBRARIES ONLINE 24/7

The integration of the Internet Technology is affecting all functions of academic libraries. The mission of library professionals, providing excellent information service to users, has not changed, but technology has added several new dimensions and opened new avenues to their tasks. Librarians are moving into dramatically different roles as new services are implemented and the rate of change is breathtaking, especially for libraries that have been accustomed to stability in organisation and in funding. The utilisation of new tools and methods for providing and collecting a variety of information to library users for diverse information needs of instructional, research, learning and entertainment activities has become common. While continuing to provide many traditional information services, librarians are developing new skills and accepting the new roles that are necessary to support technology-based services.

Acquisitions librarians still selecting and purchasing books and traditional journals, but now they are also dealing with providing user access to leased electronic databases, full-text journal articles, Internet resources etc without 'owning' the resources that are acquired only virtually. Catalogers are also moving into new roles as they attempt to provide enhanced access to the new resources like CD-ROMs, computer discs, multi-format items, and Cataloguing the Internet itself is a task that has fallen to librarians. They are making these new resources accessible and applying Metadata standards. Reference librarians, while assisting users in the library, now have an additional set of remote users, who access the reference service online, who are more demanding, less patient users who have greater expectations. This chapter discusses the methods in Online Reference service and the role of reference librarian in the digital environment.

LIBRARY REFERENCE SERVICE

Reference librarians assist users in finding, selecting and using various information sources and materials. They rely on a variety of printed and electronic sources to provide relevant and accurate information to their users. Internet is becoming more and more popular source among reference librarians and users. It enables them to search, retrieve, request, receive, and download information from sources scattered all over the world on the web.

The traditional work of reference librarians has been greatly impacted by access to electronic publications on the World Wide Web. Now Reference librarians are also using the Web to create electronic publications for in-library users and Web surfers. By creating HTML documents that provide access to Web and other electronic resources, reference service is extended beyond the physical library and designated reference desk hours, opening the building for 24-hour access.

VIRTUAL / DIGITAL / LIVE / ONLINE REFERENCE

The terms 'virtual reference,' 'digital reference,' 'e-reference,' 'Internet information services,' 'live reference' and 'real-time reference' are used interchangeably to describe reference services that utilise computer technology in some way. Whether it is e-mail reference, chat reference or an automated routing system, virtual reference is significantly influencing the delivery of high-quality library services. Digital reference techniques have been around, in one form or another, for almost a decade now.

VRS or DRS are simply defined as the provision of real-time personal assistance to users via web-based interactive software. To satisfy the information need, the librarian can 'chat' as a component of the software to answer a fairly specific or simple question, or deliver digital materials, or suggest relevant web resources to the user, and provide online bibliographic instruction. This service may happen when the library is closed, or when the user is unable to get to the library. This way, users can still be in contact with experienced reference librarians. Questions submitted via e-mail and linked web pages require attention from reference staff, and the virtual reference transaction can be more complex and time-consuming than traditional in-library service.

The Web medium that poses a new challenge for librarians offers major new tools to give us the power to control our own situation. With the expansion of reference modes to digital communication, namely e-mail and chat, there has been a delay in applying instruction to digital reference. Academic libraries started first offering e-mail reference where users could submit their questions via an e-mail address. Recently the adoption of Web forms not only changed the quality of the e-mail reference engagement for the better, but also challenged librarians to develop effective means for managing questions and responses. A digital reference transaction will usually include the following elements: the user, the interface, electronic resources, as well as print resources and the information professional.

PLANNING FOR DIGITAL REFERENCE SERVICE

Detailed guidelines for a Digital Reference Service is drafted by IFLA with a purpose to promote digital reference best practices on an international basis.

Planning should include consideration of the following:

- Physical service location.
- Virtual service location.
- Training in advanced web skills, reference interview and procedure.
- Programming and web expertise.
- Management and co-ordination of the service.
- Completion time for transactions.
- Quality control.
- Service population.
- Data collection for evaluation.
- Promotion of the service.
- Hardware and software.
- Additional equipment.

- Furniture.

The staff necessary to run such a service includes:

- Researchers to gather the information to answer questions.
- A co-ordinator to assign questions and to monitor answers; to schedule staff.
- IT support for running networks, maintaining web pages and scripts.

* Data entry staff to input and send responses.

Social Inclusion

E-mail-based and especially chat-based reference extends library services to those users with physical challenges. Not only can those users access information, but can receive real-time guidance from librarians, thus facilitating the 'human interaction' so important in reference transactions

E-government/Modernising Government

The use of real-time technology increases accessibility to all types of government services. Libraries, experts in information delivery technologies, can provide the model in local authorities for reaching out to diverse user groups

NOF Training Expected Outcomes 2-8

Services, such as Ask A Librarian and chat reference, provide excellent training for staff in simple Internet searching to more complex user interaction with state-of-the art technologies. All staff, from professional to clerical, have the opportunity to become conversant in different types of technologies while delivering real-time service.

DELIVERY METHODS OF DIGITAL REFERENCE

Digital reference services can be made through e-mail or chat. Libraries are also using a couple of different means of running an e-mail reference service: using basic e-mail or web forms. There are also a few different ways of operating a chat reference service: using simple chat software, web-based chat rooms, and web contact centre software.

E-mail

User sends the library an e-mail with a reference query, supplying whatever information he or she feels is necessary. The library may reply by e-mail, phone, fax, letter, etc. Now days the Web Pages of Libraries are coming with 'Ask a Librarian' option.

Web Forms

Here usually the user fills out an online form on the library's web site. The form asks the user to answer clarifying questions that will help the reference librarian responding to the query. The user sends the completed form to the library and the library may reply by e-mail, phone, fax, letter, etc. While e-mail reference allows the user to write down the query in his or her own words, a web form structures the user's request somewhat, prodding the user to supply additional information that will specify the request.

Chat Reference Using Simple Technologies

In this method, user exchanges short, text messages back and forth with the librarian, in a chatting environment. This way doesn't allow for all the fancy interactivity that web contact centre software allows, but it does allow for rapid, basic communication. There are three ways of running this kind of a service: with free, instant messaging software with a webbased chat room, or with chat software purchased by the library. With most of these services, the user types in an opening query or greeting to get the attention of the librarian staffing the chat reference service. The user and librarian may exchange a series of short messages to get to the heart of the user's request. This exchange of messages is live and allows for negotiation of the user's query.

Chat Reference Using Web based Contact Software

Borrowing technology from online customer service, software for web contact centres not allow for instant messaging, but they also offer give the librarian power to control the user's browser. A librarian can actually make the user's browser display a recommended web page, such as a search engine or the main page for the library's online catalogue. As the librarian pushes pages onto the user's browser, the chat window can also appear on both user and librarian's screen, allowing them to have a typed conversation about the web pages being sent to the user.

Collaborative Networks for Reference

In this model, two or more libraries team up to offer reference service using any of the above online formats. The user would send to a member library his or her request, which would be forwarded to the library best able to answer the question. A library may get a question routed to it because it has particular strengths in its collection that match the needs of the user. Or a member library might get a question routed to it because it happens to be open when the user makes his or her request. A user in New York who tries logging on at 3 a.m. Eastern time to the chat reference service of a member library in Boston could be automatically routed to a member library in Hawaii or Australia that, thanks to a time zone difference, is open.

Knowledge Base

Knowledge bases are used to retain questions and answers for reuse, in searchable database or archive. The use of previous answers to respond to new questions, knowledge bases reduce question response time and duplicated effort. If users search for and find prospective answers to their questions, knowledge bases allow libraries to meet users at their point of need. Knowledge base records will have high quality of information that users may not find on the Web. An effective knowledge base amounts to a peer-reviewed institutional memory, if only we add authoritative and reliable questions and answers to it. This is a typical way of the traditional reference service to keep all the reference questions and answers in files, through which the a 'long range reference' becomes a 'ready reference'.

FACETS OF QUALITY FOR DIGITAL REFERENCE SERVICES

The 1997 Virtual Reference Desk Expert Panel has identified eleven characteristics and features for building a digital reference service for the educational community and its fifth version is published in June 2003. The facets are divided into two main categories: *User transaction* and *service development/management*. The user transaction category includes those components that occur during the question-answering process; these features are generally visible to the user. The service development/management category involves decisions made in creating and maintaining the service that affect overall quality and user satisfaction.

User Transaction

- *Accessible*: Digital reference services should be easily reachable and navigable by any Internet user regardless of equipment sophistication, physical disability or language barrier.
- *Prompt Turnaround*: Questions should be addressed as quickly as possible. Actual turnaround time depends on a service's question-answer policy and available resources.
- *Clear Response Policy*: Clear communication should occur either before or at the start of every digital reference transaction in order to reduce opportunities for user confusion and inappropriate enquiries.
- *Interactive*: Digital reference services should provide opportunities for an effective reference interview, so that users can communicate necessary information to experts and to clarify vague user questions.
- *Instructive*: Digital reference services provide access to current information and expertise. Quality digital reference services offer more to users than straight, factual answers; they guide them in how to formulate questions, subject knowledge, and information literacy.

Service Development and Management

- *Authoritative*: Experts of a digital reference service should have the necessary knowledge and educational background in the service's given subject area or skill in order to qualify as an expert. Specific levels of knowledge, skill and experience are determined by each service and its related discipline or field.
- *Trained Experts*: Services should offer effective orientation or training processes to prepare experts to respond to enquiries using clear and effective language and following service response policies and procedures. Training of information specialists is one of the most important aspects of planning and operating a digital reference service.
- *Private*: All communications between users and experts should be held in complete privacy.
- *Reviewed*: Digital reference services should regularly evaluate their processes and services. Ongoing review and assessment help ensure quality, efficiency, and reliability of transactions as well as overall user satisfaction.
- *Provides access to related information*: Besides offering direct response to user questions, digital reference services should offer access to supporting resources and information. Services can reuse results from question-answer exchanges in resources.
- *Publicise*: Services should inform potential users of the value that can be gained from use of the service. A well-defined public relations plan can ensure that services are well-publicised and promoted on a regular basis. Publicity should not create more demand than the service has capacity to handle.

6

Knowledge Management

Knowledge management in general, tries to organise and make available Important know –how wherever and whenever its needed. This includes processes, procedures, patents, reference works, formulas, 'best practices', forecasts and fixes. Technologically intranets, group ware, data warehouses, networks, bulletin boards and video –conferencing are key tools for storing and distributing this intelligence. Knowledge management involves understanding the relationships of data; identifying and documenting rules for managing data; and assuring that data are accurate and maintain integrity. Knowledge Management involves connecting people to people and people to information. Knowledge management are realising how important it is to 'know what they know' and be able to make maximum use of the knowledge. This knowledge resides in different sources within an organisation such as databases, knowledge bases, filing cabinets and its employees and is distributed right across the enterprise. Now in this chapter discuss about what is knowledge, how it is derived. What are knowledge management, and its process, why we need knowledge management, how it's applicable in the organisation.

DATA, INFORMATION AND KNOWLEDGE

Data, information and knowledge are closely interconnected. Data lies at the lowest layer in the knowledge chain and acts as the raw material or the knowledge process.data refers to the unformatted, unstructured material freely available around us which by itself does not provide any meaning. The various signals- acoustic, visual, tactile and otherwise that are around us could be interpreted as having information. The relation between data and information formally is that, information is a structuring of data that reduces uncertainty. Information value of a message is higher if it reduces more uncertainty. In a more informal way, it could be said that information is interpreted data. Knowledge is the interpretation of information in the eye of a beholder using his own history, his experiences, insights and interpretation. It is because of this reason that the same information may lead to different knowledge for various individuals. In other words,

Data + context + Information

Or

Information = interpreted data

And

Knowledge = Interpreted Information

Or

Knowledge = Information + Experiences, Insights, Judgement (of an individual).

WHAT IS KNOWLEDGE

Knowledge is a full utilisation of information and data, coupled with the potential of people's skills, competencies, ideas, intuitions, commitments, and motivations. In the highly volatile and extremely competitive global economy of today, knowledge is people, money, leverage, learning, flexibility, power and competitive advantage.

Knowledge is inherent in ideas, judgements, talents, root causes, relationships, perspectives and concepts. Knowledge is stored in the individual brain o r encoded in organisational processes, documents, products, services, facilities, and systems. Knowledge is the basis for, and the driver of the current global economy. Knowledge is the result of learning which provides the only sustainable competitive advantage. However for knowledge to be of value it must be focussed, current, tested, and shared. There is no consensus on what knowledge is. Over the millennia, the dominant philosophies of each age have added their own definition of knowledge to the list. Science has added to this list swell.

UNDERSTANDING THE KNOWLEDGE MANAGEMENT

Knowledge Management is the explicit and systematic management of vital knowledge and its associated process of creation, organisation, diffusion, use and exploitation. Identification of Knowledge, as a recognised field of principal investigation for business use, in addition to academic research, has spurred continuing demand for information systems.

KNOWLEDGE CLASSIFICATION

INFORMATION VIEW (KNOWLEDGE AS INFORMATION)

Knowledge is derived form structured and unstructured data and information using information management systems based on information theory. IT Professional tends to follow this classification wherein knowledge is perceived as an information object.

PROCESS VIEW (KNOWLEDGE AS A PROCESS)

Knowledge comprises of ideas, judgements, experiences, know-how, Procedures, and insights and can be defined in terms of philosophy, psychology, and sociology and can be disseminated through training, education, and learning.

KNOWLEDGE SOURCES

Knowledge can be any where, and understanding knowledge can be difficult until its need and usage become clear. Knowledge sources can be classified under two major headings

STRUCTURED KNOWLEDGE SOURCE

This represents knowledge derived from structured data and information sources like databases, data marts, data warehouses and knowledge bases. These sources generally refer to the codified forms of organisational knowledge. These data form a part of the operational databases of the various departments and divisions within on organisation. Depending on the IT /IS framework within an organisation, these data may be present on multiple computing platforms and may be managed by varying and often incompatible management software. The data from such widely interspersed and incompatible sources may need to be filtered and cleaned at an intermediate stage before being moved to on organisational knowledge repository.

UNSTRUCTURED KNOWLEDGE SOURCES

This represents knowledge derived from unstructured sources like text documents, graphics, presentations, web sites, and tacit knowledge that a knowledge worker possesses. A large percentage of organisational knowledge is not in electronic form. It exists in files, notes, policy documents, and manuals. It may take the form an innocuous document pinned to the soft board of the knowledge workers, the readers of the organisation.

These resources cannot be ignored and are often the principal knowledge sources used by many people. The knowledge thus gained is never written down, be causes an immediate need, quickly satisfied, and becomes a non-need. Thesis where processes and incentives related to knowledge sharing become important. It would also become amply clear that The UN structured knowledge sources for exceed the amount of structured knowledge available. In many organisations electronic knowledge sources are not available to everyone. Access to on line knowledge repositories are often blocked by access security restrictions, disclosure or need to know policies, etc., identifying the knowledge reservoirs, its location, and who can use it is a critical KM process. It is recommended that the knowledge maps, which identify the knowledge reservoirs and the knowledge flow within an organisation be created.

KNOWLEDGE PROCESSES

The knowledge process and function play a very crucial role in leveraging the IC of an organisation. They are responsible for the extraction of knowledge from the various data and information sources within an organisation, their storage and flow within the organisation. KM implementations involve distinct and repeatable cycles or processes irrespective of the terminologies used or the path followed.

These are five distinct processes that are as follows:

- Knowledge creation;
- Knowledge acquisition/capture;
- Knowledge organisation;
- Knowledge sharing; and
- Knowledge renewal.

KNOWLEDGE CREATION

One of the fundamental questions that would arise in the minds of the readers would be 'Is knowledge created or is it discovered?' In the normal courses of an individuals or an organisations work, knowledge is created, discovered, transformed and shared. The process is cyclic and contributes to the development of the knowledge base of an organisation. The following sections would highlight the concepts. Organisational knowledge can and does take many forms.

Some of these forms are as mentioned below:

- Computer knowledge;
- Customer knowledge
- Supplier knowledge;
- Product knowledge;
- Technology knowledge;
- Process knowledge.

KNOWLEDGE ACQUISITION/CAPTURE

In today's Internet age, enormous amount of data is available to the individuals as well as organisations at the click of a mouse. This has filled a growing need to manage explosive amounts of information effectively. Although indexing and linking documents and other information sources is an important step, capturing the knowledge contained within the diverse sources is crucial for the building as well as effectively using organisational information repositories. Knowledge acquisition has been a challenging area of research.although there has been considerable work in the area of knowledge capture, activities have been distributed across several distributed across several distinct research communities.

KNOWLEDGE ORGANISATION

Knowledge organisation refers to the design and development of a knowledge base or knowledge repositories and the associated conceptual access structure in order to ensure and easier retrieval, creation and sharing of knowledge for user communities. knowledge organisation refers it the description of documents, their contents, features and purpose, and the organisation of these description so as to make these documents and their parts accessible to persons seeking them or the message that they contain. Knowledge organisation encompasses every type and method of indexing, abstracting, cataloguing, classification records management, bibliography and the creation of textual or bibliographic database for information retrieval.

KNOWLEDGE SHARING

The educational needs and skill sets of practitioners need to undergo rapid changes to accommodate increasing specialisation of knowledge and the fast pace of technological development. The sharing and reuse of accumulated knowledge would lead to increase in the productivity of the associated KM system which would be further enhanced by the incorporation of the following three mechanisms:

- Libraries of multiple layers of reusable knowledge bases that could either be incorporated in to software or remotely consulted at execution time. Layers in such knowledge bases capture conceptualisations, tasks, and problem solving methods;
- System construction will be facilitated by the availability of common knowledge representation systems; and
- The ability to translate between the various representation systems.

This new reuse-oriented approach will offer tools and mythologies that allow developers to find and use library entries useful to their needs as well as pre- existing services built on these libraries. These tools will be completed by systems that allow developers to offer their work for inclusion in the libraries.

KNOWLEDGE RENEWAL

The processes used to create, communicate, and apply knowledge results in the generation of new knowledge and resultant expansion of the organisations knowledge base. This cyclic process transforms data in to information, which is enhanced and converted in to knowledge whose application creates new data and information thereby repeating the cycle.

KNOWLEDGE MANAGEMENT ROLES

A common weakness in most knowledge programmes in the overemphasis on it at the expense of well defined KM roles and responsibilities. Traditional organisational roles typically do not address either km or the cross-functional, cross organisational processes by which knowledge is created, shared and applied. Many organisations also cluster those responsible for km into knowledge or expertise centre each being responsible for a particular body of knowledge. Their responsibilities typically include championing KM, educating the organisation, knowledge mapping, and integrating the organisational and technological resources comprising the km architecture.

WHY WE NEED KNOWLEDGE MANAGEMENT NOW

- The amount of time available to experience and acquire knowledge has diminished.
- Early retirements and increasing mobility of the workforce lead to less of knowledge.
- Competitive pressures reduce the size of the workforce that holds valuable business knowledge.
- Reductions in staffing create a need to replace informal knowledge with formal methods.

- There is a need to manage increasing complexity as a small operating companies are transnational sourcing operations.
- Change in strategic direction may result in the loss of knowledge in a specific area.

To these paraphrases of Ms-Macintoshes observations we would add:

- Most of our work is information based.
- Organisations compete on the basis of knowledge.
- Products and services are increasingly complex, endowing them with a significant information component.
- The need for life long leaning is an inescapable reality.

KM: A CROSS DISCIPLINARY DOMAIN

Library and information science we take it for granted that card catalogues in libraries will help us find the right book when we need it. The body of research and practice in classification and knowledge organisation that makes libraries work will be even more vitals as we are inundated by information in business tools for thesaurus construction and controlled vocabularies are already helping as manage knowledge.

TECHNICAL WRITING

Also under appreciated –even sneered ate s a professional activity, technical writing forms a body of theory and practice that is directly relevant to effective representation and transfer of knowledge.

DOCUMENT MANAGEMENT

Originally concerned primarily with managing the accessibility of images, document management has moved on to making content accessible and re-usable at the component level early recognition of the need to associate meta information with each document object prefigures document management technologies growing role in knowledge management activities.

ROLE OF KNOWLEDGE MANAGERS IN THE KNOWLEDGE MANAGEMENT

In this Information explosion era, the emphasis of storing an individual's knowledge, idea, views are shifting to sharing and using them with others. The major fear of an individual for sharing his/her knowledge with others is losing his/her competitive advantage over their colleagues. This fear could be removed by creating an environment of mutual sharing of this knowledge.

Most of our work is information based. Advances in technology and communication tools are expanding the opportunities and new platform for sharing, accessing and creating information. Information is just signs and numbers, while knowledge involves their meaning. What we want is knowledge. Continuous innovation is impossible without knowledge assets. Knowledge is the core competence for coping with the change. Nothing but knowledge can generate originality of services. Knowledge enables to anticipate customer needs. Knowledge grows when shared and when used, and deteriorates when not used. Knowledge is also referred to as Intellectual Capital. Knowledge when applied becomes wisdom. Knowledge is that which is distinct from both data and information.

We can understand this by following relationship:

- Data (raw symbols and facts) + Information = Knowledge (Ideas, thoughts, beliefs)

Knowledge can exist and be expressed in many forms. For ex: facts, attitudes, opinions, issues, values, theories, reasons, processes, policies, priorities, rules, cases, approaches, models, tools, methodologies, relationships, risks and probabilities. Library is viewed as an information processing house where work is done primarily with the help of an explicit knowledge base which can be expressed in words and numbers; and easily communicated or shared in the form of hard data, codified procedure or specific schedule.

While explicit knowledge is relatively easily processed by computers, transmitted electronically and stored in databases for perusal and discussions, tacit knowledge needs similar expressions before it can be understood and developed further.

TOOLS FOR HANDLING KNOWLEDGE

- Intranet
- Extranet
- Groupware
- Intellectual Asset Management
- Data Warehousing
- Workflow Management
- Electronic Document Management
- Information Retrieval

Intranet

An intranet is a corporate LAN or wide area network (WAN) that uses Internet technology and is secured behind company's firewalls:

- Intranets are developed on the same TCP/IP protocol as the Internet, they operate as a private network with limited access.
- Only authorises employees are able to use it.
- It contains exclusive and often proprietary and sensitive information.

Advantages of Intranet:

- It is fast, low-cost to implement.
- Easy to learn and use.
- Multimedia, hypertext links.
- Simple interface to information resources and services.
- Access to internal and external information.
- Improves communication.
- Can capture and share knowledge.
- Supports links with customers and partners.
- Increases collaboration and coordination.

Disadvantages of Intranet:

- Security Concerns:
  - Unauthorised access.

  - Denial of service
  - Abuse of access
  - Packet sniffling
- Productivity Concerns:
  - Overabundance of information.
  - Information overload lowers productivity.
  - Users set up own web pages
- Intranet Application:
  - This can be applied for
  - Electronic Commerce
  - Customer service
  - Training Programmes
  - Reduced time to market
  - Knowledge Sharing
  - Enhancement of Group Decision and Business Processes
  - Empowerment
  - Virtual Organisation
  - Software distribution
  - Project Management

Extranet

An extranet, or 'extended intranet,' uses the TCP/IP protocol networks of the Internet, to link intranets in different locations. Extranet transmissions are usually conducted over the Internet, which offers little privacy or transmission security. Therefore, when using an extranet, it is necessary to improve the security of the connecting portions of the internet. This is done by creating tunnels of secured data flows, using cryptography and authorisation algorithms. The Internet with tunneling technology is known as a virtually private network (VPN).

Advantages of Extranet

It provides secured connectivity between a corporation's intranets and the intranets of its business partners, materials suppliers, financial services, government and customers. It allows groups to collaborate, sharing information exclusively and exchanging it securely. It is an open and flexible platform suitable for supply chain management.

Disadvantage of Extranet

Extranet transmissions are usually conducted over the Internet, which offers little privacy or transmission security.

Extranet Application:

- Enhanced Communication
- Productivity Enhancement
- Cost Reduction
- Information Delivery

Groupware

These are the programmes that help people work together collectively while located remotely from each other by multiple LAN users. This includes software with built-in calendars, scheduling, e-mail, web navigational tools, that support the collaborative activities of work groups.

Intellectual Asset Management

It is the intellectual material-knowledge, information, intellectual property, and experience-that can be put to use knowledge management. Include patents, copyrights, etc., and allows firms to organise, analyse and manage intellectual property using an Intranet.

Data Warehouses

Data warehouses are designed as central information repositories for combining and storing vast amounts of historical and reference data from a number of different sources.

These corporate data sources include mainframe databases, client-server relational databases, spreadsheets, text reports, flat files and proprietary systems. A data warehouse, simply stated, is a physical separation of an organisation's operational data systems from its decision support systems. It includes a repository of information that is built using data from farflung and often departmentally isolated systems.

Workflow Management

As libraries convert materials into digital formats, the need for efficient work flow management tools will increase. With the addition of multimedia content, it becomes even more important to enhance the user's ability to search, identify, navigate, or browse through a collection of digital objects. The potential of digital library is great, but the substantial effort, from a workflow perspective is equally, if not more daunting. The workflow management system will reduce the manual input necessary to manage the workflow of large scale digitisation projects.

The work flow management system will also support the path from physical object and/or digitised material into a digital library repository by providing effective tools for perusing multimedia elements. The reduction of manual labour for managing the workflow of large scale digitisation efforts will encourage other libraries to move forward with the creation of digital libraries. This includes dynamic work management solutions such as document management, workflow, imaging, Computer Output to Laser Disk and network storage management.

Electronic Document Management

Information is a critical resource for all kinds of organisations either large or small, governmental or private. For effective decision making, it is necessary to have the most relevant and up-to-date information at hand at the time of the actual decision making. The amount of information to be dealt with has increased dramatically with the advent of Internet and other communication means.

The growing need to manage information abundance has given rise to fast evolution of knowledge management technology, the fundamental component of which is Electronic Document Management (EDM). The solution to the information overload problem of information intensive organisations can be found only by technologies providing intelligent information retrieval with easy access to information from anywhere to anyone. An electronic document is defined by its content and format. Content is the critical information that provides the desired knowledge, and format is the method by which the information is stored and displayed. Electronic documents may include text files, spreadsheets, presentations, scanned images, faxes, video and audio information. Electronic Document Management System (EDMS) is usually a part of a more complex work process and collaborative computing support system.

Such systems integrate knowledge intensive components for project work, workgroups, data analysis, and decision making. EDMS consists of a document ware house, document retrieval engines, and tools for document routing, imaging and publishing.

Information Retrieval

It enables text search, retrieval and document management. They are using state-of-the-art information technologies to acquire, organise, store, retrieve and disseminate Information. Online databases, CD ROM based databases and reference resources, Electronic journals, internet services, online document delivery are some illustrative Products and services of this information age.

ROLE OF KNOWLEDGE MANAGERS IN THE KNOWLEDGE MANAGEMENT

The traditional functions and services of the library are undergoing dramatic changes and a new concept of library and librarians is emerging. The librarians in this digital environment are known as Knowledge Manager. As knowledge is considered as a source of competitive advantage, knowledge managers must then know how to manage what they do know and how do they manage what they don't know. Knowledge managers should have capabilities for managing knowledge and strengthens learning.

Learning more and more and using this knowledge should be the topmost concern of knowledge manager. Knowledge Manager should create an environment and culture of openness, trust and teamwork through various interventions. The culture of knowledge sharing should be encouraged.

This can be achieved by frequent interaction. Knowledge Manager should use information lecture as enabler to leverage knowledge. They should develop the synergy between the capabilities of humans and capacities of Information and Communication Technologies. They should try to use those technologies, which are accompanied by a knowledge compatible culture.

The knowledge manager needs to understand how to:

- Acquire, develop, package, share and manage and exploit information, knowledge and understanding ad related support tools.
- Help and enable others to use and apply them efficiently.
- Develop and launch new information and knowledge based offerings and services.
- Use combinations of emerging technologies to network people, organisations and relevant sources of information, knowledge and support tools together.
- Handle knowledge to multiple formats, including animation, audio and video material.
- Lead and manage knowledge workers, network organisations and virtual team.

Knowledge managers have to know enough about systems to be able to use appropriate technologies to identify, access and exploit relevant sources of know-how. However technical understanding on its own is not enough. Communication and relationship building skills are also needed to interact with information providers and the experience and skills are required to assemble a support package.

There are new electronic tools to meet old objectives; but without the condition that librarians know how to provide, they would not be effective tools. In short, the Knowledge Manager in this digital era should possess certain characteristics, which are defined below in the table.

Characteristics	**Functions**
Information Technologist Savvy	Information expert, Technology
Effective Communicator and Negotiator	Communicate and negotiate effectively with stakeholders
Leader	Leadership skill
Manager efficiently	Managing the task and change
Vision innovation	Far-reaching vision towards
Executor effectively	Execute the information system
Delegation authority to others	Delegate responsibility with
Evaluator system	Evaluate the new information
Planner objectives of information centre	Develops plan for fulfilling
Trainer orientation programme	Conducts training and user

KNOWLEDGE MANAGEMENT AND ITS USE IN LIBRARY

Knowledge management is very essential to the success of the organisation as it not only helps is discovering the resources, but in the current scenario also help in evolving new business rules and models. When we refer to knowledge, most of us mainly tend to think of codified and documented knowledge like patents, databases, manuals, white papers, etc. There is no universal definition of knowledge management, just as there is no agreement as to what constitutes knowledge in the first place.

For this reason it is best to think of knowledge management in the broadest context. Knowledge management is the process through which organisation generate value from their intellectual knowledge-based assets. Most often, generating value from such assets involves sharing them among employees departments and even with other companies in an effort to devise best practices. It is important to note that the definition says nothing about technology, while knowledge management is often facilitated by Information Technology. Information Technology by it self is not knowledge management. Knowledge Management in libraries should be focused on effective research and development of knowledge, creation of knowledge bases, exchange and sharing of knowledge between library staff, users, training library staff, speeding up explict processing of the implicit knowledge and realising of its sharing. Knowledge management will inject new blood into the library culture. The main contents include; Mutual trust, open exchange, studying sharing and developing knowledge operations mechanism of libraries, enjoying the knowledge management process. User's delight staff's quality and enrichment as well as an all - round improvement of library starting from house keeping activities to knowledge marketing will become important objective of knowledge management in Business and Management libraries.

DESCRIPTION

Knowledge Management is not about managing or organising books or journals, searching the internet or arranging for the circulation of materials. How ever, each of these activities can in some way be part of the knowledge management spectrum and processes. Knowledge Management is about enhancing the use of organisational knowledge through sound practices of information management and organisational learning. It is the process of transforming information and intellectual assets into enduring value. It connects people with the knowledge that they need to take action, when they need it. A Reference Librarian knows something about why services are not utilised the way the organisation desires.

NEED FOR KNOWLEDGE MANAGEMENT

There is sufficient evidence of many companies who have benefited from knowledge management initiatives.

Based on these experiences, knowledge management experts argue that, for organisation and institutes to be successful and competitive today, they need to continually engage in two activities.

- Find effective way to translate the institution's on going experience into knowledge. By taxonomically structuring the knowledge and by building enterprise. Wide vocabulary through key words, which facilities effective retrieval; and
- While transferring and leveraging companies and institutions knowledge across time and space for better leverage, it is necessary to consider the following key issues.
  - Find a method for transferring the knowledge to a group or individual who can reuse it.
  - Translate what has been learned into a form that other can use.
  - The receiving team or individual adapts the knowledge for use in a particular context.

TYPES OF KNOWLEDGE MANAGEMENT INITIATIVES

Knowledge Management Initiatives are taken by organisations and learners world wide, which reveal how these companies create value from their intangible assets. There are three types of knowledge management initiatives:

External Structure Initiatives

Gaining information and knowledge from customers for example through net scape, USA, a close link via the Net for opinion leaders among customers, who are encouraged to report problems, enables it to create new generations of soft ware at a fast pace.

Internal Structure Initiatives

Building knowledge sharing culture should be done for example, 3M USA with 60,000 products of their own innovation process has an organisation that balances between creativity and conservatism. 3 M's values encourage learning and risk asking, but managers are required to link continues learning to revenues.

Competence Initiatives

Creation of careers based on knowledge management for example IBM USA and most Japanese large companies encourage dual careers, Employees are encouraged to switch between professional and managerial jobs, in order to gain holistic knowledge about the company.

SCOPE OF KNOWLEDGE MANAGEMENT

Knowledge Management is a term that has worked its way into the main stream of both academic and business arenas since, it was first coined in the 80's.

The current state of the knowledge management field is that it encompasses four over lapping areas:

- Managing organisation;
- Organisational Learning;
- Intellectual Capital; and
- Knowledge Economics.

A close look at many aspects of knowledge management practices shows that it can well be accepted that they bear a close resemblance to well established practices in librarianship and information management. This means that there is considerable opportunity for librarians to use their traditional skills to assume a new function of managing knowledge within the library which would compliment the traditional library services function. The aim of knowledge management for a library is to become more competitive through the capacities of their staff and clients to be more flexible and innovative.

VALUE OF KNOWLEDGE MANAGEMENT

Knowledge is not the same thing as a knowledge worker. And just as there is a difference between the knowledge that exists in a knowledge management systems and knowledge that exists in the mind of the knowledge worker, there is also a difference between the kind of knowledge that exist in the mind of the knowledge worker and that, which exists within a community of knowledge worker. This distinction makes is easier to account for knowledge assets. A knowledge worker is an asset that appreciates over time. Knowledge itself is more often a depreciating asset. Patents lose their value if not converted into product or licensed quickly.

KNOWLEDGE CREATION

Knowledge Creation revolves around the activities that result in conversion of knowledge. The process of conversion involves creation of tacit knowledge through informal sharing, moving from tacit knowledge to explicit, enhancing explicit content by combining codified knowledge and using explicit knowledge to create new tacit knowledge through thinking and sharing.

KNOWLEDGE SHARING

Sharing knowledge requires a different kind of environment, a unique combination of human and information system to reduce the knowledge gap.

Knowledge sharing required a different set of tools and mind set that appreciates the following:

- Knowledge /learning is by people, *i.e.*, it is a human activity;
- Thinking creates knowledge;
- knowledge is created as it gets used and is dynamic. It moves through organisations and communities in many ways.

INFORMATION TECHNOLOGY FOR KNOWLEDGE

- Connecting people to people by providing collaboration tools, that are ideally built on existing e-mail or intranet systems and introduce work flows, Intranet systems and introduce workflows. Intranet would offer a way for the community to store and share their documents.
- Connect people to information through knowledge centres. These centres will be a place to search, place to query, etc. On line training courses can be offered through this forum.

- With internet and electronic information librarians are converted to cybrarians Teamed up with knowledge managers and subjects experts, cybrarians can guide employees to internet sites that contain useful information.

KNOWLEDGE MANAGEMENT INITIATIVES IN INDIA

The knowledge management Initiatives has started in different sectors of the economy.

They may be categorised as follows:

- Initiatives at the corporate level.
- Initiatives at the Research and Development level.
- Initiatives at the NGO level.
- Financial Institutions level Initiatives.
- Initiatives at the Academic Institutions level.

KM IN LIBRARIES

Information technology is a tool for knowledge management in libraries knowledge acquisition is the starting point of knowledge management in libraries. The application of information technology enlarges the scope of knowledge acquisition. The objective of knowledge management of libraries is to promote knowledge innovation. Knowledge innovation is the core of the knowledge economy society. As basis for collection, processing, storage and distribution of knowledge and information.

Libraries represent an indispensable link in the scientific system chain, an important link in the knowledge innovation. Secondly, libraries take part in scientific research process directly. The library work is a component of knowledge innovation. Thirdly, libraries must pay attention to diffusion and conversion of knowledge. Knowledge Management in libraries is to promote relation ship in and between libraries, between library and user, to strengthen knowledge internet working and quicken knowledge flow. In the knowledge economy era, libraries will carry out research on development and application of information resources, construction of virtual libraries, protection of intellectual property rights in the electronic era etc, thus founding the base for knowledge innovation.

APPLICATION OF KNOWLEDGE MANAGEMENT IN LIBRARIES

Librarians as Knowledge Managers

Librarians have major advantage as Knowledge Management players, by enhancing the efficiency in the quality of the services they provide. Training should be provided to the end-users and the library staff to use any sources available in the library, with the help of sound IT support. Equally valuable will be constant two-way communication with all levels of management and regular interaction across disciplines.

This will lead to a fruitful cross-fertilisation of ideas and allow maximum coordination of skills and knowledge. Staff involved in the operation and maintenance of the knowledge core will need to keep themselves up-to-date with what is going on both inside and outside the organisation.

Questions to be asked include the following:

- What new projects are coming?
- Which additional areas of business might the organisation be considering?
- In the wider marketplace, what are its competitors doing?

Answers to such questions will determine the content requirement of databases with in the knowledge management function. There will also be a need to keep up-to-date with new ways of organising information in terms of creating records and making the most of indexing tools; learning about new software products and evaluating them for particular tasks. Wherever possible join the user groups, which relate to your organisation's interest; this will provide you with a network of contacts with whom to raise questions, exchange experiences and discuss areas of common concern. Tools of Knowledge Management consists 70 per cent of services and 30 per cent of Technologies. Librarians provide these 70 per cent services. This indicates the role of Librarians as Knowledge Manager.

Where their functions are:

- Providing services to the user community
- Sharing of information and understanding of user needs.
- Analysing documents, classifying and sorting them for easy retrieval.
- Building the index, etc.

Some of the Qualities of a Librarian to become a Successful Knowledge Manager

- Providing services to the user community.
- Sharing the information and understanding the user needs.
- Theoretical and practical experience in designing and implementing information systems.
- Analysing the documents, classifying and storing them for easy retrieval.
- Knowledge of current advances in information systems and technologies and their application in libraries.
- Building the index, using standard vocabulary.
- Ability to effectively teach end-users, individually and in groups.
- Having knowledge of the digital library concepts, current and new advances in the scholarly communication systems, electronic publishing, and creating knowledge databases.

Where a Traditional Librarian can Improve ?

- Focusing on the quality of information provided, which tends to lead to continuous improvement in achieving the objectives.
- Being open and acting responsive to the changing environment.
- Analysing whole library activities or systems thinking.

- Being a strong promoter of diversity in the workplace.
- Establishing trusting and respectful relationships with customers and staff.
- Developing the skills of continuous learning from the lessons learned or best practices.
- Effectively communicating with the colleagues and customers.
- Keeping track of all possible sources where one can have access to information.
- Experience in using, managing and troubleshooting computer systems and networks, MS Windows, the Unix operating system, TCP/IP protocol, other related protocols, the Internet, and World Wide Web.

Challenges

- *Intellectual Capital*: Managing of tacit knowledge is not easy. Because, we don't know what is in human mind. It is not possible to document tacit knowledge.
- *Culture*: Because of narrow mindedness or insecurity majority of people don't want to share their knowledge; some people don't want to interfere they want to stay neutral and they are away from knowledge sharing.
- *Obsolescence*: There are types of information which gets obsolete as soon as it is generated for ex: Stock market information. Because of these types of ever changing information it is difficult to give this information quickly to capable user.
- *Overloading*: Knowledge gets accumulated. If obsolete information is not removed it leads overload. And it is difficult to identify which is useful from this information.
- *Technology*: Due to rapid changes in technology it is difficult to communicate the knowledge to the user because, technology helps Knowledge Management to a large extent. Technology is tool for Knowledge Management.
- *Structure*: Structure of Knowledge management

should show overall economy. Whether to follow centralised or decentralised system.

Issues Involved

- *Knowledge maps*: This involves building an actual map of a special databases, which points towards the resource./required data.
- *Acquisition*: Acquisition along with external sources should also be extended to internal sources of knowledge. The librarian works with the knowledge team to survey the various in house documents to identify and digitise, like standards, reports, and reports of technical discussions.
- *Categorising*: The knowledge which is located inside or outside has to be represented in a way which is suitable for access or transfer on the basis of controlled vocabulary in a hierarchy.
- *Narratives*: Extracting and diffusing the success stories and technical anecdotes from resource persons.
- Managing databases.
- Capturing tacit knowledge.

7

Preserving the Information Content
Issues and Strategies

INTRODUCTION

In order to understand history, people must study its rural life, agricultural heritage, and economic, social, and cultural values. If people want to study and learn from the past, they must preserve all of their present treasures. Preservation allows them to keep materials alive, whole and available for use so that the material can be authoritatively used for the longest time possible. This will allow materials to remain accessible for their heritage, society, and for the guidance of future generations.

Preserving information content of documents is often considered important. Every organisation accumulates documents, which are required to be preserved including drawings, maps, imageries, confidential reports, etc. All these documents have different shapes, sizes and different use patterns. Everyday valuable information is increasing and to save valuable information and to fulfill the user's requirements for posterity, digital documents should be managed and preserved at a tremendous rate. The goal of digital preservation is to maintain the ability to display, retrieve and use digital collections in rapidly changing technological and organisational infrastructures. Preservation is the creation of digital products worth maintaining over time. It also refers to the various methods of keeping digital materials alive into the future.

DEFINITION

Preservation and conservation are interrelated processes. Their definitions are as follows:

- *Preservation*: A broader term than conservation. It includes all managerial and financial considerations including storage and accommodation provision, staffing levels, policies, techniques and methods involved in preserving library and archive materials and the information contained therein for access and preservation purposes by future generations.
- *Conservation*: Conservation is taken as divert intervention to prevent/make good damage to materials.

RISK ASSESSMENT FOR DOCUMENTS

The following risks can exist in document collections:

- Natural Routine Risks include relative humidity, temperature, light, pollution, and pests.
- Natural Extreme Risks include fire, flood, and earthquakes.
- Man-made Routine Risks include handling, wear, tear and erasing of material.
- Man-made Extreme Risks include war, civil unrest, and vandalism.

NEED FOR DIGITAL PRESERVATION

One of the many functions of any library is to preserve information by collecting the documents of the past and of the present and to store and maintain them so that they are available to users of present and the future.

- Problems generated by deteriorating library collection demanded the preservation of library materials, a considerable amount of time, money and efforts too.
- Some collections that a library holds become rare over a period of time, thus becoming one of few

surviving copies. Therefore, preserving it for scarcity and specimen value becomes a critical task.

- The length and breadth of recorded materials, for example books and microforms, have created problems in maintaining them. Hence, the need for preservation is even more viable.
- Due to increase in technological know how and information awareness, there seems an increasing concern for the preservation of information materials.
- The primary objective of all libraries, archives, and other custodians, is to meet the user's expectations and requirements. These organisations should preserve all materials in all formats.
- Storage media has different formats, durability and handling systems.

DIGITAL PRESERVATION ISSUES

More complex than the preservation of print collections is the preservation of digital collections. There are a number of technical, social and legal issues involved with various preservation strategies for digital objects. The following is an explanation of problems and challenges related to the different issues of digital preservation.

TECHNOLOGICAL ISSUES

There are problems associated with three aspects of digital information technology; the digital storage medium itself, the hardware configuration and software dependency.

Media Problems

Digital information can be presented using a variety of media that differ in longevity and fragility. Common formats are comprised of floppy disks, magnetic tape, cartridges, worm optical storage, and CD-ROM disks. Both magnetic and optical media have short lifetimes in comparison with media like paper and microfilm. CD-ROM and optical worm are very durable, with lifetimes of 100 yrs. For digital media longevity, digital refreshing, *i.e.,* the periodic recopying of the data on to a new medium is better. Refreshing lengthens its lifespan if the storage media is independent of any specific technology.

Hardware Obsolescence

Considering technological obsolescence of the equipment which read the media is important. Punch cards, tapes, Pc XT/AT/286, etc are almost extinct today. It would be impractical to use earlier equipment even if it was available because, the storage and handling capacity of new media is much greater.

Software Dependence

Digital information is stored in formats which are dependent upon particular software to interpret them correctly. There are many more formats than the media. As delivery mechanisms and formats change they increase their complexity. Interoperability strategy for preserving digital information involves the periodic transfer of digital materials from one hardware/software configuration to another. Its purpose is to preserve the integrity of digital objects and to use them in continuing access to information over extended periods of time by changing technology.

LEGAL ISSUES

More challenging than the technical issues related to copyright and ownership of information are the legal ones. Instead of applying copyright laws, publishers and vendors work under the terms of contract law. Libraries have quite a lot of power in deciding how information is utilised, distributed and stored under the terms of 'fair dealing'. However, there are various agencies that publish and distribute digital objects whose roles are undefined, making their legal responsibility unclear. The paper-based concept of copyright is not applicable in the digital environment because the control of copying is lost. Digital objects are flexible, easily copied, and remotely accessible by multiple users simultaneously.

STANDARD

Another challenge is the use of established standards, protocols and proven methods for preserving digital information,. *e.g.* The International Standards Organisation (ISO) has produced a reference model for an Open Archival Information System (OAIS), NEN-ISO 15489-1:2001, IDT standard, and use of Standard Generalised Markup Language (SGML) and Extensible Markup Language (XML) are some of the emerging standards suggested..

ORGANISATIONAL ISSUES

There are two distinct organisational and managerial issues. The first relates to decisions about who should preserve and what should be preserved. The second is preservation role from librarians. Sometimes lack of preservation policies and procedures, lack of technical staff and financial resources. Also, the legislation does not usually cover electronic publications. It may be more useful to physically transfer document information content, using commercial entities like vendors and publishers may also be more cost effective method of preservation.

SOCIAL ISSUES

The social dilemma to long term archiving concerns the delicate issue of trust. The economic perversities that exist in scholarly development are a breeding ground for mistrust in relationships between publishers and libraries.

PRESERVATION REQUIREMENTS

Along with the difficulties in the preservation of digital material, maintaining the accessibility of digital media is also more complicated than any other non-digital media. When a book is preserved in its original formats, all of its content, layout and format are also preserved. On the other hand, though electronic documents can be saved as a whole, it often looses its layout. Digital preservation is storing information in the appropriate environment, following storage and handling procedures that are agreed upon and copying the digital material into newer, fresher media before the old media deteriorates. For a preservation project to work smoothly, the initial task is to identify the multiple aspects of a work that has to be preserved. Simply preserving the digital information on several copies of a digital medium is not sufficient. Copying the digital information in to newer, fresher media before the old media deteriorates is the best way to ensure preservation of digital information. Make sure that the digital information can be retrieved and processed in future.

In preserving a digital object, it is important to do the following:

- *Fix the object*: A document has a fixed boundary but the boundaries of digital objects are less clear, as they are compound objects created by incorporating different media or by linking to resources from around a network.
- *Preserve the physical presence*: The physical presence here is referring to the series of one's and zero's which is the foundation of digital objects in computer files.
- *Preserve content*: This aspect refers to maintaining the ability to access the content in various formats such as ASCII text, without the establishment of font variations and layout features.
- *Preserve the presentation*: In many types of digital documents, the layout specifications are separate from the content in order to retain the original look of a document; these layout specifications must also be preserved, along with the content.
- *Preserve functionality*: Digital objects have functionality and need to be preserved. They can contain multimedia components, hypertext format. They can also contain dynamic content generated automatically from databases, or have navigation functions, such as toolbars, keyword search, or interactive tables of contents. Special efforts must be made to preserve the functionality.
- *Preserve authenticity*: It is essential to preserve the authenticity of digital objects against unauthorised changes and monitoring it to ensure that each copy is an acceptable condition of the original. Establishing authoritative depositories would also help to achieve this goal.

- *Locate and refer to the digital object over time*: Digital objects can be readily altered, copied or moved. An individual must be able to match a citation to a digital object, and to distinguish it from other versions.
- *Preserve provenance*: The digital objects place of origin and history should be saved to help in confirming that the work is original and its content is intact.
- *Preserve context*: Digital objects are partly defined by their hardware and software dependencies, their mode of distribution, and linkages to other digital objects and so preserving context is a particular challenge.

PRESERVATION STRATEGIES

Every organisation accumulates documents such as drawings, maps, imageries, confidential reports, etc. These documents come in diverse shapes, sizes and use patterns. Unless preservation strategies are actively employed, the preserved information will rapidly become inaccessible. Choice of strategy will depend upon the nature of the material and what aspects of the document are to be retained, including content and layout of the information, as well as the computer file itself. Ideally all aspects of a digital document would be preserved, but this is not always possible or feasible.

STRATEGIES FOR PRESERVATION IN ORIGINAL FORMAT

Tactics for preserving documents need to support all of the values we have come to relate with paper based materials, like their intellectual content and outward appearance. Traditionally these strategies have focused on repair and binding. Since, the mid 20th century, chemical processes, such as washing and deacidifying, have also emerged. Four preservation strategies have gained wide acceptance: increasing the use of permanent paper; climate control; collection maintenance; mass deacidification and paper strengthening.

STRATEGIES FOR DIGITAL PRESERVATION

Alternative strategies in preserving original formats include transferring it to other formats. The main strategies used are microfilming and photographic techniques. However digitisation is increasingly being considered. Several strategies try to address the initial digital preservation problem of technology becoming obsolete. These include migrating information through successive generations of technology; using software to emulate the behaviour of older machines; preserving original hardware and software to run obsolete programmes, and creating hard copies of digital objects. Using these strategies satisfies some, but not all, preservation goals. The Digital Preservation investigated three main strategies for preserving digital information.

MIGRATION

Migration has been defined as, 'A move from one hardware platform or software system to another, usually because the purchaser or lessee believes the new system to be superior. In libraries the most common example is from the catalogue or software of one to that of another. Such a change may or may not require the of data one format to another." The process of migration involves moving files from one file-encoding format to another.

It copies, converts and/or transfers files from one hardware/software environment to another or from a Macintosh environment to a Windows environment. Migration may involve copying digital information from a medium that is becoming obsolete or physically deteriorating to a newer one and/or converting from one format to another, and/or moving documents from one platform to another. Migration aids in preserving the physical presence and the content of digital material. Migration, however, may have challenges in preserving presentation, functionality and context. It usually isn't enough to stay on top of technology becoming obsolete. Migration to new operating environments can often mean that the copy is not exactly the same as the original piece of information. Decisions must be made about what parts of the data to be migrated need to be preserved. Migration is currently the most common preservation strategy for digital records.

EMULATION

Emulation has been defined as, 'In digital archiving, a preservation technique that employs special software, called an *emulator*, to translate code and instructions from an original archived software programme to enable it to run on a newer platform, obviating the need to preserve obsolete hardware and system software". One of the benefits of emulation strategy over migration is that it aids in maintaining the integrity and the 'look and feel' of the material very efficiently. This allows the original rendering programmes for obsolete digital formats to be run on future computers. Once the data is archived with appropriate metadata and software, no other action is needed except for media refreshing until access is desired. One emulator can also be utilised as a solution for several data objects requiring the same operating environment. Though this method may be expensive, it may be best for formats that are challenging to convert.

XML

This acronym stands for eXtensible Mark-up Language and is a text-based language for enhancing data with information about structure and meaning. This opens up a window for various solutions for preservation of material over a long span of time. HTML and XML are—both based on SGML, HTML describes how the data should appear. XML lets you know what the data means, Important for data exchange, XML documents can be built using text-editors or XML-editors. Therefore, it is promising to use XML an open standard as preservation strategy.

XML METADATA ADVANTAGE

An important part of XML is metadata, or data about data. The popularity of using XML for digital preservation is increasing because it protects the digital material by being platform and software independent.

The nature of digital objects is best suited to be as structured markup language for customisation and reusability:

- Platform neutrality–Transformation–XML-based digital objects can be simply changed to alternative formats, *i.e.*, all Windows platforms, and all variants of UNIX and Linux.
- Validation–complex XML-based digital objects can be easily validated with DTD. Customised presentation–different presentation of the same digital object can be served to different users.
- Searchable content–the modular nature of the digital object content can be searched to offer a higher level of search service to the users.

OUTPUT TO PERMANENT PAPER OR MICROFILM

This strategy can correct the object as a whole, preserve the content, and to some extent, preserve the layout. However the output to paper will lead to a heavy loss for hypertext documents despite these drawbacks, a 'hybrid strategy' of creating both microfilm and digital copies is gaining support as a technique for reformatting paper originals. The digital copy improves access and functionality, and the microform copy acts as an archival surrogate that can be used for later projects, keeping in mind that the original captured files should always be maintained and preserved.

TECHNOLOGY PRESERVATION

Yet another strategy for guaranteeing ongoing access to digital objects by keeping older technology available for use is by preserving technology. The strategy of technology preservation includes the preservation of a digital object with both the software and hardware needed to interpret it. It aids in the recovering of data from obsolete storage media and platform, but it requires a lot of space, and can be quite costly. Storage media, such as contemporary floppy discs, DVDs or CD-ROMs, do not ensure access to files over long periods of time. The pre-requisite in achieving this is often the timely transfer of files to new storage media. However, the availability of the hardware and software required to read the specific files must be present. For instance, imagine the disappearance of the 5 ¼ inch floppy drive. The ramifications would be great. Thus, timely transfer of files to new and contemporary storage media is suggested.

DEVELOPING DIGITAL PRESERVATION GUIDELINES

In order to preserve digital objects, libraries need to formulate proper selection guidelines for formats and standards. Effective solutions in acquiring, describing and managing long term preservation of digital resources are decided. To facilitate preservation it is essential to use current standards to create digital objects, to monitor changes incorporated in standards, migrate to new standards when they are established.

DOCUMENTING RESOURCES

A digital preservation guideline is documentation and description of electronic resources. The need for such intentional description is for the reason that digital objects do not carry the visible evidence of creation and use of non-electronic formats. Such clues guide preservation decisions. They also help users to establish that the work is whole and intact, and to understand its importance and the context in which it was created.

- NEN-ISO 15489-1:2001, IDT standard by NEN, illustrates the steps that must be taken to satisfactorily position information management according to the tasks of the organisation.
- ReMANO is a set of functional requirements for information and archives management. Two worldwide organisations, the European Commission and the U.S., Ministry of Defence, have also created proposals of requirements or specifications, they are MoReq and DoD 5015.2-STD. In addition to these, the DIRKS

METADATA

A description of a digital object is 'data about data,' or metadata. Metadata is the data that describes the content and attributes of any object in a digital library. It is utilised as the solution to resource discovery and use of any document. Metadata can be stored either as an fundamental part of the document it describes or as part of a separate file of information. A number of standards like MARC, Dublin Core have emerged. The first workshop took place at OCLC headquarters in Dublin, Ohio, consequently the name 'Dublin Core.' The Dublin Core defines a set of fifteen metadata elements—much simpler than those used in traditional library cataloguing. They were designed to be simple enough to be used authors, but at the same time, descriptive enough to be useful in resource discovery.

UNIQUE IDENTIFIERS

Digital objects can be described by allocating it a unique name and persistent identifier. An identifier is a number, like an ISBN, which is used in a conventional library. An identifier for digital objects helps to establish the authenticity of the object by confirming to a user that the resource accessed is the one cited.

Some organisations involved in digital preservation are currently using:

- PURLs (Persistent Uniform Resource Locators);
- URNs (Uniform Resource Names); or
- DOI (Digital Object Identifiers).

COPYRIGHT/RIGHTS MANAGEMENT

The achievements over the last few years of digital technologies, the rapid development of the Internet and of other communications means, have resulted in an ever increasing need for protecting of copyright and ownership of materials, *i.e.*, Intellectual Property Rights (IPRs). Due to the major impact of the Web environment on the accessibility to the material, not only the documents digitalised with very high resolution and visual quality have to be protected, but also the documents digitalised with parameters particularly suitable for the Web collaboratory must be protected. The need of data authentication is straightforward.

Once the archives make available their documents in a Web collaboratory, they need to be sure that the material has not been modified. Traditional laws on IPR protection do not seem suitable to solve all the problems raised by this technological revolution.. A system called Electronic Copyright Management Systems (ECMSs), *i.e.,* systems able to manage automatically all the issues related to trading works by protecting their IPR.

In the design of effective ECMSs, two different approaches may help to solve the problem of IPR protection:

- Wrapped is an encrypted system and integrated with an application allowing to use the work only in a controlled manner; *e.g.,* the images can just be displayed, but they can not be printed, or the audio files can be played but can not be stored in the hard disk of the user. The content can not be accessed without the proper application.
- Watermarked through digital watermarking techniques, whose aim is to firmly and robustly embed IPR related information. The objective of the integrity watermarking process is to ensure image content authentication, detecting content-changing manipulations of the documents. It is defined as: Watermarking is the art of hiding information on the internet and still keeps it from public view. This is actual software, or HTML or JAVA can do it. If you keep it hidden, only a certain sequence, code, password' software, all of them or some of them can make it possible to open. It's really complicated, but the internet is the best and the worst location to hide things. Watermarking embeds a digital signal in text, image, audio or video files, which may enclose information and evidence of rights to a product's owner or publisher.

CONCLUSION

The foremost responsibility of digital libraries and archives is to ensure the future accessibility of information and preservation of valuable materials. Objectives of digital libraries consider organising information, maintaining intellectual property rights, and presenting, retrieving and visualising digital material. Research is underway on the questions of integrity, authenticity, and user requirements for digital resources. Authenticity and integrity of digital information have been underlying concerns in digital preservation because of the ease of altering digital objects and the dynamic nature of digital information. Strategies which discuss authenticity, appraisal and retention, migration acceptable media and formats, metadata, training and awareness for staff, and monitoring of compliance are defined. Information content management needs to define procedures, including design of the record keeping system, the types of electronic records to be captured by the system and the metadata to be kept with the records.

Develop written guidelines on the criteria required for emulation and assessing the migration process and results. The Library should ensure that it has the necessary hardware and software to provide access to the digital collections. A programme of the Commission on Preservation and Access Council on Library and Information Resources supports the efforts of libraries to preserve their paper-based collections and to meet the new preservation challenges of the digital environment. We need to pay great attention to the longtime preservation and use of digital data. Trustworthy models, information systems and environments for copyright management are necessary. Technological development, good practices and successful implementations provide access to their valuable content. A widely adopted trust model for an open IPR protection and management system is still an open issue.

8

Bibliographic Control

INTRODUCTION

The future of bibliographic control will be collaborative, decentralised, international in scope, and Web-based. Its realisation will occur in cooperation with the private sector, and with the active collaboration of library users. Data will be gathered from multiple sources; change will happen quickly; and bibliographic control will be dynamic, not static. The underlying technology that makes this future possible and necessary—the World Wide Web—is now almost two decades old. Libraries must continue the transition to this future without delay in order to retain their relevance as information providers.

The Working Group on the Future of Bibliographic Control encourages the library community to take a thoughtful and coordinated approach to effecting significant changes in bibliographic control. Such an approach will call for leadership that is neither unitary nor centralised. Nor will the responsibility to provide such leadership fall solely to the Library of Congress (LC). That said, the Working Group recognises that LC plays a unique role in the library community of the United States, and the directions that LC takes have great impact on all libraries. We also recognise that there are many other institutions and organisations that have the expertise and the capacity to play significant roles in the bibliographic future. Wherever possible, those institutions must step forward and take responsibility for assisting with navigating the transition and for playing appropriate ongoing roles after that transition is complete. To achieve the goals set out in this document, we must look beyond individual libraries to a system wide deployment of resources. We must realise efficiencies in order to be able to reallocate resources from certain lower-value components of the bibliographic control ecosystem into other higher-value components of that same ecosystem. The recommendations in this report are directed at a number of parties, indicated either by their common initialism or by their general category. When the recommendation is addressed to 'All,' it is intended for the library community as a whole and its close collaborators. The Library of Congress must begin by prioritising the recommendations that are directed in whole or in part at LC. Some define tasks that can be achieved immediately and with moderate effort; others will require analysis and planning that will have to be coordinated broadly and carefully. The Working Group has consciously not associated time frames with any of its recommendations.

The recommendations fall into five general areas:

- Increase the efficiency of bibliographic production for all libraries through increased cooperation and increased sharing of bibliographic records, and by maximising the use of data produced throughout the entire 'supply chain' for information resources.
- Transfer effort into higher-value activity. In particular, expand the possibilities for knowledge creation by 'exposing' rare and unique materials held by libraries that are currently hidden from view and, thus, underused.
- Position our technology for the future by recognising that the World Wide Web is both our technology platform and the appropriate platform for the delivery of our standards. Recognise that people are not the only users of the data we produce in the name of bibliographic control, but so too are machine applications that interact with those data in a variety of ways.

- Position our community for the future by facilitating the incorporation of evaluative and other user-supplied information into our resource descriptions. Work to realise the potential of the FRBR framework for revealing and capitalising on the various relationships that exist among information resources.
- Strengthen the library profession through education and the development of metrics that will inform decision-making now and in the future.

The Working Group intends what follows to serve as a broad blueprint for the Library of Congress and its colleagues in the library and information technology communities for extending and promoting access to information resources.

BACKGROUND

BIBLIOGRAPHIC CONTROL AT THE LIBRARY OF CONGRESS

Bibliographic control is the organisation of library materials to facilitate discovery, management, identification, and access. Bibliographic control is as old as libraries themselves, and our current approaches to it are direct descendents of the librarianship of the 19th century. One of the outgrowths of standards developed in that century is that the libraries of today are able to collaborate on the creation of cataloguing and catalogue entries. In 1902, the Library of Congress began producing catalogue cards for purchase so that libraries that purchased the same book could buy catalogue cards from the Library of Congress, rather than having to catalogue the book themselves.

The service continues to this day, although now bibliographic data are in machine-readable form and are shared over networks. Today's technology facilitates the contribution by any number of libraries to the pool of available bibliographic records. This sharing of records, and of the effort that produces them, results in considerable cost savings for America's libraries. Currently, the Library of Congress serves as the primary source of bibliographic data for many libraries in the United States and beyond. LC creates a bibliographic record for its catalogue, either at the prepublication stage or when LC receives an item. From LC's catalogue, the record enters a variety of record distribution channels where it becomes available to other libraries that hold the same item. Libraries may acquire machine-readable cataloguing records from a bibliographic utility, or they may purchase them from vendors that use LC copy.

Still other libraries may, as the basis for their own records, rely on the printed CIP data that appear in some books. Library of Congress cataloguing records have traditionally been considered to represent the highest quality cataloguing. Although there is no guarantee that LC records will be perfect, they are still the cataloguing records of choice for most other libraries. Within WorldCat, more holdings are attached to Library of Congress records than to records from other sources. The widespread acceptance of LC cataloguing contributes to the consistency of access to materials across the nation's libraries, and it reduces the overall cost of bibliographic control for those libraries.

THE LIBRARY OF CONGRESS MANDATE

Creation of bibliographic records for use by others, and leadership in the area of standards development are common activities in the national libraries. LC is a recognised world leader in both endeavours. However, unlike other international players in this arena, LC enjoys neither a mandate to be a national library, nor funding concomitant with playing such a role. More to the point, it receives no funding specifically directed at providing bibliographic services for U.S., libraries. While it is beyond the scope of this report to comment on whether or not the Library of Congress should be given the statutory standing of a national library, it is necessary to observe that its lacking such status, and in particular the funding that should accompany such status, compromises its continuing ability to carry out functions depended upon by many of the nation's libraries. LC's willingness, nevertheless, to step forward and assume responsibilities beyond its designated mandate has greatly benefited libraries in the U.S., and throughout the world. It has, however, also fostered dependencies that limit LC's freedom of action in meeting changing circumstances and needs. Like other libraries, LC is now faced with the need to catalogue a growing variety of digital resources and to improve access to its unique and rare collections.

Digitisation of LC's own collections brings with it the need for major new investment in metadata creation and digital resource management. Because a large percentage of LC's cataloguing workforce is nearing retirement age, sustaining its current methods and scale of cataloguing soon will require major investment in recruitment and training. These needs and pressures cannot be ignored; they require efficient innovation and creative adaptation. Yet any major change by LC in its bibliographic services will have consequences not only for libraries and educational institutions that have come to rely on those services, but also for the entire market sector that provides goods and services to libraries.

These latter entities often make direct or indirect use of LC cataloguing as part of their product offerings. LC is permitted to recover only direct costs for services provided to others. As a result, the fees that the Library charges do not cover the most expensive aspect of cataloguing: namely, the cost of the intellectual work.. The economics of creating LC's products have changed dramatically since, the time when the Library was producing cards for library catalogues. It is now time to re-evaluate the pricing of LC's product line in order to develop a business model that allows LC to more substantially recoup its actual costs.

STANDARDS AND PRACTICES AT THE LIBRARY OF CONGRESS

In addition to producing bibliographic records, LC provides leadership in the bibliographic control standards arena. The Library is the maintenance agency for MARC21, the machine-readable record format used by libraries, and plays a key role in the creation and maintenance of the descriptive cataloguing rules used in U.S., libraries. It also manages two vital access tools, the Library of Congress Classification (LCC) and the Library of Congress Subject Headings (LCSH), both of which are used by libraries throughout the United States as well as in some other libraries world-wide. LC also hosts online sites for numerous other information standards, including METS and Z39.50. LC staff participates in the development and maintenance of literally dozens of standards related to bibliographic control and to other library functions, such as preservation and digitisation.

These standards and others that are relevant to bibliographic control are international in nature, just as the exchange of bibliographic information has become global. In recent years, development and use of MARC21, for instance, have expanded beyond an exclusively United States base to include Canada and the United Kingdom, and work is underway to enable the participation of German libraries. In this, as in so many other international standards activities, it is LC that often as not represents U.S., library interests.

THE FUTURE OF BIBLIOGRAPHIC CONTROL

What shape and form the future of bibliographic control will take is a question that the Library of Congress has investigated periodically. The motivation for the most recent investigations has been the dramatic transformation of the field of librarianship brought about by digital technologies. A report on digital strategies was conducted by the National Research Council at the behest of the Librarian of Congress in 2000. In 2001, the Bicentennial Conference on Bibliographic Control for the New Millennium—subtitled 'Confronting the Challenges of Networked Resources and the Web'—produced an action plan for the Library.

Although primarily focused on the control of networked and digital resources, the conference covered general topics of metadata creation; augmentation of library cataloguing rules to make them more suitable for describing electronic resources; support for interoperability among libraries and between libraries and other information providers; and investigation of ways to increase the efficiencies of bibliographic record creation through partnerships. Many of these topics surfaced again in a 2006 report commissioned by LC and written by Karen Calhoun. At the same time, other institutions also undertook similar investigations, including work done at the University of California on the future of bibliographic services at the University, and consideration of the future of cataloguing by Indiana University.

In 2004, the Joint Steering Committee for the Revision of the Anglo-American Cataloguing Rules began work on a new code to replace the *Anglo-American Cataloguing Rules* first published in 1967 and revised substantially since, then. The new rules, named Resource Description and Access, are ' ... being developed as a new standard for resource description and access designed for the digital world." This work is facilitated by related work done by the International Federation of Library Associations and Institutions (IFLA) on a new model for a bibliographic framework: the Functional Requirements for Bibliographic Records (FRBR) and the development of a new set of IFLA Cataloguing Principles in 2003.

THE WORKING GROUP ON THE FUTURE OF BIBLIOGRAPHIC CONTROL

The Working Group on the Future of Bibliographic Control was formed by the Library of Congress to address changes in how libraries must do their work in the digital information era.

The Working Group is co-chaired by Dr. José-Marie Griffiths, Dean and Professor of the School of Information and Library Science at the University of North Carolina at Chapel Hill, and Olivia M. A. Madison, Dean of the Library, Iowa State University.

Members of the Working Group are information professionals representing key professional organisations and information technology companies. Although a primary catalyst for formation of the Working Group was reaction in the library community to a Library of Congress decision to discontinue series authority control for the materials it catalogues, the focus of the Group's work was much broader.

The Working Group was charged to:

- Present findings on how bibliographic control and other descriptive practices can effectively support management of and access to library materials in the evolving information and technology environment.
- Recommend ways in which the library community can collectively move towards achieving this vision.
- Advise the Library of Congress on its role and priorities.

The Working Group met first in November 2006. At that meeting the Group decided to structure its process around a series of public meetings covering three specific areas:

- Users and uses of bibliographic data.
- Structures and standards for bibliographic data.
- Economics and organisation of bibliographic data.

These meetings included presentations by invited speakers, as well as testimony from members of the community. Two of the three public meetings were available as Webcasts both during and after the meeting. In addition, the community was invited to submit written testimony. The Working Group received seventy-four written submissions, of which more than fifteen were submitted on behalf of organisations or institutions. The Library of Congress mounted a public Web site for the Working Group, where it posted the Group's membership, charge, and schedule; links to background documents; summaries of the public meetings; and other information.

GUIDING PRINCIPLES

REDEFINE BIBLIOGRAPHIC CONTROL

The phrase *bibliographic control* is often interpreted to have the same meaning as the word *cataloguing*. The library catalogue, however, is just one access route to materials that a library manages for its users. The benefits of bibliographic control can be expanded to a wide range of information resources both through cooperation and through design. The Working Group urges adoption of a broad definition of bibliographic control that embraces all library materials, a diverse community of users, and a multiplicity of venues where information is sought.

The bibliographic universe today includes an enormous variety of materials: published materials that are purchased by libraries; materials that libraries licence for user access; digital materials on public networks; and materials that are unique to an individual library. It is not uncommon that these disparate materials are described and managed through different processes, and are offered separately for user access. Users would be better served if access to these materials were provided in the context of a unified philosophy of bibliographic control.

Different communities of bibliographic practice have grown up around different resource types: library collections of books and journals, archives, journal articles, and museum objects and images. As these resources and others become increasingly accessible through the Web, separation of the communities of practice that manage them is no longer desirable, sustainable, or functional. Bibliographic control is increasingly a matter of managing relationships—among works, names, concepts, and object descriptions—across communities.

Consistency of description within any single environment, such as the library catalogue, is becoming less significant than the ability to make connections between environments: Amazon to World Cat to Google to PubMed to Wikipedia, with library holdings serving as but one node in this web of connectivity. In today's environment, bibliographic control cannot continue to be seen as limited to library catalogues. Although cataloguing will and must continue to play a key role in bibliographic control, today there are many other sources of data that can and must be used to organise and provide access to the information universe.

To take advantage of these sources, it is necessary to embrace a view of bibliographic control as a distributed activity, not a centralised one. Data about collection usage—such as inclusion in curricula or bibliographies, citation links, circulation and sales figures—are all valuable bits of information in the universe of bibliographic control. User-contributed data, such as reviews or rankings, can help other users identify resources of possible interest to them. Any collection of electronic data, from library catalogues to collections of full-text works, can be mined for information through automated means. Even those resources that do not originate inside the library or its systems can be seen as tools to serve the library user.

REDEFINE THE BIBLIOGRAPHIC UNIVERSE

- The library is, of course, only one link in the supply chain of bibliographic information between author and reader. Its needs are unique, but not necessarily exclusive. All parties contribute value through the vehicle of the bib record: Creator, Publisher, Vendors/Distributors, and Stores/Libraries. To date, there is not a strong tradition of sharing data and metadata throughout the publication cycle. It may be useful, then, to think about what information is available at each stage, and how to aggregate and build on that foundation. What value is added at each stage? How can the existing value be captured and leveraged in the next?

Once considered a public good, information access is today a commodity in a rapidly-growing marketplace. Many information resources formerly managed in the not-for-profit sector are now the objects of a significant for-profit economy. Entities in this latter economy have financial capabilities far beyond those of libraries.

Further, they have the resources to engage in large scale research and development. Libraries of today need to recognise that they are but one group of players in a vast field, and that market conditions necessitate that libraries interact increasingly with the commercial sector. One example of such interaction can be found in the various mass digitisation projects in which for-profit organisations are making use of library resources and library metadata. Another is found in the increasing exchange of data along the publishing supply chain, as publishers produce data essential for online bookstores, and as library systems link to those online stores for data not traditionally carried in library bibliographic records, such as cover images or reviews. The expanding and evolving bibliographic environment is today very much Web-enabled and, as such, it crosses international boundaries. No longer is bibliographic control the domain only of libraries, publishers, and database producers. The supply chain of published and shared information and of bibliographic data and derived services, along with their current and potential users, can today be anywhere and everywhere simultaneously. The continued sharing of effort will be one of the keys to the future success of libraries.

Moreover, libraries will need to collaborate not just with each other, but with other organisations as well. For LC, collaboration can take many forms: LC can incorporate data from others into its records; it can create links to data created and held by others; it can create basic records that serve LC and allow others to enhance the records for their own purposes; and it can itself enhance basic records created by others.

These methods of collaboration are not mutually exclusive, nor do they constitute a complete list. All possible means of collaboration should be considered. Sharing, however, is not a strategy for LC alone. The entire library community and its many partners must also be part of it. Rather than relying as heavily as it has on LC, the community needs to acknowledge that in at least some areas, LC may need to be able to rely on the work of others. Moreover, the community—and LC for that matter—needs to consider carefully when it is appropriate to distribute effort and when to discontinue it.

REDEFINE THE ROLE OF THE LIBRARY OF CONGRESS

For every activity area within LC, it is important that the community ask itself whether there is some other institution or group that might take on that work so that LC can reallocate resources. Is there duplicate effort being expended? Are there possible partnerships that could reduce the burden on the Library? Since, LC is not funded for the role of national library, are there any national library-type functions that LC currently performs that could be collectively fulfilled by the community? The Library must analyse its tasks to identify areas where work is being done primarily to benefit other libraries.

If these tasks are not of direct and substantial benefit to the Library, they should be considered for divestment. In working towards divestment, LC must work with the members of the community that benefit from the work to develop a plan for its transition. The immediately affected community should be encouraged to consider if those tasks still return value. If so, and only if so, the community must devise mechanisms to ensure their management and fulfillment outside LC. Even in areas where work currently being done by LC is not done primarily to benefit others, LC may still conclude that the work can no longer be supported, or that it no longer repays the effort. Again, decisions to cease work previously performed must be taken only after engaging interested and affected parties.

Because no one has full knowledge of all of the activities and skills within the community at large, there needs to be a mechanism for other institutions to approach LC with proposals for collaboration or even for transfer of responsibilities. This need to divest extends to the creation of bibliographic data.

Since, the time that the Library of Congress first began distributing catalogue cards, it has had a role as the primary source of bibliographic records for libraries in the United States. In addition, for libraries around the world, LC has also become a primary source of bibliographic records for materials published in the U.S., The Library of Congress took on this role at a time when it was uniquely positioned to provide these services, but circumstances have changed. Participation in bibliographic networks and initiatives such as the Programme for Cooperative Cataloguing (PCC) have led to the library community as a whole having at least as much bibliographic expertise as LC. The Working Group urges LC to identify areas where it no longer need be the sole provider of bibliographic data and to create partnerships to distribute responsibility for data creation.

Although the Library of Congress will undoubtedly remain a major producer of cataloguing copy, LC can and should begin to see itself as one of many peer institutions that can contribute bibliographic data to the community. Determining how much and what work might be shared more broadly will require discussion and evaluation of what other members of the bibliographic community can contribute. It will also require coordination and management so that all participants understand their respective roles. The goal should be that of LC's deriving increasing benefit from the work of other libraries.

The Library has long accepted a leadership role in the areas of standards development and maintenance. The range of standards that applies to the digital environment is broad and growing. No single institution can understand, much less participate in the development and maintenance of all standards relating to information management. In addition, the standards landscape in the library field is murky, with many different organisations working on similar standards in a non-coordinated fashion. LC should consider sharing the standards effort within the community and collaborating with other interested institutions to create a rational and efficient means of managing the standards needed for information exchange.

This includes sharing the management of the primary data standard for bibliographic records, which should belong to the community rather than to a single institution. More than most libraries, the Library of Congress has incredible untapped value in its unique and rare holdings. These remain largely outside of bibliographic control while the Library puts most of its effort into managing modern, traditionally published items of the sort commonly found in many other libraries. Great benefit to scholars and citisens could result from a shift in the relative level of attention accorded the Library's unique and rare materials. The Working Group urges that greater bibliographic attention be paid to the primary resources within the Library, recognising that their nature and quantity is such that they will not realistically lend themselves to the application of traditional cataloguing practices.

FINDINGS AND RECOMMENDATIONS

INCREASE THE EFFICIENCY OF BIBLIOGRAPHIC PRODUCTION

Eliminate Redundancies

Some of the interest in looking for new ways to effect bibliographic control is based on the current costs of that activity. Because the incredible growth in information resources is not matched by a related growth in library funding, it is necessary to re-examine the efficiency with which the work of bibliographic control is performed.

The Working Group identified three primary areas of redundancy in the bibliographic production process:

- the supply chain, wherein some data are created by publishers and vendors and later re-created by library catalogers.
- the modification of records within the library community, wherein such modifications are not shared, even though they could be useful to others.
- the expenses that are incurred when individual libraries must purchase records because the sharing of those records is prohibited or restricted.

Until very recently, bibliographic control has been an artisan activity, as there was no alternative for providing access except to transcribe, by hand, data from the objects being described. Now, however, publishers and vendors are working in an electronic environment, and print material generally originates in electronic format. Publishers can provide some elements of descriptive metadata in electronic format for much of their output and libraries need to capitalise on those metadata. The abstracting and indexing industry has the capability to utilise existing products to disaggregate the data they compile to supply metadata at the article level. Despite the fact that descriptive metadata are being created in venues, however, libraries have so far taken minimal advantage of them. Given the explosion of material requiring some level of bibliographic control, the model of item-by-item manual transcription is no longer sustainable.

Libraries must find ways to make use of the data created by others in the supply chain, including data that can be derived from algorithmic analyses of digital materials. The redundant modification of records in libraries results in unnecessary costs to the library community as a whole. Redundancies occur when individual libraries make changes to records in their local library systems but do not share those changes with the broader community.

Their reasons for not sharing record modifications may be operational, technical, or economic. OCLC's business model has a real impact on the distributed system of bibliographic data exchange. While OCLC policies allow some libraries to enrich WorldCat records centrally, some consider these policies to be overly restrictive. Another area of redundancy relates to vendor-supplied records that are corrected by libraries that receive them, but outside the mainstream cataloguing workflow.

As a consequence, local changes are not re-distributed. In still other cases, re-distribution of records may be forbidden by the licence agreement between the vendor and the library. This leads to duplication of effort on the part of other libraries that own the same titles. Some unnecessary changes to records could be eliminated if there were a persuasive body of evidence that indicated what parts of the record are key to user access success.

Such data would enable catalogers to make informed judgements about how best to spend their time on each record. Cataloguer judgement and institutional policies are applied with care, but without metrics it is difficult to determine or justify changes in practice.

Consequences of Maintaining the Status Quo

Redundant work means wasted resources. Time and money are spent redoing work that has already been done, rather than creating new records for materials not yet cataloged. This leads to delays in providing access to materials, and to users being unable to locate materials that, though owned, are not yet accessible. Duplication of work may also lead to duplicate records being input into consortial databases or into OCLC. These duplicate records—with or without minor inconsistencies that make it difficult to identify duplicates from true variants—lead to more wasted resources as libraries have to examine multiple records in order to find the best matches for the items they are cataloguing.

Recommendations

Make Use of Bibliographic Data Available Earlier in the Supply Chain:

- *All*: Be more flexible in accepting bibliographic data from others that do not conform precisely to U.S., library standards.
- *All*: Analyse cataloguing rules and modify them as necessary to ensure their ability to support data sharing with publisher and vendor partners.
- *All*: Develop standard crosswalks for the conversion of vendor data to library system formats.
- *All*: Develop managed processes for creating and sharing conversion programmes so that programming is not done redundantly at multiple institutions.
- *All*: Work with resource providers to coordinate data sharing in a way that works well for all partners.
- *All*: Demonstrate to publishers the business advantages of supplying complete and accurate metadata.

Re-purpose Existing Metadata for Greater Efficiency:

- *All*: Develop workflow and mechanisms to use data and metadata from network resources, such as abstracting and indexing services, Amazon, IMDb, etc., where those can enhance the user's experience in seeking and using information.

- *All*: Use metadata supplied by sound recording, motion picture, and other audio-visual distribution sources.
- *All*: Use descriptive cataloguing provided by book vendors and non-U.S., libraries whenever available.

Automate the CIP process:

- *LC*: Require publishers participating in the CIP programme to supply ONIX or other equivalent standardised XML metadata.
- *LC*: Develop fully automated mechanisms to accept descriptive data in ONIX format from book publishers and transfer them to the MARC format for use as CIP records.

Re-Examine the Current Economic Model for Data Sharing in the Networked Environment:

- *LC*: Convene a representative group consisting of libraries, vendors, and OCLC members to address costs, barriers to change, and the value of potential gains arising from greater sharing of data, and to develop recommendations for change.
- *LC*: Promote widespread discussion of barriers to sharing data.
- *LC*: re-evaluate the pricing of LC's product line with a view to developing a business model that enables more substantial cost recovery.

Develop Evidence about Discovery Tools to Guide Decision-Makers:

- *All*: Make use of existing, and gather additional evidence on user behaviour to establish empirically the correlation between user behaviour and the content of bibliographic records.

Desired Outcomes

LC's increased use of publisher- and vendor-supplied data for bibliographic description will signal to other libraries that effective record creation can be achieved by using these data.

Catalogers' time will be freed to enable increased focus on the intellectual work of providing controlled access points for discovery and retrieval of more material. More records will be shared, thus enabling reallocation of time and effort to the processing of materials and collections that are currently not described and therefore not readily accessible to the public. With a body of evidence-based research data, decisions about changes to current practices can be made based on known impact. Libraries can confidently eliminate or retain various types of record editing based on knowledge of the actual effect they have on user success in the catalogue.

Increase Distribution of Responsibility for Bibliographic Record Production

Libraries of all types rely heavily on the Library of Congress for the original cataloguing records on which they base the bibliographic control of their own collections. They obtain these records from various sources: they use LC's Cataloguing in Publication records; harvest bibliographic records from LC's online catalogue; use LC-supplied records from OCLC; or purchase records from vendors that obtain their records from OCLC or directly from LC.

These same libraries also rely on LC for substantive aspects of their authority work, either because the LC bibliographic records they are using include LC-performed authority control or because the authority records they otherwise use are supplied by LC to OCLC and other vendors. The long history of LC's supplying cataloguing and authority data has supported this reliance on LC on the part of the nation's libraries, but the burden on LC has become increasingly heavy as funding has not kept pace with demand. For well over twenty years, the Library of Congress has recognised the need to share with other libraries in the community the work of creating bibliographic and authority records.

The Programme for Cooperative Cataloguing—and its component programmes, *Bibliographic Cooperative* (BIBCO), *Name Authority Cooperative* (NACO), *Subject Authority*

Cooperative (SACO), and *Cooperative Online Serials* (CONSER)—attempts to distribute the load of original cataloguing and authority work required in an expanding information universe by accepting contributions from libraries across the country to the national bibliographic and authorities databases. These libraries' personnel are trained by LC and by PCC members to produce records at certain levels of quality and in certain quantities.

Unfortunately, there are a limited number of library participants in the cooperative programmes, which limits the extent to which these programmes relieve Library of Congress of some of its bibliographic control production responsibilities. Because many libraries provide bibliographic control to their collections chiefly via copy cataloguing and the loading of LC authority files into their online systems, over the past century these libraries have not only reduced the number of staff in their cataloguing operations, but also have reduced the proportion of staff who are professionally educated to catalogue. Cataloguing personnel in most libraries are predominantly paraprofessionals whose training often does not include the creation of authoritative name forms, subject analysis, or in-depth description.

Thus, when LC makes decisions that have a substantive impact on the flow of authority work or bibliographic records, these libraries are unable to compensate for the loss without the addition or reallocation of resources. The libraries that are most dependent on LC for bibliographic data are often the smallest and least well funded, and are therefore the most vulnerable to any LC cutbacks, since, they do not have the resources to pursue other options such as joining OCLC or outsourcing work to a service vendor.

One of the lessons learned from LC's announcement that it intended to stop series authority control was just how vulnerable libraries can and do feel when faced with peremptory change on LC's part. The dependency on LC for bibliographic data goes beyond libraries to the market segment that makes use of library bibliographic data and that creates library applications. Even though they are heavy users of LC data, these parties often do not participate in decision-making about bibliographic records and are also not considered in the creation or modification of cataloguing standards and practices.

Consequences of Maintaining the Status Quo

Long-term dependence on Library of Congress bibliographic services leaves the users of those services increasingly vulnerable to any changes in them. Long-term reliance on Library of Congress leadership and on its provision of cataloguing records leads libraries—even some large libraries with relatively plentiful staff—to think that they bear no responsibility, individually or collectively, for sharing substantively in the work of bibliographic control. System-wide redundancies result in higher overall costs and lower effectiveness.

Financial pressures on library operations make this increasingly unsustainable. It is important to achieve greater efficiencies within the overall system so as to release effort to higher value activities. As a consequence of management decisions relating to PCC, BIBCO, NACO, SACO, and CONSER, and of the rigorous membership requirements of those programmes, libraries that might have participated are discouraged from contributing significantly to the effort of creating bibliographic records.

Share Responsibility for Creating Bibliographic Records:

- *LC*: Library and publishing communities: Share responsibility for creating original cataloguing according to interest, use and ability. Consider categories of materials for which responsibilities can be distributed and categories of metadata that can be appropriately provided by each of the participants.
- *LC*: Analyse the Library's use of PCC-produced data and determine how to take full advantage of the shared product.
- *LC*: Recognise the impact of LC practice on other libraries. Changes in practice must be openly arrived at with sufficient opportunity for public input, and

widely announced with sufficient time to allow other libraries to consider the ramifications, if any, for their own practices and workflows.

Examine Current Original Cataloguing Programmes and Sub-Programmes at the Library of Congress:

- *LC*: Identify all distinct cataloguing programmes and operations within the Library of Congress; determine the relative importance of each to the Library of Congress and other libraries; use these determinations to inform management decisions as to priority, continuation, etc.
- *LC*: For those aspects of operations that extend beyond the Library's immediate mission as the Library of Congress, identify other entities or groups with the interest and ability to assume responsibility for them.
- *LC*: Work with interested entities such as PCC, ARL, professional organisations, publishers, etc. to plan transition to new distribution of responsibilities.

Expand Number of PCC Participants:

- *PCC*: Assess barriers and incentives to participation by more libraries, including PCC's and LC's abilities to manage a larger scale effort of collaboration.
- *PCC*: Reduce personnel and other costs to PCC participants and to LC.
- *PCC*: Actively recruit new participants. Develop a 'marketing programme' for PCC, publicising its work and benefits.

Increase Incentives for Sharing Bibliographic Records:

- LC, PCC, and OCLC: Explore ways to increase financial or other incentives for contributions of new bibliographic records and of upgrades or corrections to existing records to the national shared bibliographic and authority databases.

Desired Outcomes

Rather than continuing to occupy the position of the 'alpha library,' LC will become a true partner with many other libraries and organisations in creating bibliographic control in the future. Greater efficiencies will enable libraries to redirect effort from enhancing the cataloguing of mainstream materials to other activities that contribute to bibliographic control.

These might include more broadly-based authority work and greater attention to cataloguing collections of unique and rare materials. LC will have more resources to devote to making its own collections accessible to the American public. All types of libraries will contribute to the best of their abilities and resources to the 'public good' that comes from bibliographic control and resource sharing. More libraries will participate in PCC, BIBCO, NACO, SACO, and CONSER.

Collaborate on Authority Record Creation

The Working Group received substantial input concerning the present state of and future possibilities for authority control. Testimony consistently bore out the fact that both libraries and their users rely on the Library of Congress to provide catalogue records with current, valid, and unambiguous access points. Although there is much speculation that improvements in machine-searching capabilities and the growth of databases eliminate the need for authoritative forms of names, series, titles, and subject concepts, both public testimony and available evidence strongly suggest that this is not the case.

While such mechanisms as keyword searching provide extremely useful additions to the arsenal of searching capabilities available to users, they are not a satisfactory substitute for controlled vocabularies. Indeed, many machine-searching techniques rely on the existence of authoritative headings even if they do not explicitly display them.

While the creation of authoritative headings is critical to user success in finding and identifying resources, it definitely adds significantly to the cost of bibliographic record creation. Although costs can be managed to some degree by sharing the burden of authority record creation, the need for authoritative forms for names, titles, and series is driven by the resources themselves and by the high rate of increase in the production of intellectual resources. In a time when anyone can be an author, the number of new creators is growing rapidly. As libraries expand their application of bibliographic control to include more digital materials, the number of name authority records that must be created for new authors will only increase, placing an added burden on cataloguing departments.

To continue to provide effective authority control, a variety of strategies must be pursued. One strategy might be to develop automated means to assist in authority control, for example to assist in disambiguation among authors; another might be to engage publishers and authors themselves in the process of unambiguous creator identification. Subject analysis—including analysing content and creating and applying subject headings and classification numbers—is a core function of cataloguing; although expensive, it is nonetheless critical.

While subject headings are recognised as essential for collocating topical information, the complexity of LCSH creates difficulties for heading creation and use. At present, the process of maintaining LCSH and of creating new or revised headings can be slow to meet the needs of those working with emerging concepts in both published and archival materials. The Working Group identified a number of areas that might lend themselves to greater cooperative attention. First, there may be opportunities to work with the abstracting and indexing community, which is increasingly interested in the ability to identify more precisely the authors represented in its indexes.

It may also be possible for LC to work with foreign national libraries that are engaged in similar activities. Internationalisation of bibliographic data requires heading equivalencies in different languages, reflecting different national practices. The work begun on a Virtual International Authority File is a step in this direction. Finally, work needs to be done to create data structures that identify resources irrespective of language choice and, thus, to reduce reliance on terms and headings that are language-based.

Consequences of Maintaining the Status Quo

Authority control will be limited to library applications, and often only to well-established or large systems that can afford to acquire the data. Erosion of authority control will impede users' abilities to retrieve desired information in a timely fashion. As keyword searching becomes increasingly prevalent, works in languages other than English are at risk of becoming less accessible, or even inaccessible.

Increase Collaboration on Authority Data:

- *LC, PCC*: Identify ways to promote wider participation in the distribution of responsibility for creating, enhancing, and maintaining authority data.
- *LC, PCC, and library community*: Work with other interested parties to enhance, expand, and make more affordable training opportunities in the area of authority data creation.
- *LC, PCC, and OCLC*: Explore ways to increase financial or other incentives for contributions of new authority records and of upgrades or corrections to existing records in the national shared bibliographic and authority databases.

Increase Re-Use of Assigned Authoritative Headings:

- *LC, ILS vendors, publishers, etc.*: Investigate convergences of name authority and identity management in various contexts, such as libraries, publishing, and repository management.
- *LC*: Bring together other communities working on problems of author identification; map the issues; and investigate possibilities for cooperation.
- *LC*: Make the LC Name Authority file available as a Web resource, for downloading or linking to through various Web service interfaces.

Internationalise Authority Files:

- *LC, OCLC, and National Libraries*: Pursue more aggressively the development of internationally shared authority files.

- *LC, OCLC, and National Libraries*: Work actively to advance a uniform approach to linking national and international authority records that represent the same entity.
- *All*: Create a file structure that will enable institutions to determine which forms of headings are authorised for use in various languages.

Desired Outcomes

There will be increased sharing of authority data between libraries and between library systems and systems from other communities, with library authority data available to anyone working with bibliographic data. Economies will be realised by minimising the number of times the same entity needs to be researched. Exchange of information about the same name from one system to another will be made simpler and more reliable. Access to data will be unimpeded and barriers to using data will be minimized. New partnerships will result from collaboration and coordination among a wide array of stakeholders. This will realise workflow efficiencies and minimize redundancies among the entities that create and use both authority and bibliographic data. Better access to materials in a more seamless search environment will mean fewer failed searches and fewer faulty search results.

Internationally shared authority files will enhance access to non-English language materials, including those in non-Roman alphabets and scripts, and will encourage international sharing of information and data.

ENHANCE ACCESS TO RARE AND UNIQUE MATERIALS

Special collections are of great value to scholars for research purposes. In addition, as educators seek to engage more students, including undergraduates, in research that utilises primary sources, these materials are increasingly important for teaching and learning. Non-textual special collections are of particular interest to scholars as they make increasing use of images and sound in their teaching and research. Special collections also reflect the unique identity of a particular library, and are often considered showcases of community cultural and intellectual life. Processing of unique and primary source materials has not kept up with acquisitions for decades. The result is that there are backlogs of unprocessed collections of these materials at libraries and repositories across the country that are not accessible through the libraries' online discovery tools.

The situation is especially critical for materials in non-textual formats. The 1998 survey of ARL special collections libraries illustrated this problem quantitatively. Even when materials are fully processed, past practice has often been not to share bibliographic data for unique and archival materials, in large part because the value of sharing data has been equated with its potential for use by cataloguers in other institutions. The need for trade-offs between broad access and detailed description is increasingly recognised by special collections librarians and archivists, and there is substantial debate in the profession about these issues.

Few models exist, however, for how such trade-offs might be made. Moreover, it is difficult to quantify the value differential between trade-offs, because too little is known about use patterns and users' needs. The ability to digitise special collections materials has the potential to greatly enhance access to and use of these materials, and there is growing understanding that wherever possible these collections should be made public and accessible in digital form.

This raises a number of questions, including how the strong interest in providing source material in digital form may change the economics and practices of processing collections. Full text indexing of textual materials via optical character recognition is a powerful alternative to many traditional descriptive practices, but given the current state of the various technologies for indexing and retrieval, optical character recognition techniques are much less usefully applied to images and sound recordings.

Other questions involve the integration of access to the

full range of special collections, either within the total array of information resources held at a single institution, or at a national or international level; and the need for libraries and archives to share, exchange, and consolidate information about special collections material.

CONSEQUENCES OF MAINTAINING THE STATUS QUO

Uncatalogued collections of unique and rare materials are inaccessible because, in addition to not being available via a library's primary discovery tools, they are likely to be in closed stacks, eliminating the possibility of discovery by browsing. Research and teaching are hindered because researchers cannot locate these materials without suspecting such a collection might exist and without highly labour-intensive efforts to identify and locate materials.

Access to unprocessed collections is highly staff-dependent and therefore a cost burden to the institution. Access to or awareness of materials by information seekers outside the institution is limited. Without straightforward access to special collections materials, service is severely compromised. The promise of digitising special collections material is limited in the absence of a concomitant ability to discover them.

RECOMMENDATIONS

Make the Discovery of Rare and Unique Materials a High Priority:

- *LC*: Direct resources to support the discovery of rare and unique materials, including resources freed by the institution of economies realised in other areas.
- *All*: Gather and share data on access paths that guide researchers to unique materials as a means to inform best practices for access in a Web environment.
- *All*: Make finding aids accessible via online catalogues, and available on the Internet.

Streamline Cataloguing for Rare and Unique Materials, Emphasising Greater Coverage and Access to a Greater Number of Items:

- *LC*: Adopt as a guiding principle the provision of

some level of access to all materials, rather than comprehensive access to some materials and no access at all to other materials.

- *All*: Establish cataloguing practices that are practicable and flexible, and that reflect the needs of users and the reality of limited resources.
- *LC*: Encourage adoption of current rules and practices for cataloguing of unique and rare materials, including options for streamlined cataloguing, and shared use of and creation of authority records across collections, as applicable.
- *All*: Consider different levels of cataloguing and processing for all types of rare and unique materials, depending on institutional priorities and importance and potential use of materials, while still following national standards and practices.

Integrate Access to Rare and Unique Materials with Other Library Materials:

- All: Integrate access tools for unique and rare materials into the information access structures that serve the institution as a whole.

Encourage Digitisation to Allow Broader Access:

- *LC*: Study possibilities for computational access to digital content. Use this information in developing new rules and best practices.
- *All*: Study usage patterns to inform digitisation priorities.

Share Access to Unique Materials:

- *All*: Encourage *inter*-institutional collaboration for sharing metadata records and authority records for rare and unique materials.
- *All*: Encourage libraries and archives to submit records for rare and unique materials to shared databases such as OCLC.
- *All*: Examine financial and other incentives and disincentives to the sharing of records for rare and unique materials. Modify systems, practices, and

agreements as necessary to increase incentives and decrease disincentives.

DESIRED OUTCOMES

- Discovery, accessibility, and use of rare and unique materials in all formats are comprehensive.
- Learning, research, and creation of new knowledge are enhanced.
- Reputations of individual institutions are enhanced as information about special bodies of resources becomes more widely known.
- Greater value is realised from an individual institution's investment in acquisition and housing of rare, unique, and archival materials.

POSITION OUR TECHNOLOGY FOR THE FUTURE

THE WEB AS INFRASTRUCTURE

Today, many information access and bibliographic workflows are moving to the Web. Data that were once stored in databases and used only for search and display of bibliographic information are now being used to interact with services outside the databases, such as connecting to full text or interacting with Web-based resources such as maps and reference works. Data that are stored in separate library databases often do not disclose themselves to Web applications, and thus do not appear in searches done through commonly used search engines. Such data are therefore invisible to information seekers using these Web applications, even though a library's catalogue may itself be openly available for use on the Web.

The library community's data carrier, MARC, is based on forty-year old techniques for data management and is out of step with programming styles of today. No community other than the library community uses this record format, severely compromising its utility to other communities as a data transmission tool. Bibliographic applications being developed outside of the library environment are not making use of, and may not be compatible with, records encoded in MARC. New and anticipated uses of bibliographic data require a format that will accommodate and distinguish expert-, automated-, and user-generated metadata, including annotations and usage data. Flexible design should allow for the selective use of metadata in different environments. Libraries have defined many standard vocabularies such as gazetteers, controlled terminologies, and authority lists that help them independently create compatible resource descriptions. Some of these vocabularies, however, are generally available only as textual documents, and are often buried within lengthy standards, for example the General Material Designation list contained in the *Anglo-American Cataloguing Rules,* and the MARC Code List for Languages, contained in the MARC standard.

These vocabularies have great value within the library community but because of how they are made available, that value cannot be shared with other communities. The use of language strings such as personal or corporate names as identifiers hinders data exchange across languages and across different information communities. Emphasis on textual strings as identifiers binds entries to a single language and thus hinders efforts to internationalise both authority files and bibliographic files that carry the authoritative forms of headings.

Text strings also do not serve as useful identifiers because strings may change over time to reflect changes in display or access forms. The more that data are used by different applications, the more important it is that they be clearly identified using language-neutral identification schema. Ideally, such schema should also provide contextual information as well as links to additional information about the data element and its meaning.

Consequences of Maintaining the Status Quo

Use of library data is limited to library systems and services. The data are not accessible in a form that integrates with Web applications. Unless the library community confirms its role in the evolving and expanding environment, and develops arrangements with new participants to take advantage of what each has to offer, library data will be isolated from the many non-library communities, such as publishers, authors, information service providers, and end-users that are engaged in accessing and making use of bibliographic information.

Recommendations

Develop a More Flexible, Extensible Metadata Carrier:

- *LC*: Work with the library community and other interested communities to specify and implement a process for the development of a carrier for bibliographic information that is compatible with Web technology and standards, is flexible and extensible, and is not limited to library data practices.
- *LC*: Contribute resources to support the work of coordinating the definitions and linkages of the data elements in nationally and internationally accepted bibliographic standards.
- *All*: Work with vendors to raise awareness of the need to begin developing products that can accept input of data utilising a variety of metadata formats.

Integrate Library Standards into Web Environment:

- *All*: Express library standards in machine-readable and machine-actionable formats, in particular those developed for use on the Web.
- *All*: Provide access to standards through registries or Web sites so that the standards can be used by any and all Web applications.
- *LC*: Begin transitioning LC-managed vocabularies to a platform that is both Web services-friendly and allows files to be downloaded for incorporation into other applications. These vocabularies include the many lists that are used in bibliographic records such as language and geographic codes, resource format codes, etc.

Extend Use of Standard Identifiers:

- *LC*: Generate standard Web-based identifiers for all data elements and vocabularies that LC maintains.
- *All*: Work to include standard identifiers for individual data elements in bibliographic records, both prospectively and retrospectively, wherever such identifiers are defined, and work to identify changes in metadata carrier standards necessary to incorporate and use such identifiers.

Desired Outcomes

Library bibliographic data will move from the closed database model to the open Web-based model wherein records are addressable by programmes and are in formats that can be easily integrated into Web services and computer applications.

This will enable libraries to make better use of networked data resources and to take advantage of the relationships that exist among various data sources on the Web. In coordination with a broad group of interested parties, especially creators of bibliographic data outside of libraries, the library community will develop a record carrier that can interact seamlessly with library data and library systems, and that can be used both by libraries and by other communities that deal in bibliographic data.

The carrier format will support a variety of bibliographic control practices and resource types. The vocabularies developed by the library community will be available for Web discovery and easy reuse by applications developers. Vocabularies will be managed in registries or other structures to facilitate more rapid updates than are possible with centrally managed lists.

Knowledge organisation systems will facilitate multilingual versions of vocabularies and cross-walking between them. All data points in the networked environment will be clearly identified, primarily with Uniform Resource Identifiers (URIs). Registration of data points will include information about meaning and usage. The library community will share identifiers of authors, works, and other controlled elements of bibliographic data to enable interchange of data between different communities of use, while still allowing display and indexing of data elements to vary according to the particular needs of the communities concerned.

STANDARDS

Although usually cast in technical terms, the institution of standards for bibliographic data is in reality a business issue. It is through the consistent application of standards that the full value of bibliographic data can be released across many potential use environments.

Standards remove barriers. Barriers exist when it is difficult to use or reuse data, either because standards do not exist, because they are not fit for the intended purpose, or because they are inconsistently applied. Two types of barriers are of particular importance: inefficiencies in performance, and processing costs. To work effectively, discovery, request, resolution, and delivery systems need to communicate effortlessly. Standards are especially vital in the current environment wherein we want to make data work harder to support a growing number and variety of applications. Data exchange between systems is increasing and systems are interacting with data from many different sources, including exchange with non-library partners.

Library systems increasingly exchange data internationally and with non-library partners such as Google and Amazon. Data are reused along publisher/bookseller/library/aggregator chains. Data are increasingly being used all along the discovery-to-delivery chain to facilitate more streamlined services. New discovery environments are emerging that extract and merge data from several library systems. The classic library standards 'stack' may not provide the best means to interact with data from other information ecologies.

The library community has a long tradition of creating standards. Recently, there has been a proliferation of standards—both officially registered and *de facto*—prompted by the needs of digital materials and digitising initiatives. While it is useful to continue the explorations embodied in such standards development, the library community needs to be much more focused on identifying and addressing real needs with workable solutions. Too much development is based on unvalidated assertions or professional ideology. Our metadata environment is becoming extremely complex, comprehending AACR2/RDA, MARC 21, MARC XML, MODS, Dublin Core, and ONIX—amongst others. Our retrieval protocol environment is also complex, with Z39.50, SRW/U, MXG, and the need to work with OpenSearch and other protocol approaches.

This standards proliferation is a distraction to national bodies, a confusion for practitioners, and a vexation for developers. The standards processes for the library community take place in a variety of organisations which sometimes have overlapping participants. In particular, the FRBR and RDA initiatives are currently moving forward within different organisational structures—to the extent that they are moving forward. Because the Library of Congress is a major player in both efforts it could well use its influence to help coordinate these initiatives more closely and to introduce a stronger cost/benefit perspective into the work. Over and above our concerns about RDA development proceeding in parallel with FRBR and its related activities, the Working Group has additional concerns about RDA, including:

- The promised benefits of RDA are not discernable in the drafts seen to date.
- Unclearness on how metadata created according to RDA will align with existing metadata.
- The business case for moving to RDA has not been made satisfactorily.
- The financial implications of adoption in terms of changes to workflow and supporting systems may prove considerable.

Consequences of Maintaining the Status Quo

Data exchange and reuse is hindered by inconsistencies in the data, and by data encoding that is not designed for the current and emerging machine environment. Consequently, costs increase across all parts of the bibliographic control ecosystem, and service to users diminishes.

Recommendations

Suspend Work on RDA:

- *JSC*: Suspend further new work on RDA until:
  - More, large-scale testing of FRBR has been carried out against real cataloguing data, and the results of those tests have been analysed.
  - The use and business cases for moving to RDA have been satisfactorily articulated.
  - The presumed benefits of RDA have been convincingly demonstrated.
- *LC, JSC, and DCMI*: Work jointly to specify and commission exploratory work to model and represent a Bibliographic Description Vocabulary, drawing on the work of FRBR and RDA, the Dublin Core Abstract Model, and appropriate semantic Web technologies. Some preparation for this work has already been done in joint discussion of JSC and DCMI.

Develop Standards with a Focus on Return on Investment:

- *All*: Design data standards with a view towards maximising machine-processing of data.
- *LC*: Review record creation practices to ensure that as many data elements as possible are controlled.
- *All*: Analyse and assess costs and benefits of new or revised standards before undertaking a standards-development process.
- *LC*: Take a system wide perspective when moving into new areas of standards work, with a strong focus on improving the efficiencies of the library community generally.
- *All*: Design data standards with data reuse as a goal. This means that all members of the supply chain must be considered during the standards development process.

Incorporate Lessons from use into Standards Development:

- *All*: Modify standards development processes to include

standards validation against planned deployment.

- *All*: Include software engineers and user services experts in the development processes for all information technology standards.
- *All*: Develop an evidence base that enables the community to validate the assertions that are being made about the need for a standard.
- *LC*: Fund analysis to identify the descriptive practices that are needed to support emerging uses of bibliographic data, such as those seen in new discovery environments.

Desired Outcomes

Assurance that RDA is based on practical realities as well as on theoretical constructs will improve support for the code in the bibliographic control community. The suspension of work in as-yet-undeveloped areas of RDA could be used by the Joint Steering Committee to address outstanding issues of language, organisation, usability, etc. Further development of standards will be based on evidence arising from changing use patterns.

The library community will realise that bibliographic data need to support a variety of user, management, and machine needs. In particular, it will be recognised that human users and their needs for display and discovery do not represent the only use of bibliographic metadata; instead, to an increasing degree, machine applications are their primary users. Data will be designed and developed with this in mind. Libraries will be mindful of the total life-cycle cost of using data, including the additional processing that may be required if the data are reused in other environments. They will also be aware of the costs of the proliferation of data types and search protocols, and will work to consolidate standards.

POSITION OUR COMMUNITY FOR THE FUTURE

DESIGN FOR TODAY'S AND TOMORROW'S USER

The metadata created by libraries' bibliographic control activities serve multiple types of users. These include the customers of our libraries and of our catalogues, other libraries, and the library service industry. 'Users' are not only people, but the systems and software that interact with metadata to provide services. Metadata are used within both a consumer environment and a management environment.

Each of these groups and uses poses somewhat different requirements. Users of library materials are diverse, and a single individual will exhibit different needs, expectations, and behaviours as the purpose of his/her research changes. There is no 'typical user.'

Library users can vary widely in their knowledge both of library systems and of the subject domains they are investigating. Studies indicate that over three-quarters of users have low knowledge of how to use the library catalogue as well as low subject knowledge of their immediate topic of interest. By contrast, less than 1 per cent of users have high skills in both using the catalogue and subject domain knowledge. This disparity in user skills and needs makes it difficult for libraries to focus their bibliographic control efforts.

Users are making new demands on metadata. Thanks to the ubiquity and utility of Web search engines, in combination with rapid innovations in Web technology, most users now conduct their research in multiple discovery environments: search engines, online booksellers, course management systems, specialised databases, library catalogues, and more. They prefer to have simultaneous access to information in many physical and digital formats, beyond traditional print. A significant change in the searching behaviour of library users has occurred in the past decade, with users often bypassing library catalogues and going first to search engines and other Internet resources.

The content of these discovery systems is becoming more blended and diverse; materials formerly managed through separate standards and practices are now being mixed in both general and domain-specific systems. As experienced users of Internet search engines, library users expect increased capabilities in our online systems. They value features and data that help them make sense of results by ranking, organising, and clustering. Library catalogues have consciously presented a neutral and authoritative view of the bibliographic universe. Evaluative information, such as reviews and reading lists, has not traditionally been part of the library catalogue. Today, bibliographic Web sites like Amazon.com and LibraryThing provide users with information about resources, as well as information that help them evaluate those resources. They also allow users to share reading lists, add reviews and ratings, and supply their own subject tags. Both Amazon and LibraryThing embody a combination of bibliographic and social networking systems.

LibraryThing, in fact, is largely based on library-produced data. Library systems are responding to changes in user expectations with new collocation and display methods, including clustering all versions of a work, and faceting retrieved results sets by subject, format, classification, and language. Few library systems, however, currently allow users to add or manipulate catalogue data. Libraries have tended to equate bibliographic control with the production of metadata for use solely within the library catalogue. This narrow focus is no longer suitable in an environment wherein data from diverse sources are used to create new and interesting information views.

Library data must be usable outside of the catalogue, and the catalogue must be able to ingest or interact with records from sources outside of the library cataloguing workflow. The tightly controlled consistency designed into library standards thus far is unlikely to be realised or sustained in the future, even within the local environment. Any given library will, of necessity, serve users with different levels of sophistication in library use and in subject knowledge.

The challenge to libraries, then, is to produce metadata that will serve this broad range of users well. Many libraries have chosen to produce metadata to satisfy the needs of their most sophisticated users, despite the fact that such users are but a small percentage of their total user base. They do so on the increasingly dubious assumption that all users will benefit from the greatest detail in cataloguing.

Consequences of Maintaining the Status Quo

Library users will continue to bypass catalogues in favour of search engines. Some studies have found that over three quarters of library users start with a search engine and not the online catalogue. The resources needed to catalogue at a sophisticated level are increasingly difficult to sustain. Libraries face a trade-off between doing detailed cataloguing for regularly published materials, and doing less-detailed cataloguing for a wider variety of information types.

Recommendations

Link Appropriate External Information with Library Catalogues:

- *All*: Encourage and support development of systems capable of relating evaluative data, such as reviews and ratings, to bibliographic records.
- *All*: Encourage the enhancement of library systems to provide the capability to link to appropriate user-added data available via the Internet.

Integrate User-Contributed Data into Library Catalogues:

- *All*: Develop library systems that can accept user input and other non-library data without interfering with the integrity of library-created data.
- *All*: Investigate methods of categorising creators of added data to allow informed use of user-contributed data without violating the privacy obligations of libraries.
- *All*: Develop methods to guide user tagging through techniques that suggest entry vocabulary.

Research Use of Computationally Derived Evaluation:

- *All*: Make use of holdings and circulation information to point users to items that are most used and that may potentially be of most interest.
- *All*: Compare user tags with controlled vocabularies and identify correlations between them.

Desired Outcomes

Library bibliographic data will be used in a wide variety

of environments, and interoperability between library and non-library bibliographic applications will increase/improve. Library catalogues are seen as valuable components in an interlocking array of discovery tools. Library resource discovery and evaluation will be enhanced by contributions from users.

REALISATION OF FRBR

Since, the 1998 publication of the final report of IFLA's Functional Requirements for Bibliographic Record (FRBR) study, the FRBR framework has served as an international catalyst for reconceptualising bibliographic data and bibliographic relationships. FRBR suggests alternatives for analysing intellectual content for bibliographic control. Recent data modeling exercises in library and other arenas have provided sophisticated models that highlight important areas for attention.

At the same time, the emergence of resource-oriented architectures in the Web environment has made the bibliographic community alert to the benefits of providing access to data resources using simple Web-based protocols and schema. The combination of these two strands suggests an important future direction for the Library of Congress and for Web-based, network-level bibliographic control. The Working Group envisions a bibliographic infrastructure wherein data about entities of interest are encoded in agreed-upon ways and made available through agreed-upon Web protocols for ready and efficient use by other applications and services.

LC and the library community need to find ways of 'releasing the value' of the rich historic investment in semantic data onto the Web. System implementations experimenting with the FRBR 'Work' concept to cluster materials in the user interface are proving the value of the model at the Work definition level. However, clustering at the Work level exercises only a minor part of the FRBR model, which redefines the full range of bibliographic entities and their relationships. At the same time, the impact of the FRBR model on cataloguing practice and on the machine-readable bibliographic record has not been extensively explored. There is no standard way to exchange Work-based data, and no cataloguing rules that yet support the creation of records using the FRBR model. The work of the Joint Steering Committee to ready RDA for publication in 2009 is using FRBR for guidance. Unfortunately, that means that RDA is being based on a framework that has not yet received substantial testing on live data, in real libraries, at scale. The Working Group feels strongly that until FRBR has been tested, it will not be possible to usefully evaluate its applicability in the context of RDA.

Consequences of Maintaining the Status Quo

The library community is basing its future cataloguing rules on a framework that it has only barely begun to explore. Until carefully tested as a model for bibliographic data formation, FRBR must be seen as a theoretical model whose practical implementation and its attendant costs are still unknown.

Recommendations

Develop Test Plan for FRBR:

- LC, OCLC, IFLA Working Group, and Representative System Vendors: Identify what agreements are necessary to support Work-based views in bibliographic systems.
- LC, OCLC, IFLA Working Group, and Representative System Vendors: Develop and agree upon a schema for the exchange of Work-based data.
- LC, OCLC, IFLA Working Group, and Representative System Vendors: Clarify the status of the Expression entity and, if appropriate, carry out work similar to that described in 4.2.1.1 and 4.2.1.2 for that entity.
- LC, OCLC, IFLA Working Group, and Representative System Vendors: Use the results of the activity as the basis for promulgating and evaluating FRBR implementations.

Desired Outcomes

The study, refinement and validation of FRBR will

provide a more robust framework for the creation of the resource description and access rules that will be used in the future to support a broad range of relational searching options. The final product will be a bibliographic environment with clearly defined elements and relationships that can be used in a variety of bibliographic control situations.

OPTIMISE LCSH FOR USE AND REUSE

The Working Group recognises that subject analysis is a core function of cataloguing, and that Library of Congress Subject Headings have great value in providing controlled subject access to works. LCSH is used widely in the community and is often the only searchable subject term set in library catalogues. However, while it is recognised as a powerful tool for collocating topical information, LSCH suffers from the double disability of a structure that is cumbersome from both administrative and automation points of view.

For cataloguers and users alike, the LCSH vocabulary is often out of synch with common terminology. While thesaural relationships are available as lead-in vocabulary to some authorised subject headings, the lead-in terms are often no more intuitive than the established terms. LC does update subject terms as warranted and encountered, but from outside LC the results often appear to be arbitrary and unexpected. Library of Congress cataloguers and members of other institutions can notify LC regarding the need to update a term to more current language, but not all change requests are acted upon.

Some changes, albeit greatly needed, are refused because of the impact they would have on previously cataloged items, or because they would benefit one portion of the community that uses LCSH while disadvantaging another. The creation of pre-coordinated subject strings is a time-consuming and inexact process.

Creation of these strings, for which there are four volumes of instructions is generally assigned to senior and/or professional cataloguing staff not just because analysis of subject content is a difficult task, but also because navigating the thesaurus is difficult, and the rules for heading construction are complex. While pre-coordination can offer users an implicit indication of the relationship between subject terms, the SCM rules for applying subdivisions do not always enable those relationships to be made manifest.

In addition, the complexity of the rules regarding the order of subdivisions may result in strings that represent term relationships poorly or not at all. Moreover, the SCM rules can in fact hinder subject access because they limit the number of specific subject terms that are supposed to be attached to a bibliographic record and because they restrict the application of subject terms to the level of specificity of the resource.

Subject specificity benefits both expert and novice user by collocating items with the specific topics of which they are examples. However, as Karen Markey noted in her paper for the Working Group's February meeting, the novice user—especially the 'double novice' —maybenefit additionally from more general subject access to overcome his/her lack of knowledge of the subject matter s/he is researching. Unfortunately, the SCM does not allow for the use of broader or equivalent terms in bibliographic records.

Instead, it relies on the LCSH reference structure to lead to those terms, and on the user interface of online catalogues to provide guidance through references or redirected searches. The structure of LCSH, moreover, as an alphabetical list does not facilitate browsing of authorised headings within a particular discipline or topic.

Catalogers who may be unfamiliar with the topic of the resource in hand or novice users trying to find an authorised subject term cannot browse through LCSH by topic to search for the term that satisfies their information need. Rather, they must come to LCSH with a subject heading in mind and hope that they will find it has already been established or that they will be led to other useful established terms.

Searching for authorised terms within a particular subject area might be facilitated if there were more thorough correlation between LCSH and the Library of Congress Classification.

Consequences of Maintaining the Status Quo

The complexity of LCSH, in combination with its idiosyncratic updating and the seemingly capricious limitations on its application, have negative consequences for both cataloguers and catalogue users, and mitigate against its use by stakeholders outside the library community. The non-topical, non-hierarchical organisation of LCSH makes systematic, coordinated updating of the vocabulary difficult. The complexity of rules that guide the creation of subject strings leads to errors in string construction, which in turn create inconsistencies in the controlled vocabulary, interfere with retrieval of relevant materials, and ultimately defeat the purpose of a controlled vocabulary.

LCSH headings are utilised by information seekers who have prior subject knowledge, while subject novices turn to other tools such as Internet search engines that do not penalise them for their lack of subject expertise.

Recommendations

Transform LCSH:

- *LC*: Transform LCSH into a tool that provides a more flexible means to create and modify subject authority data.
- *LC*: Provide LCSH openly for use by library and non-library stakeholders.
- *LC*: Provide LCSH in its current alphabetical arrangement, and enable its customised assembly into topical thesauri.
- *LC*: Increase explicit correlation and referencing between LCSH terms and LCC and *Dewey Decimal Classification* (DDC) numbers.

Pursue De-Coupling of Subject Strings:

- *LC*: Work with OCLC and/or other appropriate partners to identify a scheme or product that could take advantage of the power of LCSH's controlled vocabulary and serve as a base to take advantage of terminologies that function in a more accessible environment with broader audiences. The FAST is an example of such an attempt.

- *All*: Evaluate the ability of LCSH to support faceted browsing and discovery.

Encourage Application of, and Cross-Referencing with, Other Controlled Subject Vocabularies:

- *LC and providers of subject vocabularies*: Provide references within LCSH, where appropriate, and between LCSH and other established sources of controlled subject headings, such as MeSH, the NAL Agricultural Thesaurus, Sears, and the Getty Art and Architecture Thesaurus. Make vocabularies cross-searchable and interoperable.
- *All*: Apply terms from any and all appropriate sources of controlled subject headings in bibliographic records to augment subject access.
- *All*: Explore mechanisms to exploit cross-vocabulary linkages to enhance retrieval, without limiting to the headings explicitly provided in individual bibliographic records.
- *LC and OCLC*: Explore ways of reducing creation costs and improving effectiveness by working more closely between DDC, LCSH, and LCC, the main 'universal' library approaches to subject analysis.

Recognise the Potential of Computational Indexing in the Practice of Subject Analysis:

- *All*: For works where full text is available in digital form, study the extent to which computational analysis and indexing of the digital text can supplement or substitute for traditional intellectual subject analysis.
- *LC*: Based on the results of the previous recommendation, examine the tradeoffs and potential resource savings of using computational analysis and indexing to substitute for some subject analysis.
- *All*: Initiate a standards process that allows the various results of computational analysis and indexing to be interchanged and shared as part of bibliographic records, in order to permit sharing of

metadata without necessarily sharing the underlying resource.

Desired Outcomes

LCSH will be easier to update and to apply. Terminology will be more current and consistent. The subject cataloguing process will be more straightforward. An easier, more intuitive application of subject terminology will save time and free catalogers for other work. Restructuring LCSH will make it useful to a wider range of users, as well as facilitate navigation and manipulation in user interfaces. The addition to bibliographic records of subject terms from other thesauri will provide more, and more varied, subject access to resources.

STRENGTHEN THE LIBRARY AND INFORMATION SCIENCE PROFESSION

BUILD AN EVIDENCE BASE

Bibliographic control occurs in a complex system of participants, information resources products and services, and technological capabilities. There are increasing numbers of participants, information formats and media, and information technologies. Contributors of bibliographic data and services may have different and sometimes conflicting agendas. Multiple user communities may have changing and expanding needs and expectations.

In this increasingly complex environment, the actions taken by key players can have downstream impacts on others. Unfortunately, there are still inadequate measures of the costs, benefits, and value of bibliographic information and almost no information on the interdependencies within the broader bibliographic control environment, including the impact of internationalisation. Although the use of cost-benefit analysis for service organisations such as libraries is problematic, all organisations must achieve goals and provide value. Bibliographic control may be considered by many to be a public good, but it has real costs attached to it, and presumably it has real value. The Library of Congress currently does not have sufficient quantitative data about its bibliographic control operations to present a business case for the actions that it wishes to undertake to modify its operations. Too often, decisions appear to be made based on simple cost-cost comparisons, without apparently adequate consideration of the tangible and intangible benefits of various options.

Consequences of Maintaining the Status Quo

With more participants in the bibliographic control environment, decisions are often made independent of any reliable data. These decisions can perturb the system in unanticipated and undesirable ways. Duplications and gaps may arise. Finite resources—especially human resources—may not be optimally applied from the perspective of the overall system.

Recommendations

Develop Key Measures:

- *LC*: Bring key participants together to agree to implement a set of measures of:
  - Costs, benefits, value of bibliographic control for each group of participants; and
  - Interdependencies among participants.
- *LC*: Develop a statement of value of LC's service that includes benefits to libraries and to the marke sectors that provide services to libraries.
- *LC*: Analyse changes in LC service levels in terms costs and savings within LC and potential effects the larger community.

Support Ongoing Research:

- *All*: Encourage ongoing qualitative and quantit research about bibliographic control, for va types of libraries and over a protracted per time.
- *All*: Through LIS and continuing education, greater understanding of the need for resear quantitative and qualitative, into issues of bibli control.

- *All*: Work to develop a stronger and more rigorous culture of formal evaluation, critique, and validation, and build a cumulative research agenda and evidence base. Encourage, highlight, reward, and share best research practices and results.

Desired Outcomes

The community will have an improved understanding of the real costs and benefits of various aspects of, and choices to be made within, today's system of bibliographic control. A business case will be articulated that includes data points to be used over time to assess the consequences of change. A statement of goals for LC will be developed that includes a broad vision of the value of its services. Included in this should be all of the types of organisations that benefit from the Library's data services, including those in the for-profit sector. A growing evidence base will be created that can be used to monitor erformance and effectiveness of the system and its component rts and inform future decision making by system participants.

IGN LIS EDUCATION FOR PRESENT FUTURE NEEDS

e educational preparation for cataloguers, indexers, and brarians and information professionals is not ised across programmes or curricula. Many LIS es have shifted from teaching cataloguing to rganisation of information, although some continue to offer both. There is an impending and e of cataloguers, indexers, etc. as these positions etirements, resource reductions, and a dearth ty to teach them.

ree decades, it has been assumed that the sionals in these positions will decline as on acquiring bibliographic control data ty, there has been a shift in demand from ion industry, but LIS programmes tend rather than the latter. As in so many ve key to the profession's capability to address new challenges in bibliographic control. As changes take place in policies, standards, processes, and practices for bibliographic control, these need to be incorporated into the educational system for LIS professionals—both in library schools and continuing education programmes—in a timely manner.

Consequences of Maintaining the Status Quo

If the educational programmes do not stay up to date, they will further stress the system by producing professional librarians whose skill sets do not match the needs of the marketplace they will enter.

Recommendations

Communicate with LIS Educators:

- *LC and ALA*: Convene a biennial meeting with LIS educators and trainers, perhaps in coordination with ALA and ALISE, to discuss changing policies, procedures, processes and practices, the levels of demand for qualified professionals in the area of bibliographic control, and base levels of knowledge required, in the first instance, of those who will work in bibliographic control and, in the second instance, of all professionals.
- *LIS programmes and library community*: Accept that base levels of knowledge for all professionals include: Understanding the role of organising resources in information control, transfer and access processes; Being familiar with basic principles and practices for organising resources in libraries, archives, museums and other information resource centres; Skills for organising resources and understanding description and subject analysis as fundamental components of this activity; Understanding the basic role of metadata for organising digital resources; Being aware of new developments that have an impact on the organisation of resources, such as the Dublin Core, FRBR, etc.

- *LIS programmes*: Make available curricula covering advanced knowledge and skills to those who intend to specialise in bibliographic control. These could include traditional cataloguing, knowledge organisation theory, database design, metadata for unique materials, indexes and thesauri/fact analysis, computational linguistics, philosophy of information, managing e-resources, systems librarianship, etc.

Share Educational Materials Broadly via the Internet:

- *All*: Make educational materials available over the Internet, free or at reasonable cost.
- *All*: Use network capabilities and other distance learning technologies to increase the availability of education for all library staff. In particular, encourage the creation of courses that can be taken at the learners' convenience.

Develop Continuing Education for U.S., Library Profession:

- ALA and ALA-APA: Consider development of a U.S., wide continuing education programme in bibliographic control which could be hosted by a professional association or academic institution.
- ALA and ALA-APA: Develop an economic model that can ensure sustainability of the continuing education programme.

Desired Outcomes

There will be sufficient numbers of qualified professionals to participate actively in the current and to help shape the future bibliographic control environment. They will have a thorough understanding of current practices and upcoming challenges. These librarians will be productive and effective professionals while remaining open and adaptive to change.

Bibliography

Adiseshiah, M.: *Starting, Managing, and Promoting the Small Library*, New Delhi: Institute of Library Sciences and Concept Publications, 2005.

Agnihotri, V.K.: *Information Management in Archives and Libraries*, New Delhi: Vikas Publication, 2000.

Cernea, M.M.: *Digital Libraries: Philosophies, Technical Design Considerations*, New York: Oxford University Press, 2000.

Chambers, R.: *Public Libraries*, New Delhi: Oxford & IBH, 1999.

Crook, R.: *Evaluating the Twenty-first Century Library*, UK: Cambridge University Press, 2004.

Grandin, B.: *Engineering Libraries: Building Collections and Delivering Services*, UK: Intermediate Technology Publications, 2008.

Jain, S.P.: *Electronic Resources and Services in Sci-tech Libraries*, Hyderabad: National Institute for Rural Development, 1999.

Kempton, J.: *Advanced Indexing and Abstracting Practies*, London: Macmillan Press, 2002.

Mill, Cyril R.: *Library Users and Reference Services*, California: University Associates, 1998.

Mitra, S.: *Library Science Abstracts*, New York: Routledge, 2008.

Mukherjee, A.: *Dictionary for Library and Information Science*, New Delhi: Vikas Publication, 1997.

Mukherjee, N.: *Digital Libraries: Principles and Practice in a Global Environment*, New Delhi: Concept Publication, 2005.

Parikh, K.S.: *Library Work*, New Delhi: Oxford Publication, 2007.

Punia, R.K.: *The Application of Expert Systems in Libraries and Information Centres*, New Delhi: Northern Book Centre, 2006.

Raju, M.R.: *Magazines for Libraries*, California: University Associates, 2007.

Rosenstone, J.: *Handbook of Abstracting Practices in Libraries*, New York: Macmillan, 2001.

Verba, S.: *Collection Evaluation in Academic Libraries, Cambridge*, MA: Harvard University Press, 2006.

Index